D1558811

THE HIG

PENN STATE'S
GRIDIRON LEGACY:
THE BOB HIGGINS &
STEVE SUHEY FAMILIES

RICH DONNELL

OWL BAY
Publishers

Owl Bay Publishers
Post Office Box 6461
Montgomery, AL 36106

Design by George Littleton

Owl Bay books are available as premiums or fundraisers, and are sold at discounts for educational use.

Manufactured in the United States of America.

ISBN 0-9638568-2-0

To my father,
Thomas Marshall Donnell, Sr.

Blest are those whose blood
and judgment are so well
commeddled.

—William Shakespeare

Acknowledgments

I REMEMBER VIVIDLY the sunny winter's day in State College, Pennsylvania when I walked down the steps into the basement of the Suhey family home on South Sparks Street. My host, Larry Suhey, and hostess, Larry's sister Betsy, apologized for the disorganization of the dozens of tattered boxes they had brought into this chilly room from the darkness of the attic of their mom's home. But I could only grin at the things I saw peeping out of those boxes — an original, slightly scarred photograph of a football game in which none of the players wore helmets; a yellowed newspaper clipping in which the headline referred to Harvard as a gridiron power; an old prep school yearbook dated 1913.

Two thoughts entered my mind. One was that the material in these boxes would save me a year's worth of excruciating research in various archive departments. The other thought was that I must treat the material with the utmost respect — not necessarily out of concern for physically damaging it, but simply because of what it was. I had before me the heart of Penn State football. Heck, I had before me the story of college football.

"You might be interested in this," Larry said, handing me a piece of paper he had plucked from one of the boxes.

I read it and felt for perhaps the first time in my life that I was actually holding history in my hands: a letter from the legendary college football pioneer and coach, Amos Alonzo Stagg, to Penn State's Bob Higgins.

"Yes, I might be interested in this," I whispered.

A humbling realization came over me then that never left as I worked in that basement room: I have a Football Hall of Fame all to myself.

As I began my research it didn't take me long to discover that I had even more than football here — I had the story of a 20th century American family that represented everything that was good about America.

During the course of my interviewing to go along with my research, a former Penn State football player who was an All-American on the field and has remained an All-American off of it, Dave Joyner, stated simply the theme of this book: "Higgins-Suhey are the kind of people that made America great," Joyner said. "They epitomize Penn State through their work ethic, their integrity, their honor, their love of family and their feelings of tradition."

How did I get into the Suhey basement? A year ago I wrote a biography entitled *Shug: The Life and Times of Auburn's Ralph 'Shug' Jordan*. Jordan, who died in 1980 at the age of sixty-nine, was head football coach at Auburn University for twenty-five years, 1951-1975. His team won a national championship in 1957 and he fielded many other great teams, but for most of two decades he coached in the shadow of cross-state rival Paul "Bear" Bryant and the University of Alabama. The Jordan story hadn't been told. As one who loves college football, I took on the privilege of telling it.

The enjoyment and success that my publisher and I experienced from *Shug* left us on the lookout for another college football story. One morning, as I was growing anxious over not having another sports book to write, George Littleton of Owl Bay Publishers phoned and asked, "Do you want to do it again?" Of course I did. "What's the school?" I asked. "Penn State," George replied.

Of course, Penn State. It doesn't get any better than Penn State. I had received a master's degree in journalism from Penn State in 1983, and was in school when Penn State won the national championship in 1982.

George mentioned the Higgins-Suhey families as the subject of a new book. He had gotten wind of the idea from a friend named Charlie Smith, who is a print consultant for EBSCO Media in Birmingham, Alabama. Smith had previously worked for L.G. Balfour Co. and knew Steve Suhey, who also worked for Balfour in central Pennsylvania. Smith became friends with Steve's son Larry, who took over his dad's territory after Steve died in 1977.

Charlie and Larry had much in common. Charlie played football at the University of Alabama until an injury ended his career prior to his sophomore year of 1970. Larry played fullback for Penn State from 1972-1976. Charlie and Larry became best friends and rendezvoused annually for the classic Alabama-Penn State series between 1981-1990. Larry introduced Charlie to Coach Joe Paterno, and Charlie returned the favor by introducing Larry to Coach Bryant.

Charlie was the one who suggested that a great topic for another football book would be this remarkable family which had played and coached at Penn State for three generations, as far back as World War I.

I have always been attracted to the old days of college football, and of course I knew of Bob Higgins, the former Penn State All-American end and head coach. I also knew of Steve Suhey, the All-American guard who played for his future father-in-law at Penn State and spearheaded in 1947 the greatest defense against the run in the history of college football. I was a young sportswriter in the 1970s and therefore I knew of the three Suhey brothers — Larry, Paul and Matt — who had played for Paterno, and that the youngest brother, Matt, went on to a great pro career with the Chicago Bears.

But only when the voices of the past spoke out to me from those boxes in the Suhey basement, and only when so many family members and friends and former teammates without hesitation opened themselves up to me, did I come to know and truly appreciate what is certainly Penn State's — and to a large extent all of America's — greatest gridiron legacy.

Rich Donnell
July 15, 1994

Foreword

By JOE PATERNO

THIS BOOK BRINGS WARM and wonderful memories. Memories of unique individuals and a unique family started by a true patriarch. These are special people who established a special relationship with a great University — a committed family who joined together for three generations and influenced for good thousands of individuals who would be bound together by being Penn Staters. "We are Penn State!" is a cheer that denotes pride in our school and there are many traditions, accomplishments and individuals rooted and nurtured in this pride.

It would not be an overstatement to say that Bob Higgins, "The Hig," his daughters, their husbands and children — and in particular his daughter Ginger, who mirrored her father in her leadership and charisma — synergized those intangible qualities that inspire people; that make people want to be with them; and whose common sense and commitment to their traditional values and their families carried over into their loyalty to friends and institutions. They displayed a loyalty and pride that constantly portrayed itself in a fierce, combative nature that refused to allow themselves and their coterie to be anything but the best.

This book is a modern history of Penn State football. It starts with a young hero, a great athlete, the Frank Merriwell of the 1919 Penn State Football team. And the book carries on through his progeny to where we are today.

But to think of this as a football book would be to deprive us of the richness and inspiration of the lives and families of people who truly cared and truly wanted to make a difference. We who love Penn State owe Rich Donnell much for bringing to life one of our true heroes — that wonderful patrician gentleman, Robert Arlington Higgins — a great human being, a great player and a great coach whom we love as "The Hig."

August 2, 1994
State College, Pennsylvania

THE
HIG

§ 1 §
Present Meets Past

THE BLUE LINCOLN DRIFTED around the practice field and slowed to a halt near the dozens of sweating young men trying to become a part of the Chicago Bears professional football team. The owner of the car — bald, bespectacled, wrinkled — sat deep in the back seat and lowered the humming electric window. He caught the eye of an assistant coach who had been leading the running backs through their drills. The assistant hustled over to the old man's window.

"Good morning, Mr. Halas," the coach said eagerly to the long-time owner of the Bears.

"Which one is Suhey?" the old man asked.

The coach pointed him out. Eighty-five-year-old George Halas watched Matt Suhey as the workout continued. He was impressed by Suhey's compact build, his powerful legs and enormous calves. Bears' General Manager Jim Finks was excited about Suhey and had told Halas as much. The Bears had drafted him in the second round out of Joe Paterno's legendary Penn State program.

Suhey had lettered four years for the Nittany Lions while becoming one of the greatest runners in the school's history. When he stripped off his blue and white uniform and plain black shoes for the final time, Suhey's 2,818 yards rushing placed him just behind Lydell Mitchell on the school's career rushing list. Suhey had carried the ball 633 times and scored twenty-six touchdowns. He mainly played fullback at Penn State, but came to Paterno recognized as perhaps Pennsylvania's best-ever high school tailback. He played at State College Area High School, within walking distance of the Suhey family home. Suhey's speed made him an obvious choice to return kickoffs and punts for Penn State, a fact which had not escaped the Bears. Two of Matt's older brothers, Larry and Paul, also played under Paterno, with all three playing together on Penn State's 1976 Gator Bowl squad.

General Manager Finks played pro ball with Matt's father at Pittsburgh in 1949. George Halas coached the Bears against that Pittsburgh team and he remembered Steve Suhey: a rock-hard guard with halfback speed; a kid who came up the hard way and made himself an All-American at Penn State after service in World War II. A knee injury shortened Suhey's pro career. It occurred to Halas that Matt Suhey had his father's legs.

Halas marveled at the Suhey family's football tradition. Matt was about to become a third generation pro football player, following not only his dad but also his grandfather, Bob Higgins.

"The Hig," as he was known, had been the head coach at Penn State when his future son-in-law Steve Suhey made All-American. That Suhey-led team in 1947 went undefeated and played SMU and Doak Walker in the Cotton Bowl. The Hig had steadily built up the Penn State program during his nineteen years there, and fielded his greatest teams just before illness forced his retirement in 1949. And he had done all this in spite of a "Purist Policy" rule then in effect that prohibited the awarding of football scholarships at Penn State.

But Halas remembered Higgins as much for his playing days as for his coaching career. The Hig was an All-American end at Penn State in 1919 following his distinguished service in the Great War. In 1920, the first year of organized professional football, Higgins played with Jim Thorpe and the Canton Bulldogs. In 1921 Chicago won its first professional championship. During that season Chicago played Canton, and Halas lined up one-on-one against Higgins.

"Get Suhey over here," Halas snapped as he stepped out of the car.

The coach moved toward the field and called for Suhey.

One of the running backs perked up. He looked at the coach and pointed to himself, unsure whether he had heard correctly.

"Mr. Halas wants to meet you," someone told Suhey.

Suhey removed his helmet and ran toward the car. He was a handsome young man with dark hair and a strong chin.

"Mr. Halas, this is Matt Suhey," said the assistant.

Halas offered his hand.

"I played against your grandfather," Halas said.

"Yes sir," Suhey replied. "I knew you had."

"I was an end with Chicago and your grandfather was an end with Canton. Your grandfather was tough and quick."

"Yes sir," Suhey said.

"But I whipped him pretty good," Halas added with a smirk.

"Are you sure about that?" Suhey retorted, trying to force a smile.

"I handled him," Halas nodded.

Suhey felt his face flush. He knew George Halas was a great man; that he was the one man most responsible for the success of pro football. But Suhey wasn't intimidated by him. Matt Suhey had been raised with legends and All-Americans and great football traditions at Penn State. The Higgins-Suhey trophy collection was Hall of Fame caliber. The family clipping collection was like a university archive. Who was this old man to insult Bob Higgins?

"Knowing what I know about my grandfather's playing days, sir, I don't think you whipped him," Suhey said.

The eyes of the legendary Bears' owner locked into those of his second-round draft pick.

"Suhey, get back to work!" the assistant ordered, growing uneasy with the potential clash of proud traditions.

"Yes sir," Suhey mumbled. He strapped on his helmet and trotted back to the field.

Halas watched him return to the action and climbed back into the Lincoln. He was satisfied that the Bears had found their fullback of the future. Football was in this kid's blood.

§ 2 §
A Stonecutter's Son

MATT SUHEY'S FAMOUS GRANDFATHER, Robert Arlington Higgins, was born in Corning, New York on December 24, 1893. Bob Higgins did not share the eccentric nature of his father, Michael Hennessy Higgins. The son certainly possessed his father's wit and appreciation for life and camaraderie, but the son played between the lines, unlike his father. Michael Higgins definitely enjoyed stepping out-of-bounds.

Michael Higgins was born in Ireland, immigrated with his family to Canada, and ran away from home at age fifteen to join the Twelfth New York Volunteer Cavalry as a drummer boy during the Civil War. He settled in Corning after the war, married Anne Purcell, and they had twelve children: eight boys and four girls. One of the boys, Henry George McGlynn Higgins, died of croup and congestion when he was only four. Anne Higgins became mired in depression as the face of her son quickly slipped away from her memory. One evening Michael and one of his daughters, Margaret, pushed a wheelbarrow and a bag of plaster two miles to the cemetery. With his daughter holding a lantern above him, Michael Higgins dug up the grave and made a death mask of the boy's face. From this he sculpted a bust of the child and presented it to his wife. The gift lifted her out of depression and soothed her sadness for the remaining years of her life.

Higgins was a stonecutter and sculptor by trade. He often said a person's head was a sculptured expression of their soul. As Higgins walked through the cemetery that night he recognized many of the large marble and granite angels and saints because he himself had chiseled them. He performed his labors for the predominantly Roman Catholic community which was best known for its famous "Corningware" glass industry. Higgins also built furniture. He was an artisan and his companions were cabinet makers, masons and carpenters. He was also a philosopher and a champion and friend of the American economist Henry George, who espoused the single-tax movement and for whom Higgins named the boy who died so young. Higgins was also known as a rebel. Religious dogma irritated him and his strong opinions frequently cost him precious tombstone and sculpture customers.

Higgins preached on the freedom of expression. He emphasized that life was a treasure not to be squandered. He told his children, "You should give something back to your country because you as a child were rocked in the cradle of liberty and nursed at the breast of the goddess of truth. Leave the world better because you, my child, dwelt in it."

He was quick to offer a visitor a glass of whiskey and a place to stay; many mornings Anne Higgins rose to find a tramp asleep on her kitchen floor. And Michael Higgins too frequently allowed his passions to stand before financial reality, as when he co-sponsored a speaking engagement for Henry George at a local hotel. He funded the event with money he needed to buy coal for the winter. The Higgins family suffered as a result.

While poverty constantly threatened the large family, the domestic toilings of the mother and the eldest daughter, Mary, helped them survive. But Anne Higgins died of consumption at age forty-eight in March 1899. Bob Higgins, the youngest of the eleven living children, was then only five years old. His sisters — Mary, Nan, Margaret and Ethel — became surrogate mothers both to him and his next oldest brother, Dick. Michael Higgins, meanwhile, lost much of his spirit following his wife's death.

The daughters eventually sent Bob to Highfield School in Hamilton, Ontario. The siblings scattered throughout the country and by the time of their father's death in 1926, only son Joe remained in Corning. Bob Higgins kept in touch with his father through the years, though he communicated more frequently with his sisters, especially Mary.

Bob Higgins came into his own as an athlete at Highfield.

He played rugby, cricket and hockey, boxed and competed in track. In rugby he played left wing in 1907 and left half the following year. *The Highfield Review* stated, "Murray and Higgins are more like boys of eighteen than of fifteen. They are big, strong, clever players." He was captain of the rugby team in 1909, playing center half, and in the team photo sits in the middle with the rugby ball in hand. "He has a thorough knowledge of the game and the necessary control over his men," the school paper wrote. Higgins relished his leadership role and was later captain of his football team at both Peddie Institute and Penn State.

Of his cricket endeavors, the paper said, "Highfield gained their total with five wickets still in hand, thanks again to Higgins, who played very well, getting 32."

Higgins won the finals of the annual boxing tournament in the heavyweight class. The report of the bout said, "In the first round Higgins did all the aggressive work. In the second round Higgins made some very vicious uppercuts which almost invariably found their mark. In the third, Sweeny being winded, Higgins began to show up better and got the decision on straight boxing."

Higgins also won the "All-Round" track and field championship, his best event being the pole vault.

The young Higgins wrote of his accomplishment in May 1909 to his sister Mary. "Don't faint or anything, but brace yourself against the wall...I won the championship of the school. Are you still alive? It was the greatest surprise of my life. I did not even try to win it...When Mr. Collinson said Higgins is the winner of the Championship, I thought he had made a mistake, and then he said it again so I went up and got the cup."

The school paper predicted Higgins's future on the field of play: "He is a powerful and well built lad and capable of great success in athletic work."

Higgins's sisters gathered the necessary funds to send him on to Peddie Institute, a boys' Baptist prep school of three-hundred students in Highstown, New Jersey, just southeast of Princeton University. Higgins enrolled as a sophomore and listed his sister Margaret's New York City address as his own. Higgins was forever grateful to his sisters and later wrote,

"As the baby of a large family, no one can really appreciate sisters more than I do. In a nutshell, had it not been for my four wonderful sisters our family would never have made it — not even to first base. In fact we could have never had a chance for the first time at the plate."

The tender care of his sisters instilled in Higgins an appreciation for correct behavior toward women and an allegiance to proper manners in general. Many of the football players he coached at Penn State would learn from Higgins "how to act," and long after their playing careers would praise their old coach in this light.

Higgins learned the game of football at Peddie from his coach, Morris Midkiff, who was the first great influence on Higgins outside of his family. Midkiff taught clean football, which was not a common practice in the game's early years. He tried to use the sport as a foundation on which to build character in his players.

Midkiff stressed the fundamentals of blocking and tackling. Higgins later incorporated this simple philosophy unlike some of his less successful coaching peers. Midkiff once said, "Any coach whose boys are well grounded in those fundamentals will be sending players to college who will compel the best coaches to notice them, but no college coach is going to notice the boy who knows a hundred tricky formations, but whose blocking merits a fine for criminal negligence and whose tackling looks as if he were trying to give somebody a shampoo."

Midkiff's first year as the football coach at Peddie, 1910, was the season before Higgins arrived on the varsity scene. One loss and a tie were the only blemishes on Midkiff's debut. The senior captain of the squad was Dave Paddock, who went on to letter four years as a quarterback at the University of Georgia and make the All-Southern Conference team in 1914. Paddock was captain of the 1914 Georgia team. A center on that Peddie team, Kenneth Sprague, played ball at Brown. Three other linemen played ball for Lafayette and another at Yale. Midkiff had plenty of talent returning, but felt he needed someone to provide a spark. Midkiff recalled meeting Higgins:

"The day before school opened in 1911, I walked down to

the ramshackle old Highstown station to watch the trains come in with the newly arriving students. None of the new boys looked like good football prospects. Disappointed, I had started to return to the campus, when a most peculiar individual stepped from the train. First, there was a derby hat at least half a size too small to cover the bronze curly locks which propelled luxuriantly at the rear over a collar surrounding a neck somewhat the worse for coal dust. The collar was set off by a cravat which exposed the collar button, but the wrinkled coat seemed to cover a pair of lumpy shoulders and the baggy trousers bulged at the calves. Furthermore, the canvas-covered telescope suitcase swung from a hand like the hand of Providence, attached to about six feet of what didn't look like a student, but did appear to be considerable of a man.

"In the hope against belief that this fellow might be coming to school, I accosted him. He admitted that he was looking for the school and had ridden all night by day coach from Toronto to find it. No, he had never played our American game of football; he had played a little rugby in Canada. 'But you see, sir, I expect it will take all my time for my studies.' Great grief! All this in soprano! He looked like a football player, but he dressed like a farmer at a county fair and he talked like a female impersonator.

"However, after I had wheeled him over to the gymnasium, seen him stripped, and watched John Plant, our physical director, take his measurements, I began to dream dreams and see visions. That afternoon, with the exception of little George Dunning, whose record of ten flat for the hundred still adorns our gymnasium walls, the newcomer outran every other man on the squad in a fifty-yard sprint. The first time this ladylike person kicked the ball it spiraled over fifty yards. So, before two days had passed, despite the fact that the boys dubbed him 'Mamie' because of the soprano voice, I knew who was going to play right end for me that year.

"My second year at Peddie was, to say the least, a salubrious one for my reputation as a coach. Three of the players — Endicott, guard; Garrett, fullback; and Higgins — later captained their college teams. Garrett led one of Foster Sanford's best teams at Rutgers. Endicott, as captain at Swarthmore, was rated by many as an All-American tackle.

By the time we had scored our last touchdown in 1911, on a pass to Bob Higgins, we had won all nine of our games and had rolled up 180 points to our opponents' zero for the season. I was now, as are all coaches to whom the gods award such material, locally rated a football genius."

Higgins fell in love with football, but he excelled at all sports. He stood just over five-feet, ten-inches tall and graduated with nearly 180 hardened pounds. He was the school's champion heavyweight boxer for two years. He played center on the basketball team for two years, one year in which the squad went undefeated and won the state championship. He played baseball for two seasons and he was captain of the hockey team. He competed in track for three years and ran on the Peddie relay team, which was one of the best prep foursomes in the state. It ran in events held at many large universities such as Princeton and Rutgers. But no relay event was bigger than the annual Penn Relays in Philadelphia, and Higgins and the Peddie team twice competed in that famous meet. The Penn Relays so impressed Higgins that he attended every year while a student at Penn State.

A part of the tradition was for Higgins to hop a freight. Once he was nearly nabbed by soldiers who were guarding bridges, tunnels and railroad crossings throughout the state in response to the turbulence of World War I. At Lock Haven, a guard threatened to shoot Higgins when he failed to heed a "Hands up!" order. Higgins slipped off the other side of the train and scampered to freedom. But he still made it to the meet.

Along with Midkiff, two other men influenced Higgins while he was a student at Peddie. One was headmaster Dr. Roger Swetland, who was said to be a man of "vision, judgment and action." There was no questioning his authority or the rigid disciplinary penalties he handed down. One boy calculated that Peddie students had walked for 2,731 hours along the guard path behind the gymnasium in the fall of 1912. The young, exuberant Higgins contributed his fair share of footwork to the total.

However, the headmaster was also said to have possessed "a sympathetic kindness under his outward austerity." Most importantly, "he was perceptive in sizing up the worth of a boy."

John Plant had played football at Peddie in 1904 and became athletic director in 1906. He served in that position until 1924. "The Old Roman," as he was called, emphasized clean play and sportsmanship above all else. Higgins and the other Peddie athletes so admired Plant that when fire destroyed his Chalmers automobile in 1912, the students raised enough money to buy him a new car of the same make. Plant's favorite line was: "A Peddie sport for every boy." Plant coached Higgins in basketball, track and boxing.

In 1994, at age ninety-eight, the oldest living alumnus of Peddie Institute, Guy White, recalled his friend Higgins. White was two years younger than Higgins. He and the other underclassmen admired Higgins for his athletic accomplishments and almost considered him a member of the faculty. The younger boys tried to hang out with "The Hig" as much as possible.

White was a small boy and somewhat stoop-shouldered. Higgins in his good-natured manner habitually gave White a playful slap on the back to straighten him up.

"The problem with that was he was a real big guy and I was a little guy," White said. "He didn't realize that some of those slaps had a sting to them. One day I put some thumb tacks through a thin piece of cardboard, put the cardboard on my back and put on my blazer. Next time he slapped me on the back he tore his hand up pretty good."

"You shouldn't have done that," Higgins said in a threatening tone as he flexed his punctured hand.

"You shouldn't hit me so hard," White squeaked.

Realizing that the smaller boy had been suffering and that his blazer was now ruined, Higgins smiled and shook hands with his buddy.

"He was a wonderful person," White said. "He would do anything for you. He played all of the sports and was very strong and husky, but he was never a rough kind of guy."

White recalled that Higgins's end play on the football field stood out every game. "He was always making a long run or doing something that had us cheering for him," White said. "We didn't see how we could ever be beat with Bob Higgins on our side."

Even classmates the same age as Higgins looked up to him. He was wise and responsible, and especially fun to be with. His classmates referred to him as a "tramp" because he always stayed near the school, even during holidays. Higgins had little choice: he had to work to match his sisters' funds for his schooling, which approached three hundred dollars a year for tuition, room and board. His friends more sympathetically saw him as "alone in the world" for he really had no other home. He had no desire to return to Corning and impose upon his father's distressed spiritual and financial situation. In the spring of 1912 Higgins wrote to his sister Mary: "I wish you a very happy Easter. I am at school working a little now. All the fellows have gone home again for the Easter holidays. As I am waiting on tables I get my board free. I was over to the Baptist Church last night and the school children from the town had a few exercises and the children did awfully well. I am going to try and get a job as a life saver on the beach this summer. I think it would be better than to drive a car. There are four fellows here who do that every summer. Do you ever hear from (brother) Dick? I never do. Is he still in NY? All the Kellogg Farm burnt on one side of the road. You know that is the place I worked last summer. I hope you have had a pleasant Easter. The school is going to build a new house next year and in five years expects to be the largest school in the country. Your loving brother, Bob."

In May he followed up to Mary: "Your letter received today and also the check which I thank you for very much. I am going to be a life saver at a hotel where people go in bathing. It is easy work and with good nice people. The fellow I am going with was down there last year and he said he made $200, so I think I shall be able to get along all right don't you. The reports for the last six weeks just came out and I am glad to say I passed in every subject, although not high marks but nevertheless I passed. School lets out on the 12th of June then I think I will go to New York and stay there until the 17th, then to the ocean until September. I hope you can come down because it would seem good to see you again. It seems about five years since I last saw you. This fellow I am going to work with is studying for the ministry. So every time I say a word that is not fit for the drawing room he tells me about it. I am glad I am not in Corning. Your loving brother, Bob."

When the summer came and went, Higgins starred once again on the gridiron as an end and punter as Midkiff's Peddie squad won six and lost two. But even as late as the winter of his junior year in December 1912, Higgins had yet to imagine playing football in college. He expected to attend Cornell University in Ithaca, New York. His sister, Mary, wanted him to go there.

That December he wrote Mary: "I don't think I will be able to get into Cornell next year and if I am not I will finish here and go there in '15. I am working very well now and my lessons are becoming easier to me. I spent Thanksgiving at one of the fellow's houses and he showed me a very nice time, but you know I never have the kind of times I had when in Canada, and when I get out of Cornell that's where you and I are going. I hope you had a pleasant Thanksgiving? I think I will try and get some kind of a job for the Christmas holidays as I haven't a cent and (sister) Nan is helping Dick this year so I can't look to her. But you remember I don't look to you for anything, so this is not a gentle hint. I had some kidney trouble and the doctor bill was $12, so when I got that paid my Xmas presents looked few and far between. We haven't had any snow as yet and the grass is as green as ever. Your loving brother, Bob."

Higgins, now called "Hig" by his schoolmates, was elected senior captain of the football team in 1913. He soon began to hear from colleges and universities. Playing right end and again demonstrating his powerful punting form, Higgins led the squad to a 6-1 record. Peddie won by such lopsided scores as 53-0, 61-0, 60-0, 93-0 and 91-0. The notion of holding down the score against weaker foes was not yet in vogue. Only Lawrenceville scored against Peddie in the only game Peddie lost, 15-7. Higgins was recognized as "one of the best schoolboy ends in the east." Midkiff said, "Higgins is a player who is always cool and is constantly thinking."

The school paper reported that following the season at the football banquet, "Captain Higgins spoke of the loyalty toward him as captain, and it was here first made public that under his direction a prayer meeting had been held by the team before entering on the field during the entire season."

The Peddie paper also reported that Penn, Penn State, Harvard and Yale had asked Higgins to consider them before he selected a college. The prospect of student-aid while attending college attracted Higgins, who for too long had relied on his sisters to share the burden of his education.

Still, Higgins didn't know where he was going when he graduated from Peddie Institute on June 14, 1914. He was one of twenty-three to graduate. He would miss the frequent "sings" on the steps of old Wilson Hall, and the playful but aggressive class rivalries that usually resulted in bruises and torn clothing on class banner day. He would miss Peddie and he would never forget it, returning often in later years.

But the time had come to move on, and many events were unfolding in the world abroad and close to home. Higgins prepared to embark on the most exciting years of his life.

§ 3 §
Football Comes Of Age

ON JUNE 28, 1914, two weeks after twenty-year-old Bob Higgins graduated from Peddie Institute, a nineteen-year-old student named Gavrilo Princip shot and killed Austrian Archduke Francis Ferdinand and his wife as they left the Town Hall in Sarajevo, capital of Bosnia. The murder was the spark that set off World War I. Tensions had been smoldering since the Franco-Prussian War of 1870, when Germany began building a military power. Testy nationalist feelings had as far back as 1882 resulted in the Triple Alliance of Germany, Austria-Hungary and Italy. And in 1907, concerned over Germany's intentions, France, England and Russia overlooked their own differences and formed the Triple Entente. A month after the assassination, Austria-Hungary declared war on Serbia. Russia began to mobilize its military. On August 1st, Germany declared war on Russia and two days later declared war on France. By the end of the month, following Germany's conquest of Belgium, England had entered the war.

But Bob Higgins in 1914, like most people in America, was not yet overly concerned about developments across the Atlantic. That summer, as he weighed his growing number of college options, Higgins was more interested in an event gaining attention on the domestic front. In New York City, Higgins's sister Margaret, the girl who had once gone with her father to dig up her brother's grave for a death mask, had become an international figure as she founded and pioneered the birth control movement. She had married years earlier and was now well known as Margaret Sanger.

After leaving Corning, Margaret had taken up nursing

and attended training school in White Plains, New York. She received post-graduate nursing education in Manhattan. She married Bill Sanger, an architect and painter, and they associated with a liberal group then living in New York, including journalist Jack Reed and feminist Emma Goldman. In 1912, as a visiting nurse in the city's lower east side, Sanger cared for a seriously ill woman who had given herself an abortion. The lady begged Sanger for advice on how to prevent more pregnancies. Sanger had no answers for her. Later that year the same lady aborted herself again, only this time the woman died. Sanger became committed to the cause of contraception. She began to study methods used in Europe.

In early 1914, as colleges were contacting prep sensation Higgins, his older sister announced a national campaign of contraception education based on the grounds of economics and feminism. She called the current situation of the married woman "biological slavery." She coined the term "birth control" and published a monthly magazine, *The Woman Rebel*, to disseminate her message. But the postmaster declared the magazine obscene and refused to mail it. The government arrested and indicted Sanger, who fled to Montreal and then to London.

The following year, authorities arrested Bill Sanger for distributing Margaret's birth control pamphlet entitled "Family Limitations." Margaret returned to the U.S. in 1915 and the obscenity charges were dropped, largely as a result of public sympathy over the death of her daughter, Peggy. A few months later Sanger organized the National Birth Control League, which later became the Planned Parenthood Federation of America.

In October 1916, Sanger, along with her sister Ethel Byrne, opened America's first birth control clinic in Brooklyn. They were arrested for distributing contraceptives. Ethel was convicted and began a hunger strike at Blackwell's Island Prison. The governor released her after eleven days. Sanger was convicted and imprisoned for thirty days in 1917. But in an appeal of the case in 1918, the New York Court of Appeals judge, while upholding the conviction, gave physicians the right to give advice for "cure and prevention of disease," which was the birth control movement's first legal breakthrough.

Certainly Bob's sister Margaret, who was ten years his senior, had inherited their father's inclination toward freedom of expression and battling the status quo. Many years later, one of Bob Higgins's three daughters, Mary Ann, asked him what he had thought of Margaret's rise to national notoriety. "Oh it was very embarrassing," Higgins replied. Higgins agreed with his sister's cause, however, and years later would help her seek support of birth control legislation. But the topic was not one to bring up during a dinner party in the era of the Great War, and as a young man starring on the Penn State gridiron, Higgins naturally preferred to sidestep the red-faced discomfort brought on by its mention.

Higgins, meanwhile, decided on Penn State College and enrolled in the fall of 1914. The man who reeled him in was Dick Harlow, a former Penn State tackle (1910-1911), who was an assistant coach for head coach Bill Hollenback. As the recruiting pressure mounted on Higgins, Harlow invited the young man on a trip to the Pocono Mountains in northeast Pennsylvania. Harlow basically isolated Higgins until school opened. In addition to hiding Higgins from other college recruiters, Harlow may have been keeping him away from his sister Mary, who apparently wanted him to attend Cornell.

College football by 1914 was beginning to surge in popularity. The game was not yet fifty years old, dating back to the first officially-recognized intercollegiate football game between Rutgers and Princeton on November 6, 1869. But only since 1906 had major rule changes modernized the game. President Teddy Roosevelt, in October 1905, had seen a photo of a bloodied and beaten Swarthmore lineman named Bob Maxwell who was the victim of an onslaught from the Penn team. Roosevelt summoned representatives from Harvard, Yale and Princeton to the White House and told them to clean up the game and give it some structure. Eighteen players had died by the end of that season. Ganging up on the opponent's best player was an all-too-common scheme. The Maxwell Award, begun in 1937 and given annually to college football's outstanding player, was named for Swarthmore's Bob Maxwell, who later became a sportswriter.

Football officials and college delegates met twice in December in New York City. A rules meeting, from which came an organization that would become the National Collegiate Athletic Association (NCAA), was held January 12, 1906. Walter Camp of Yale and Captain Palmer Pierce of Army spearheaded the rules movement. They legalized the forward pass; established a neutral zone the length of the ball between the opposing lines; required a minimum of six players on the offensive line; raised first down yardage from five to ten yards in three downs; reduced game time from seventy to sixty minutes and divided the game into halves.

From 1907 to 1912 the college game implemented additional rules which served both to make it more exciting and reduce the number of serious injuries. Outlawed were the flying tackle and interlocking interference (a form of the wedge). It became illegal to use one's hands, arms or body to push, pull or hold upon his feet the player carrying the ball. Seven men were required to be on the offensive line. Points for a field goal were reduced from four to three and a touchdown was increased from five points to six. Halves were divided into two fifteen-minute quarters. Number of downs to keep possession of the ball went from three to four. A player withdrawn from the game could return in an ensuing quarter, instead of having to remain out for the duration of the game. The playing field decreased from 110 to 100 yards, but ten-yard end zones were created in which a forward pass could be caught.

Other rule changes slowly liberalized the forward pass. At first the pass had to cross the line of scrimmage within five yards from where the ball had been put into play. In 1910 the five-yard restriction was removed and the pass could cross the line of scrimmage anywhere. In 1912 the receiver became protected by rules prohibiting defensive players from interfering with him. The receiver had previously been fair game.

Thus, when Higgins entered Penn State, college football was largely recognizable as the game we know today.

College football was producing legendary figures and teams by 1914. Walter Camp starred as a halfback for Yale from 1876 to 1881 and served Yale as an advisory coach for the next eighteen years. Pudge Heffelfinger would be recognized as one of the greatest linemen ever long after he played at Minnesota in 1889-1891. Amos Alonzo Stagg was a star end for Yale in 1888-1889 and began a 41-year coaching career at Chicago in 1892, which included unbeaten teams in 1899, 1905, 1908, 1913 and 1924. A great innovator, Stagg invented the center snap, the huddle, the man in motion, the backfield shift, the principle of option pass or run and various defensive schemes.

Fielding "Hurry Up" Yost coached Michigan to four consecutive unbeaten seasons from 1901 to 1904. Michigan didn't lose until Stagg's Chicago team beat the Wolverines 2-0 in the final game of the 1905 season, which gave Chicago a 9-0 record and a share of the mythical national championship with Yale. The largest college football crowd to date, 43,000, watched Yale preserve its unbeaten season that year by nipping Harvard 6-0. Yale remained undefeated through the 1906 and 1907 seasons. Penn, coached by Sol Metzger, was the best team in the country in 1908 with an 11-0-1 record. Its best running back was Wild Bill Hollenback, who in a few years would coach Penn State into the national picture. Penn's 6-6 tie in 1908 came against Pop Warner's Carlisle Indians. A sophomore running back named Jim Thorpe made third team All-American for Carlisle that season.

Coach Howard Harding Jones, an end at Yale from 1905-1907, coached Yale to a 10-0 season in 1909. The Bulldogs featured six first-team All-Americans. Percy Haughton, who played fullback and tackle at Harvard, coached the Crimson to an unbeaten season in 1910, one of his five undefeated Harvard teams.

Thorpe, 6-1, 185 pounds, left Carlisle for two years to play semi-pro baseball but returned in 1911 and 1912, making All-American both years. Warner's eleven went 11-1 in 1911. Thorpe had his greatest afternoon against Harvard as he booted four field goals in an 18-15 win. Carlisle played an amazing fourteen games in 1912, going 12-1-1 and scoring 505 points with Thorpe accounting for 198 of them and scoring twenty-five touchdowns. Only Penn, which had lost its first four games of the season, beat Carlisle, 34-26. Between the 1911 and 1912 football seasons, Thorpe took time out to capture the Pentathlon and Decathlon events at the Winter Olympics in 1912 in Stockholm, Sweden. Though they barely missed each other in college, Thorpe and Higgins later met on the professional field of play.

The best team in the nation in 1912 was Haughton's Harvard, going 9-0.

The following season, 1913, is best remembered for the coming of age of the forward pass in the Notre Dame-Army clash. Notre Dame was an underdog when it invaded West Point, but the Irish prevailed, 35-13. Quarterback Gus Dorais completed thirteen of seventeen passes for 243 yards in what was reported as the greatest passing exhibition ever seen. His primary receiver was the team's captain, senior end Knute Rockne, who hauled one in for a 35-yard touchdown. It was Army's only loss of the season. Notre Dame, coached by G. W. Philbrook, went undefeated, as did Stagg's Chicago and Haughton's Harvard.

Penn State, which had fielded its first football team in 1887, first gained national respect in 1906. Coached by Tom Fennell, who had played at Cornell, Penn State won eight, lost one and tied one and was considered one of the nation's top ten teams. The only loss came to undefeated Yale, 10-0. These were the only points the Penn State defense allowed all season. Penn State also placed its first player ever on Walter Camp's All-American first team in 1906 — center W.T. "Mother" Dunn.

Penn State returned to national prominence during the 1911 and 1912 seasons under head coach Bill Hollenback. He had become head coach in 1909 and went 5-0-2 in his debut. The team christened its new campus playing site for the 1909 season New Beaver Field. The previous site, Old Beaver Field, which consisted of a 500-seat grandstand, was first used in 1893 and named for James A. Beaver, a Civil War brigadier general, superior court judge, governor of Pennsylvania and at intervals from 1874 to 1914 president of the University's board of trustees.

Following the successful season in 1909, Hollenback left for a one-year coaching stint at Missouri in 1910. His brother, Jack Hollenback, filled in and coached the Lions to a 5-2-1 record.

Hollenback didn't like Missouri and returned to Penn State as head coach for the 1911 season. The Lions went 8-0-

1 in 1911 and 8-0 in 1912. Both teams were considered among the five best in the country. Dexter Very, captain of the 1911 team, made second team All-American at end both years. Pete Mauthe, captain of the 1912 team, was a triple-threat fullback. Sophomore Shorty Miller, at five-feet, five-inches tall, was the quarterback both seasons, with Dutch Hermann backing him up in 1911. Hermann would become the school's first full-time freshman football coach in 1915 and serve on the staffs of Dick Harlow, Hugo Bezdek and Bob Higgins.

The 1911 season included a 5-0 win over Cornell with tackle Harlow blocking a punt that Dad Engle picked up and ran for the only score of the game (touchdowns went from five to six points after the 1911 season). Also in 1911, Penn State beat Penn 22-6 before fifteen thousand fans in Philadelphia. Miller returned the opening kickoff for a touchdown and scored again a few minutes later on a 32-yard run. The tie in 1911 came against Navy, 0-0, in Annapolis.

The 1912 team, led by Miller, Mauthe and Very, was perfect, allowing only six points while scoring 285 in eight games and whipping the likes of Washington & Jefferson, Cornell, Penn, Ohio State and Pittsburgh. Mauthe, an outstanding punter and placekicker in addition to his great skills at fullback, scored 119 points, including eleven touchdowns. Mauthe paced Penn State to a 38-0 win at Pittsburgh by kicking a 51-yard field goal with Miller holding. Mauthe also connected with Very on an unheard-of sixty-yard pass that set up a touchdown in the Pitt game.

The 1912 team featured Very and Al Wilson at the ends; Engle and Red Bebout at the tackles; Levi Lamb and Al Hansen at the guards; John Clark at center; Miller at quarterback; Dan Welty and Punk Berryman at the halfbacks; and Mauthe at fullback. Very was named first team All-American at end on several newspaper teams, but for the second year in a row had to settle for second team on the more prestigious Camp All-American squad.

Mauthe, Miller and Very would be inducted into the National Football Foundation College Football Hall of Fame, respectively, in 1957, 1974 and 1976.

Though Miller returned as captain for his senior season in 1913, Penn State fell to 2-6, losing the final six games of the season. One of the losses came against Notre Dame, 14-7, in State College, which marked Penn State's biggest home game up to that time. Notre Dame was led by senior captain Rockne.

This, then, was the era of American football into which Bob Higgins first stepped as a Nittany Lion in 1914. He unpacked his bags at the Track House, a three-story structure for varsity athletes built in 1903 adjacent to Old Beaver Field.

The season marked Hollenback's last as head football coach at Penn State. He would be the first of three head coaches for whom Higgins would play at Penn State. Higgins remembered Hollenback's fairness with his players and his disdain for swearing.

Despite the poor season in 1913, and the loss of quarterback Miller and tackle Bebout to graduation, and the academic ineligibility of Berryman, Hollenback felt he had enough material to field a successful team, particularly if Higgins lived up to his potential. Higgins started as a freshman in 1914, which preceded by a year the rule that made freshmen ineligible to play varsity ball.

Though just a freshman, Higgins's leadership and knowledge of sports prompted head coach Hollenback to seek his assistance. In an effort to spruce up the offense, Hollenback had Higgins instill many of the wide-open features of rugby into the offensive game plan. Higgins had played three years of rugby while attending Highfield in Canada. A newspaper report stated, "Under the direction of Higgins and Hollenback, Penn State's varsity has spent most of the week hurling the ball to all corners of the field, until the heads of the scrub and freshman teams were whirling."

The season started with four easy home wins over Westminster, Muhlenberg, Gettysburg and Ursinus. In his debut against Westminster, Higgins ran forty yards to set up a score in the 13-0 win.

Then it was time to travel to Cambridge, Massachusetts to play Harvard. Head coach Percy Haughton had put together another powerful Crimson team in 1914. Harvard had gone undefeated in both 1912 and 1913 and was unbeaten going into the Penn State game on October 24. Almost 22,000 fans turned out for the battle of the unbeatens, including Higgins's sister Margaret Sanger, who was on the lecture circuit in Cambridge. This was the only football game she ever saw her brother play. Inspired by Margaret's presence and taking on mighty Harvard, Higgins was at his best.

Penn State scored first on a 33-yard field goal by Levi Lamb, and scored again in the opening period on fullback Jeff Clark's thirteen-yard touchdown run, capping a long drive spearheaded by quarterback Don James. Harvard pulled close before halftime, scoring on a pass from All-American Fred Bradlee to Jeff Coolidge. The halftime score was 10-6.

Penn State continued to outplay Harvard in the third quarter as the defense, paced by 185-pound freshman Higgins, shut down the Harvard offense. A Tobin field goal gave Penn State a 13-6 lead and the game appeared in the bag with less than two minutes to play. But Penn State fumbled a Harvard punt and Harvard recovered near midfield.

Haughton promptly substituted a speedster named Westmore Wilcox, better known for running track than playing football. He took a lateral at the line and jetted for the touchdown. A newspaper account of run stated: "It was the culmination of one of the most exciting games witnessed in the stadium in many years. The life saving run of Wilcox will go down in history as one of the greatest runs that have taken place on the gridiron." The extra point tied it 13-13, which is how it ended. That same score would visit Higgins again — almost forty years later — in the biggest game of his coaching career. Penn State held Harvard to just two first downs and ninety-five yards rushing, half of that coming on Wilcox's touchdown.

"The visitors outrushed, outkicked and outmaneuvered the Crimson," a game story reported. "Higgins's end playing was the best seen in the Harvard stadium all season."

Coach Hollenback began comparing Higgins to former Penn State end Dexter Very. Higgins would always remember the Harvard game not for his outstanding performance but as one of the cleanest games he ever played in.

Penn State's lineup for the game included Higgins at left end, George Kratt at left tackle, Ran Miller at left guard, Bill Wood at center, Cecil McDowell at right guard, Lamb at right tackle, Whitey Thomas and A.M. Barron both seeing action at right end, James the quarterback, Welty and Edgerton running at left half, captain Yegg Tobin at right half and Clark at fullback.

On the same day Penn State tied Harvard, Yale lost its first game of the season to Washington & Jefferson. One paper the morning after the games announced, "Yale and Harvard Disgraced!"

The pep rally bonfire the Monday night following the game literally exploded with excitement. Most of the school's enrollment of nearly two thousand students and almost that many locals assembled around the fifty-foot high woodpile, which had been saturated with gasoline. Captain Tobin tossed on the torch and the ensuing explosion knocked him off his feet, severely burning his face and hands. Windows shattered more than a hundred yards away. Tobin was hospitalized and the season soured. Penn State, without Tobin, won the following week 17-0 over Lafayette, which gave Penn State a 5-0-1 record. But the Nittany Lions, still without Tobin, lost to Lehigh 20-7. Michigan State shut down Penn State 6-3 and Pittsburgh beat the Lions 13-3 to close the season despite a great defensive performance by Higgins in which he sacked six Pitt runners for losses. Tobin attempted to play the final two games with bandaged hands, but he wasn't up to speed. The 5-3-1 record was a disappointment after a beginning that had Penn State bound for a high national ranking. Army, coached by Charlie Daly with Bob Neyland playing end, and Bob Zuppke's Illinois were considered the two best teams in the land, followed by Harvard which finished undefeated, albeit with two ties.

Freshman Higgins had lived up to his reputation. The following March (1915), Higgins received a letter from Parke Davis, one of the country's most respected football historians:

My dear sir:

You will recall me perhaps as Princeton's member of the Intercollegiate Football Rules Committee.

I have been asked by a magazine of national circulation to write for it an article on the greatest football players in the entire United States who will be playing next fall. Now you are one of my selections for this national galaxy of stars, provided that you will be playing next fall. If you will be, please send me a full sketch of your athletic career, all sports, but with particular reference to football, giving me all of your greatest exploits and achievements. I also would like to have a picture of you in football suit, and an action picture of you in a game, if available. Do not be modest in your sketch for I shall keep it confidential and will transcribe its words into my own.

   Thank you for your courtesy, I am,
   Parke H. Davis

   Despite the acclaim, a nasty rumor surfaced concerning Higgins. A newspaper reported that Higgins would leave Penn State and enter Rutgers, following his roommate who had already done so. The roommate had wired Higgins to come on.

   But the rumor was ill-found and Higgins was too busy playing other sports at Penn State to transfer anywhere. He boxed and played baseball his freshman year. He was in splendid physical condition when the 1915 season opened.

   Hollenback opted to enter private business following the 1914 season, which opened the door for assistant Dick Harlow to become head coach. Higgins played for Harlow in 1915 and 1916. Harlow's devotion to fundamentals and his skillful handling of personnel made a strong impression on Higgins.

   Penn State won seven and lost two in 1915. Harlow won his first five games, including a 13-3 whipping of Penn at Franklin Field in Philadelphia. Penn led 3-0 at half, but a forty-yard touchdown run by Punk Berryman (back from academic ineligibility) in the third quarter put Penn State ahead. The Lions scored again in the third quarter on a forty-yard pass from quarterback Stan Ewing to Higgins. Sophomore Higgins led a dominating defense that shut out Penn in the second half and preserved the win.

   Newspapers billed the upcoming game as Harvard versus Higgins. A report stated, "Higgins, the star end who came near defeating the Crimson last year, is still playing and will bother the Crimson just as much as ever."

   Higgins turned in another outstanding game, but the Penn State bubble burst in the road match as Harvard won

41

13-0. Penn State led in total yardage, but fumbles and penalties killed the Lions' chances. Harvard scored first when it recovered a dropped punt in the end zone. Penn State scored on a 39-yard run in the second quarter but it was called back.

"Penn State outclassed and outplayed Harvard so far in every department of the game, that the wonder is she did not smother the Crimson by at least three touchdowns," an account of the game said. "The work of end Higgins of Penn State was as brilliant a piece of end play as the year has produced. He slowed Eddie Mahan down to a walk. That in itself is a feat worthy of immortality."

Harvard's Mahan was one of the great all-time fullbacks.

Penn State rebounded to defeat Lehigh and Lafayette, but dropped the season finale at Pittsburgh 20-0. Pop Warner had left Carlisle for Pitt prior to the season. All-American center Bob Peck and backs Jimmy DeHart and George McLaren drove the Panthers to an 8-0 season.

Following the season Walter Camp named Higgins to his All-American second team. Everybody else picked Higgins on their annual first teams, including Michigan head coach Fielding Yost, Navy coach Jonas Ingram, International News Service sportswriter Frank Menke, and the Boston Post newspaper, which wrote: "Higgins has a wonderful knowledge of end play. He is a great tackler, fast down the field under kicks, a quick fathomer of interference, and a spectacular receiver of forward passes."

Of course college life wasn't all football for the gregarious Higgins. For example, once a year the athletes at the Track House held a dinner party. The catch was that every piece of food and china had to be stolen. This led to some interesting expeditions around campus. Chickens were had in the wee hours from area farms; salt and pepper procured from professors; silverware rounded up at local eateries. Higgins himself led a mission to nearby Bellefonte and secured the dinner wine from the parish priest.

One of Higgins's best buddies was Ben Jones, better known as "Casey." He played with Higgins on the 1916 team and then entered the service as a pilot with Captain Eddie Rickenbacker's squadron in France. Higgins and Jones teamed up several times behind the front lines in Europe for a night out when they could arrange a leave. Higgins always kidded Jones for the preferential treatment he and other of Rickenbacker's pilots received. "You get a bed to sleep in and get to eat ice cream," Higgins said. "I sleep in a ditch and eat mud."

The two remained friends for life. The importance of Jones's recruiting support for head coach Higgins in the 1930s will be explored in a subsequent chapter.

Higgins became a brother in Beta Theta Pi fraternity, the same fraternity his wife, Virginia, served as house mother years later. Several of Higgins's teammates were also members of the frat and during a game they might be heard formally addressing each other as in, "Nice tackle, brother Bob."

Higgins appeared destined for Camp's first team his junior season in 1916, and Penn State, with several returning starters, appeared ready to establish itself as a national power. But Higgins lost Camp's endorsement and Penn State fell from grace with losses to traditional rivals Penn, 15-0, and Pittsburgh, 31-0. Penn State won the other eight games on its schedule but the victories, mostly against weak opposition, paled beside the two losses. Penn State supporters winced once again at Pitt's success under Warner. For the second straight season the Panthers went undefeated. Pitt and unbeaten Army, coached by Daly and led by All-American Elmer Oliphant, rated as the best teams in the nation.

During the off-season Higgins kept one eye on his books and the other on the war in Europe. He stayed in shape by joining the wrestling team with the season in progress in early 1917. Penn State had won its first two meets against Cornell and Princeton when Higgins became a regular in the 175-pound class, filling in for a wrestler who had withdrawn from school. Higgins wrestled in the final four matches of the season, winning two with pins, taking another in a decision and wrestling to a draw to finish 3-0-1 in a sport absolutely new to him. The Penn State squad finished the season with a 6-0 record. A newspaper reported, "To Ed Lewis, the coach, goes the bulk of the credit for State's performances. He developed the 1917 squad from green material. Five of the seven men to win wrestling honors were new on the team." The season marked Penn State's eighth with a wrestling squad, with just four losses in those eight seasons.

Higgins looked forward to playing his senior year of football and had by now tossed around the idea of becoming a coach. His teammates elected him captain for the 1917 season. But Higgins wouldn't be playing football come September. America was going to war, and Bob Higgins was going with it.

§ 4 §
A Yankee In Europe

I N THE FALL OF 1918 during a lull in the allied offensive along the Western Front, a U.S. soldier nestled in a trench heard another soldier singing from a nearby dugout. The soprano voice rang familiar.

"Where do you think you're going, Bob Higgins?" asked the soldier in the trench.

The singing ceased. The soprano voice replied, "I don't know who you are or where you're going, but I'm going to Berlin!"

In May of 1917 Higgins attended First Officers' Training Camp at Fort Niagara on Lake Erie. Commissioned a Second Lieutenant after ninety days there, he went to the Massachusetts Institute of Technology for special training in trench warfare and on to Camp Lee, Virginia. He was assigned to Company I, 318th Infantry, 80th Division, composed of Pennsylvania, West Virginia and Virginia men. The 80th wore the insignia of the Blue Ridge Mountains. Higgins and his division boarded the *Leviathan* at Hoboken, New Jersey and arrived in France on May 30, 1918.

The United States had declared war on Germany on April 6, 1917. German aggression in starting the war and the brutal invasion of Belgium in 1914 had turned many Americans against Germany. Then in May 1915 a German U-boat torpedoed the British passenger ship *Lusitania*. Of the twelve hundred passengers who were killed, 128 were U.S. citizens.

In an effort to cut off supplies from England and France, German submarines had orders to fire on any ships approaching or departing French and British coasts. Attacks on unarmed merchant ships caused the loss of a number of American ships and lives. President Woodrow Wilson warned Germany against future attacks, but Germany only increased its assault and additional American lives were lost in early 1917. Wilson asked Congress for a declaration of war and stated that America was "going to make the world safe for democracy."

The two major fronts at the beginning of the war were the Western Front in northern France and southwest Belgium, and the Eastern Front from the Black Sea to the Baltic. By the end of 1914 the war in the West had assumed the character it would retain through more than four years of brutal conflict — a static front with armies bogged down in trenches and dugouts behind snarls of barbed wire.

The war expanded as more countries entered the fray. Japan joined the Allies in 1914. Turkey joined the Central Powers, which was the Germany and Austria-Hungary alliance. But this alliance was now without Italy which dropped out of that pact and, in May 1915, entered the war on the side of the Allies. A new front was formed against Austria-Hungary from the Adriatic to Switzerland.

On the Western Front a series of bloody battles ensued. The number of casualties was mind-numbing. The French lost 125,000 men in an unsuccessful attempt to retake the city of Saint-Mihiel near the French-German border. Another 240,000 French lives were lost in an offensive near the cathedral city of Reims. The British sustained overwhelming losses in courageous fighting at Ypres in the northwest. The French defended the city of Verdun in 1916, sacrificing 542,000 in casualties while inflicting 434,000 casualties on the Germans. In the Battle of the Somme, British and German dead numbered a horrific 420,000 and 650,000, respectively.

The Allies prayed that the U.S. entry into the war would lift their spirits and break the deadly stalemate along the five-hundred-mile Western Front. Under the command of General John Pershing, the first wave of American soldiers came ashore in late June 1917 at the French port of Saint-Nazaire. By the end of June, American soldiers numbered just over sixteen thousand. On Armistice Day, November 11, 1918, the American Expeditionary Forces (A.E.F.) had surpassed two million.

Higgins and the 318th Infantry saw front line action

during the Meuse-Argonne offensive which began on September 26, 1918. It was one of the climactic battles of the war and followed the successful allied victory at Saint-Mihiel.

The Meuse-Argonne offensive was directed at the French city of Sedan, which Germany had captured early in the war. Sedan was a major railway hub through which German armies were supplied in the West.

Pershing's First Army planned to push north with the dense Argonne Forest on its left flank and the north-south flowing Meuse River on its right. Approximately 225,000 American troops in three corps, each with three divisions, stretched along a twenty-five mile front. Sedan was forty miles away.

Of the nine divisions, the 80th Division, including Higgins and the 318th Infantry, was second to the far right, between the Montfaucon hills to the west and the Heights of the Meuse to the east. The 80th Division along with the 33rd to its right and the 4th to its left, were part of the Third Corps under Major General Robert Lee Bullard.

The German army had four years of built-in entrenchment that rippled several lines deep with barbed wire, machine guns, cannons and concrete shelters. The Germans knew every inch of the countryside the Americans sought to take. Low country laced with swamps and brooks marked the terrain for Bullard's three divisions. The target of Higgins and the 80th Division was the town of Brieulles, in the bend of the Meuse River. Following three hours of shelling on the German lines, the U.S. soldiers advanced at 5:30 a.m. on September 26th and continued to advance until noon. But German artillery from the towering Montfaucon in the west and the high domes east of the Meuse River closed in on the exposed men of the 80th. They inched ahead all day, suffering nearly one thousand casualties while taking as many prisoners. The American drive to Sedan had advanced several bloodsoaked, precious miles. Higgins would later refer to the drive as a "foot race."

For the next six weeks the American First Army slowly pushed the Germans back to Sedan. It was during this action, on the left wing of the American advance, that Corporal Alvin York of the 82nd Division captured 132 Germans, kill-ing twenty-five, while taking an important hill. Near the center of the line, Colonel George Patton, destined to become one of the great generals of World War II, led the 1st Tank Brigade during the assault of the 37th Division

A week into the offensive Higgins's leadership and bravery earned him a promotion in the line to First Lieutenant. When not leading his men in the charge, he guided raiding parties that took out German snipers and captured dozens of prisoners.

Red Smith, perhaps the greatest sportswriter of all time, wrote of one incident depicting Higgins's fortitude at the front:

"It's hard to say where this story rightly begins but probably as good a place as any is a boisterous sector in the Argonne, about 15 miles from Verdun on October 5, 1918, the day they dragged Lieutenant John K. Hammitt, of Philadelphia, back out of the shellhole where he had lain for 27 hours.

"Jack Hammitt, of the 318th Infantry of the 80th Division, used to spit at machine-gun bullets when he heard the high-pitched 'Hyyonnning' beside his ear, but while leading an advance on October 4 he walked into a couple that didn't give him spitting notice, and he wasn't a hopeful case when they hauled him out the next day.

"His best friend, Lieutenant Robert Higgins, looked him over and told a pal, 'Well, I guess Jack's done,' and a few hours later went out to lead the advance himself.

"French tanks were supposed to precede the infantry, screening the charge, but things got a trifle overheated and the chauffeurs of the iron forts clambered out and started crawling back toward their lines, using the tanks as shields. That was when they heard a thin soprano voice, cracked with weariness and shaking with rage.

"'Gentlemen and soldiers of France,' the voice screamed, only it used synonyms not favored in diplomatic circles, 'get back in those things before I blow your eternally valiant guts out!'

"The Poilus may not have understood the English words, but the meaning of the tone was unmistakable and the figure that towered in their path, a hand grenade in each big fist, reduced doubt to a minimum. There they were, the imperial army of Germany behind them and Bob Higgins of Penn State, directly ahead. They made the obvious choice. They got back in their tanks, and the 318th drove on to a touchdown."

Another story involving Higgins concerned a lone German plane that repeatedly attacked an allied trench. When the plane returned yet again the Allies were ready and met it with a terrific barrage. The only weapon Higgins had was a six-shooter. He pulled it out and fired six times. The plane crashed and the British officers congratulated Higgins for downing it. "I believe I did get that plane," Higgins always joked.

The 80th Division captured more than eighteen hundred prisoners during its seven weeks on the front line. It suffered 1,241 dead and 4,788 wounded. American forces had nearly 53,000 killed and 203,000 wounded in the war.

In later years Higgins rarely spoke of his experience in combat, preferring instead to recall the better moments. "They say 'an old soldier never dies,' and I've often wondered if it isn't his memory that keeps him alive. For a soldier's memory does some peculiar things. As time passes he forgets the hardships — the empty stomachs, the sore feet, the mud and the rain, and all the nerve-wracking incidents of war — and remembers the carefree hours on leave, the rests behind the lines, and, above all, the easy comradeship with the best guys that ever lived."

Indeed, Higgins developed deep and lifelong friendships with a number of his World War I service buddies. They formed what they called "The Last Man's Club" and met annually for forty-six years at various locations in the Eastern U.S.

Vince Smith and Jack Hammitt, soldiers in the 80th Division, were in on the club's founding in Northern France in August 1918. In 1964, Smith, an attorney in Greensburg, Pennsylvania, recalled the momentous occasion:

"The 80th Division was brigaded with the British in Northern France. Our troops manned the trenches and were officered by the British. The American officers were observers — with no responsibilities.

"Elsie Janis, sweetheart of the American Expeditionary Forces, was entertaining in the area with headquarters in the only hotel in Doullens, about ten kilometers away from where we were quartered.

"Jack Hammitt said, 'I know Elsie Janis. Let's go to Doullens and see her.' We hopped in a lorry and went to the only bar in Doullens and learned that Elsie Janis, her mother and General Cronkhite, the commanding general of the 80th Division, with a couple of aides were having dinner in a private dining room. Hammitt sent a note in to Elsie, and she came into the bar, threw her arms around Hammitt and gave him a big smooch.

"Just then a French interpreter came into the bar and, after noticing the blue-ridge insignia on our sleeves, said, 'One of your officers was just killed.' All of us said, 'Who?' He got out his notebook and said, 'Frank Clemmer of Staunton, Virginia.

"We were proposing a toast to Frank Clemmer, and the interpreter said, 'Most of you fellows will be killed. You should have a bottle of rum for the last man that survives. I'll buy it. Bartender, how much is that bottle of Negrita Rhum?' The bartender said it was $2.40. Elsie Janis said, 'Let me present it,' and she made a little speech and presented me with the bottle for the last man who survived in the Last Man's Club."

Twelve soldiers originally formed the club and they posthumously recognized Clemmer as one of the original thirteen members. Ten of the original members were: attorney Smith; Hammitt, who would sit on the board of governors of the Philadelphia Stock Exchange; Sidney King, who would practice law in Virginia and serve as legal counsel for the N & W Railroad; Charles Sweeney, a career military officer who served in numerous high-ranking capacities for several allied countries in both world wars and other skirmishes around the globe; Edward Crane, who became president of a publishing company; Henry McWane, who became president of the Lynchburg Foundry and Machine Co. in Virginia; Guy Dirom, who became president of the A.S. White Co. of Lynchburg, Virginia; James Douglas, a real estate dealer of Alexandria, Virginia; Earl Shively, who became a politically influential attorney and counsel for the Pennsylvania Railroad Co.; and Higgins, bound for the National Football Foundation Hall of Fame.

Two original members never returned from the war. Frank "Ting" Culbertson of Sewickley, Pennsylvania and

Clovis Moomaw, a law professor at Washington & Lee in Lexington, Virginia, were both killed in action.

Twenty years after the war, club member Hammitt vividly recalled Culbertson's final moments in a letter to Higgins.

"On October 3, 1918 the Second Battalion was withdrawn from the lines for a rest, after having gained their objective. We pitched camp in the rear and were preparing a meal when Captain Moore was summoned to Battalion Headquarters. He returned in a few minutes and said we had to leave again for the front. Off we went on empty stomachs.

"We arrived in Nantillois between one and two a.m. October 4. We were instructed there that we were to go east on the road and report to a captain of the 4th Infantry of the 3rd Division and he would show us our position. I placed all the men and told them to lie down and rest. I went back to the dugout where Captain Moore and Ting were waiting. I promptly crawled in an old packing box to try to get some sleep. When Ting saw me do this, he got in the other half of the box with the remark, 'This is damned uncomfortable,' Ting being about six feet, three inches. I said to him in a kidding way, 'Don't worry, Ting, we will probably be dead tomorrow night and won't have to worry about a place to sleep.' To my surprise, a strange look appeared on his face and he said, 'Jack, please let us not talk about it.' I knew then that he felt he was going to get it.

"We were just dozing off when a runner came dashing up and asked Captain Moore to report to headquarters in Nantillois at once. He did so and returned in a few minutes all excited and stated that something phony had been pulled on us. That we had been placed in the wrong direction by this unknown captain. Later, I was interviewed by a Colonel of the 4th Infantry in Washington, and it developed the supposed captain was a German spy.

"We had to get our troops turned as we were facing the 4th Division A.E.F. instead of the Germans. Ting and I immediately got to work and turned our men, barely in time. While we were in the dugout, Ting stated that he wanted to lead the attack, but I said that inasmuch as the 2nd and 3rd platoons had been chosen to lead the attack, that I should lead because I had handled these platoons before. After some discussion, Captain Moore agreed with me and we proceeded that way.

"We attacked about 5:25 a.m. and, according to what I heard, Ting only got forward a short distance when he was hit. A couple of men picked him up on a stretcher to carry him back, but in the confusion and semi darkness drifted over into the 4th Division lines who were on our left. Shortly after this, another shell came along and blew the three of them to pieces. That is the reason, at first, that Ting was reported missing, as he could not be found among our dead and wounded. Sometime later he was finally identified as one of the 80th Division."

Hammitt was seriously wounded himself on the same day and lay in the field for twenty-seven hours. He spent forty months in the hospital.

First Lieutenant Moomaw of the 318th Infantry was killed the next day, October 5. Sweeny remembered Moomaw's heroic last moments:

"The First Battalion, 318th Infantry, Eightieth Division had been attached for duty since the preceding September 26th to the General commanding the Eighth Brigade, Fourth Division in line of battle on the right flank of the 80th Division. Early on the morning of this day, in compliance with orders from brigade headquarters, I ordered First Lieutenant Clovis Moomaw to report with his platoon for duty to brigade headquarters.

"On arrival there he was instructed that his platoon was to be organized into liaison groups for service with the units of the front line and that as soon as he had completed this organization he would be at liberty to rejoin his battalion. At the same time he was informed that orders had just been issued for his battalion to advance and occupy the south west corner of the Bois de Faye where, as the result of a German counterattack, liaison had been lost between the first line elements of the Fourth and Eightieth Divisions.

"Once his liaisons organized, Lieutenant Moomaw would have been perfectly justified in rejoining his battalion in passing by Brigade Headquarters and then in comparative safety behind the lines. Instead of which from the front lines of the Fourth Division he decided to attempt to reach his command in passing by the fought- over zone of the Bois de Faye, realizing that any information he might obtain would be of the greatest value to his battalion commander. He reported to me at the southern edge of the Bois de Faye shortly after my arrival there. The information which he had gathered proved afterwards to be extremely accurate and of the greatest value. Shortly afterwards he was killed by a shell.

"The judgement, initiative and courage displayed by this officer in reconnoitering the Bois de Faye instead of rejoining his battalion by the longer and safer route were of the highest order."

The annual "Last Man" gatherings usually lasted two or three days and were eagerly anticipated by Higgins and the others. Many of the members, including Higgins, wrote frequently to each other in letters that were referred to as "broadcasts," in that a letter directed to one individual was copied and sent to the other members. As the annual meeting neared, the letter writing multiplied and so did the exchange of barbs and hints at memorable moments of meetings past. Spouses such as Virginia Higgins could only sigh and wait for the occasion to pass. Often three or four members met en route to the larger meeting which always included plenty of bourbon, singing, golf and swimming. These light times aside, the memories of war prevailed during the commemorative dinner. The members set places for their deceased comrades and sat around the table with the bottle of unopened Rhum Negrita as the centerpiece. Tears flowed with the stories.

Higgins held The Last Man's Club dear to his heart. He kept the correspondence from the years when the club was at its roaring best, in the 1930s and early 1940s, as the members aged into their forties. While some of the men regularly wrote about the politics of the day, Higgins filled his letters with humor and good-natured kidding, along with the occasional poem or song, and the latest tidbits on his three beloved daughters. He also wrote about coaching the Penn State football team. The letters reveal a solid person who took losing and winning in stride. Throughout Higgins's letters was a theme that life should be enjoyed rather than fretted over. War had shown the members of the Last Man's Club how fickle life could be.

§ 5 §
Football For The Brass Hats

FOLLOWING ARMISTICE DAY on November 11, 1918, another operation was put into motion — the formation of a football tournament involving division teams from throughout the A.E.F. The event became highly-publicized both in Europe and in the U.S. Legendary sports writer Grantland Rice covered many of the games for the *Stars and Stripes* military publication and his articles were reprinted by newspapers throughout the country. It was this series of games that really threw Higgins into the national sporting limelight.

The divisions quickly searched their ranks for coaches and football players and weren't shy about pulling in stars from other units. Unbeknownst to Higgins, his excellent record on the gridiron at Penn State surfaced and he received sudden orders to transfer out of the 80th Division. Only when he reached the 89th Division at Coblenz, West Germany did he realize why he had been transferred.

From February 14, 1919 to March 29, 1919, Higgins and the 89th Division won seven consecutive games to capture the A.E.F. Championship. The team scored 108 points to their opponents' eighteen.

An article in *The St. Louis Post-Dispatch* newspaper called the 89th Division team "without doubt one of the greatest aggregations of college football talent ever assembled and equally, without doubt, the best coached team in the world."

Indeed, an amazing number of great college players and coaches filled the 89th roster. Grantland Rice selected five players from the 89th squad for his All-A.E.F. team. One of the selections was Bob Higgins, who obviously hadn't forgotten how to play end while entrenched in the Argonne. The other Rice picks from the 89th were left guard Paul Withington, captain of the team, from Harvard; fullback Potsy Clark from Illinois; halfback Adrian Lindsey from Kansas; and left end Howard Laslett from Kansas.

The other divisions also fielded excellent teams as it became apparent how many current and former college football stars had entered the service. Higgins always considered his participation on the 89th Division championship team as one of the greatest accomplishments in his football career. Near the end of his coaching days at Penn State, Higgins provided a lengthy, colorful recollection of the bruising battles on the overseas gridiron.

"After the Armistice, the brass hats thought it would be advisable for every division to organize a football team — something to do to keep the men out of mischief. Thirty or forty 'old soldiers' who made up the 89th Division football squad have a choice collection of memories to keep them young. And I am absolutely sure that not one incident from the time they started pre-season drills until they whipped the 36th Division at Paris to win the championship of the A.E.F. has ever been forgotten.

"I have often been asked whether the thrills of Army football were comparable to those in college competition. My answer is that almost every football game is alike to a player who really loves the game. You want to win every one, no matter how unimportant it is. Of course, the crowds and color of the college game add to the excitement of the contest for any young kid. But let me tell you, those Army games had everything. Why, we were only continuing the war a little beyond the Armistice with just a few holds barred and a time limit on the action!

"I have often been accused of being a 'ringer' with the 89th. Actually, I was. I served in France with the 80th Division of which I am now national commander. Following the Armistice I received orders, much to my disgust, to report to the 3rd Corps School for Small Arm Firing. For some reason, after a month's course, I was put in command of the school — a job nobody else wanted.

"My heart wasn't in the work and I must have done a

pretty terrible job. I passed everybody. This was unheard of in the Army and I was on the carpet in no time and then ordered to Blois (we called it 'Bloohey'). However it was pronounced, its function was definite. In 'Bloohey' soldiers were examined for mental defects. After three or four days cooling my heels I was ushered into an office to face two elderly colonels.

"I took my hat off and stood at attention for a few minutes, but they paid very little attention to me. After awhile one of them looked up and said:

"'Are you a first lieutenant or a second lieutenant?'

"'First Lieutenant, sir,' I answered.

"'Why don't you wear an insignia?'

"I was a little bit peeved by this time, so I answered: 'I have an insignia on my hat and I generally take it off when I'm inside. I'm also usually invited to take off my trenchcoat, and I have an insignia on my uniform.'

"This stopped him for a minute, but the other colonel began to ask me questions about small arm firing. At that time I could quote the book used at the school and even told him what page of the text the answers were on. After about twenty minutes of questioning I began to feel pretty satisfied with myself. Then one of them said:

"'What are you here for? What's wrong with you?'

"'I have been with the 80th Division, I Company, 318th Infantry since the start of the war and I want to go back to my company. I didn't want to be in the 3rd Corps School.'

"'Very well, Lieutenant, you'll go to the 89th Division, C Company, 355th Infantry, Army of Occupation, Coblenz.'

"I learned right then that in the Army you can't win an argument with your superior officers. At the time I was pretty sore about the whole thing, but it turned out to be the best break I ever had.

"Football was in the air when I arrived at Coblenz, and I didn't mind that a bit. My playing days at Penn State had been cut short by the war. It had been a great disappointment to miss my final season of 1918. Later, I returned to captain the Nittany Lion team in 1919, but I couldn't foresee this turn of affairs and football in the Army seemed like a fitting climax to overseas duty.

"What a crowd we had! Our coach was Captain Paul Withington, who served for ten years at Harvard under Percy Haughton. He was also head coach for a few years at Wisconsin. Paul loved football more than any man I have ever known and the way he coached that tough group of Army men — most of them former college stars — was amazing. He weighed 227 pounds, was 6 feet, 2 1/2 inches in height. A great guard, he worked out with the team every morning, made up all of our plays, conducted practice sessions, gave pep talks before the games and between halves, and led the team in all of its encounters. He left a lasting impression with me, and I often find myself imitating him.

"Paul was an M.D. before the war but did not apply for a commission in the medical corps. He got his captaincy and finally his majority in the infantry, and tried to get in all the fighting he could. He was really a powerful man. Had he not taken exercise every day (he carried iron dumb-bells around with him) and watched his diet he would have become enormous. There were three Withingtons at Harvard, I understand, and all played football. Paul was the oldest, and it was quite a coincidence that he played against his younger brothers in the A.E.F.

"The 89th was loaded with fine athletes who didn't confine their activities to football alone. This Division also won the A.E.F. championship in baseball. There were nine big leaguers on the ball club and two ex-college stars — Potsy Clark from Illinois and Ad Lindsey from Kansas — who were also leading members of the football squad. The Norfolk Naval Reserve team may have its Bob Fellers, but the boys in the 89th didn't feel bashful when they were a couple of runs ahead with old Grover Cleveland Alexander in the box.

"Charlie Gerhardt, our quarterback, is now General Charles Hunter Gerhardt, commanding general of the 91st Division, Medford, Oregon. Charlie played at West Point under Charlie Daly, whose systems, like Haughton's, was to keep the ball in the opponent's territory and let the other fellows make the mistakes. With Lindsey's great kicking and Gerhardt's field generalship, we were hard to beat.

"Withington was All-American and Clark was All-Big Ten Conference. Carl Schweiger (Colorado College tackle) made the All-Rocky Mountain Conference team, and both Lindsey and Poge Lewis (Washington University center) were All-Missouri Valley Conference selections. Boy, would I like to have a handful of these players now!

"The 89th was composed largely of men from Missouri, Kansas, Oklahoma and Illinois. The commanding officer was General Leonard Wood. There was a great deal of tradition and spirit connected with the division which contributed no small bit to the success of its athletic teams.

"Our first series of games was arranged to decide the championship of the Army of Occupation in Coblenz, the little town where the Moselle and the Rhine come together, about 60 miles from Cologne. The 89th went into action against the 90th on February 14, 1919 on the 7th Corps football field at Wittlich. Although we had much the better of the game during its early stages and Marsh Wilder (Kansas halfback) went across for one touchdown, the 90th drove to our 12 yard line in the last few minutes of play. We were saved when our opponents made an illegal substitution and were penalized half the distance of the field. We won 6 to 0.

"Next we played a practice game with the 3rd Army and won easily, 30 to 0. The big game coming up was between the Marines and the 4th Division, to be played at Coblenz, with the winner playing us. Congressman Hamilton Fish from Duchess County, New York, former All-American tackle at Harvard, was captain of the 4th, and Harry Lagore, star halfback at Yale, was sparkplug of the Marines. The 4th won handily, and gained the right to meet the 89th in Coblenz for the championship of the Army of Occupation.

"All the soldiers in our division knew about a telephone conversation which took place between Colonel Hipple of the 4th, who called up our chief of staff, Colonel Lee. These two gentlemen were classmates at West Point. Colonel Hipple said:

"'We would like to have a little wager on the outcome of the game next Saturday, and we think anything under 10,000 francs would be a piker's bet.' Without waiting for a reply, he hung up.

"Colonel Lee, being from the South, was not only proud, but had a pretty sharp temper. He sent out a division order urging everyone to back the team with hard cash. He put a captain on special duty to collect the funds. I have forgotten how much was actually collected, but it was well over 100,000 francs. He kept it in a little black bag. To our surprise the 4th covered every cent.

"I'll never forget the pageantry that took place before the encounter. Eddie Rickenbacker's Airplane Circus gave an exhibition which included tailspins, nose dives, falling leaves, and every other sort of thriller known to airmen at that time. An observation balloon went up with a great American flag floating from it, and our 200 buglers sounded forth with marvelous teamwork. It was impossible to estimate because there were no tickets sold, but there must have been 10,000 people on hand. It was a high ranking crowd. General after general was there and colonels were extraordinarily plentiful.

"With Fish of Harvard leading the 4th and Withington of Harvard directing the 89th, the game was pretty much (Harvard) Crimson in more ways than one. The first quarter was all even, but we began to get stronger as the game progressed. With only 20 seconds of the first half remaining the ball was near the 4th's goal after one of Lindsey's high, twisting punts had been caught and the man downed in his tracks. A kick out of danger was their only play. It came, but it was hard luck for the 4th. Poge Lewis broke through and blocked the punt and Scrubby Laslett (Kansas end) fell on the ball for a touchdown.

"Out came the 89th banner with the division insignia and then that crack Bugle Corps of ours blasted out with Pay Call. Our players began to hug one another and I can remember seeing guard Sergeant (Harry) Flannagan hopping up and down with joy. No college team had ever felt any better about a touchdown. When the cheering that could be heard far up the Rhine had died down, Lindsey kicked the goal.

"During the remainder of the game the 4th fought for every inch, but if there had been any idea in the minds of our opponents that this first touchdown was a stroke of luck, number two soon dispelled it. We flashed down the field with the same spirit which took us across the Meuse in the Argonne. Clark, Lindsey and Grover Padfield (St. Louis U. fullback) made steady gains. Then Potsy uncorked one of those long runs which used to break the hearts of the opponents of Illinois University. He was down and up three times on a 35 yard gallop to the three yard line. Then Clark was given the ball around left end for the touchdown. Lindsey kicked the goal to make it 14 to 0 and there was no more scoring. After the game our players were unanimous that they had never engaged in a harder or cleaner contest. There was never a moment when the fighting wasn't furious, but there wasn't one dirty spot on it.

"There were many factors contributing to our victory, but not the least was the fight talk delivered by General Frank L. Winn, commander of our division. Half of this talk was made in our hotel prior to the game. The general was pretty well wound up and Captain Withington was stewing around, afraid we were going to be late. Finally he could stand it no longer. He herded us into big Army trucks, general and all, who delivered the last half of his pep talk en route. After the game we rode back to the hotel in Army trucks. Conversation was light and running high. Someone said the game wasn't half as tough as the practice Withington had given us the Wednesday before, with the first team backfield and a second team line against the second team backfield and the first team line. He would put the ball on the 20 yard line and make us carry it over and over again by straight line smashes. It was kept up all afternoon.

"It was on to Paris for our team now — it was there that the final series for the A.E.F. championship would be held. Along with our squad went that same captain with the little black bag, who had been placed in charge of our wages. This captain was a sort of an advance man — not a press agent — but a taker of all bets. As I remember it, the betting was not limited to officers or even the men in the ranks. Most of the players were eager participants, and since we won every game, we had nearly 1000 francs a week coming in besides our regular pay. We were literally rolling in wealth, and Paris isn't such a bad place to spend money — particularly when you are in your twenties and neighborhood criticism is missing.

"Fresh from our conquests on German soil, we were rarin' to go. We licked the 88th Division, 14 to 9, at Trier in a practice game arranged as a warmup for the championship battles. The King and Queen of Belgium attended this contest, and I remember feeling pretty good after it was over because I had scored one of the touchdowns on a pass play.

"On March 14 we were scheduled to play the crack S.O.S. (Service of Supply) team from Saint-Nazaire. It happened to be one of the greatest games on our entire schedule, but I doubt if any member of the 89th squad recalls that contest at the Paris Velodrome as clearly as a riotous dressing room incident which occurred before we went out on the field.

"Captain Withington was one of the old school. He was trained in Haughton ways and he believed in whipping his team into a frenzy of excitement before each game. Now, most of us were old-timers who had played three or four years of college football. The fight talk was aged stuff to us. Not so with Sergeant Flannagan, the Omaha policeman, who would stand spellbound while Withington reared up and down in front of us, waving his arms, and orating in splendid style. When it was over, Flannagan was always first out of the door. If someone hadn't always remembered to open it we felt that he would tear right on through.

"Well, it was one of the captain's customs to wind up his pep talk with something like this:

"'And if we lose this game, it will be *your* fault, and *yours*, and *yours*, and YOURS!' Withington would go down the line, picking out certain players and shaking his finger in their faces. But he'd always end up with Flannagan. When he'd get to the big sergeant he'd let him have one right on the jaw, and Flannagan would tear out on the field in a blinding rage which usually meant curtains for the guy who played opposite him on the line.

"On this particular occasion the Nebraskan was cagey. When the coach got to him, he ducked. Right behind him was Poge Lewis, nursing a sore shoulder. Withington's blow caught Poge where it hurt the most, and out came the shoulder joint. Poge let out a roar that nearly blew off the roof, but as I remember it, we patched him up and he played anyway. There were no softies in our outfit.

"We licked Saint-Nazaire, 13 to 0, on the great bicycle race course, which provided a beautiful spot for an American football game. It was the scene of a great outpouring of officers and doughboys, of men and women welfare workers, and many Frenchmen in uniform and civilian clothes who had never seen a game called football where you carry the ball around in your arms. This puzzled them.

"We always said that Saint-Nazaire had the best backfield in the A.E.F. It consisted of Red Maloney of Georgetown, John Barrett of Washington & Lee, Red Hastings of Pittsburgh, and Eddie Mahan of Harvard. But we scored the touchdowns, the first one on a 60-yard march in the second quarter. Lindsey scored the touchdown (set up by a long pass from Lindsey to Higgins).

"What Captain Eddie Hart, the old Princeton star and coach of the Saint-Nazaire team, must have said to his men between halves appeared to have a telling effect, for they came on the field full of ginger. Barrett returned Lindsey's punt 20 yards and then Eissler, Mahan and Barrett bent the 89th line back yard by yard. It became first down on our 11-yard mark, and then Eissler and Mahan went through a yard or so at a time to make another first down by inches on the one. Here our great line held with the same die-in-the-trench spirit that marked the Third Army's fame on the battlefield. Eissler twice, Mahan, and finally Barrett assaulted our forwards but we held the enemy every time. Talk about the old college try!

"Our second and final touchdown came as a sort of anti-climax. After a series of short gains, Potsy Clark finally broke away for a 16-yard touchdown run. Actually it was Lindsey's punting that turned the battle in our favor. Ad got away with one punt of 70 and another of 66 yards, and had the satisfaction of outkicking Mahan, one of the greatest punters of all time.

"After the Saint-Nazaire game both Eddie Mahan and Eddie Hart joined our coaching staff. I have often remarked that the 89th Division had the greatest coaching staff ever assembled. Certainly it would cost some college a pretty penny today. We ended up with almost as many coaches as players in the starting lineup. In addition to Withington, Hart and Mahan, we had Spike Denny, All-American end at Brown, who was our original assistant coach; Trumbull and Souci of Harvard; Major Pritchard and Captain Redfield, old West Point stars; and I'm sure there must have been others.

"Coaching us was no easy task. We needed every last one

of them. We had one training rule. Everyone was supposed to be in bed at 10 p.m. Friday night, and we kept this rule — most of the time. The rest of the week the players were allowed to use their own judgment. There were a few real escapades. Those that occurred did little harm and left only fond memories. I'll never forget the time Ad Lindsey, who came from Kingfisher, Oklahoma, first saw the Cafe de la Paix. He said, 'Boy, this is a swell place. It reminds me of the Busy Bee in Kingfisher.'

"A week after our victory over Saint-Nazaire we were to play the Supply Corps outfit which was quartered at Tours. Our million dollar coaching staff was determined to prevent a letdown, so they drove us hard. We often remarked that our games were a cinch compared with some of the practice sessions directed by Withington and Hart. This pair could take it as well as give it. One day these giants — Paul was taller but Eddie was broader — were talking in the center of the practice field. Charlie Gerhardt took a flying dive at Eddie from the rear. He bounced off without even making an impression. Eddie turned around casually and looked at Charlie on the ground. He said, 'Oh, is that you, Charlie?' and kept on talking with Withington.

"We had a comparatively easy time with the team from Tours, and succeeded in beating them 17 to 3. Shortly after this game we heard that our opponents in the championship game would be the 36th Division. For the last three weeks the 36th had been trying to eliminate the 28th. The first two games were ties, so it was finally decided that the team making the most yardage would win in case the next contest was deadlocked. It did end up in a third tie, but the 36th won by a few yards.

"Saturday, March 29, 1919, was selected for the big game to be played in Paris. The *Stars and Stripes* A.E.F. newspaper (Grantland Rice) wrote:

'The American Army football championship will be fought out this afternoon at the Velodrome, Parc des Princes, Auteuil, before the most important military and diplomatic gathering ever known to the great American college game. General John J. Pershing himself will attend and yesterday the Commander in Chief personally invited President Wilson and Secretary of Navy Daniels to be present. It is hoped that the President may find relief from his Peace Commission duties long enough to be present. Secretary Daniels, it is expected, will be there. Important members of the Peace Commission also will attend. Other military notables who, it was made known yesterday, will attend include Lieutenant General Hunter Liggett, commander of the First Army; Major General Edwin R. Smith, commander of the 36th Division of the First Army; Major General Frank L. Winn, commander of the 89th Division.

'The opposing teams in the final struggle for the A.E.F. championship rested quietly in their hotels last night, having been conditioned to the pink for the efforts of their lives. The game will begin at 3 o'clock sharp. Admission is free to soldiers and civilians of the Allied Nations, French in particular being welcome.

'Six thousand soldiers from all points of the theater of war are on their way by special trains to Paris for the spectacle which is certain to be of the Army-Navy aspect.

'Captain Paul Withington and his staff of advisers put the finishing touches on the 89th squad yesterday at Longchamp. The men had only a light workout with a final rehearsal of signals.'

"Of course our coaches had scouted the 36th and we were familiar with their personnel. They depended a great deal on the kicking of Big Chief Massett, an American Indian, and they hoped he would out-punt our Lindsey. Another Indian, Bellieu, played right end for the Arrowheads. Spitz Clarke was their outstanding runner.

"Massett attended Oklahoma University, as did Sergeant Frye, the 36th Division center; Sergeant Tolbert, a tackle; and Lookabaugh, fullback. Three of our opponents had Texas University for their alma mater — Sergeant Gray, tackle; Lieutenant Clarke and Sergeant Cranfield, halfbacks. Bellieu went to Kendell College; Brown, a guard, to Sewanee; and McCuller, left end, attended the University of Missouri. And of course fair Harvard had its representatives in the person of Captain Whitney, the quarterback. Somehow he had crashed the monopoly of the Southwest.

"The usual tenseness prevailed among our players but I think we were pretty cocky, too. I remember seeing Grantland Rice in the press box, covering the game for the *Stars and Stripes.*

"We were all interested in a cablegram Paul Withington received from the Governor of Hawaii. Paul was born on this island, and the message expressed the hope that a son of Hawaii would lead his team to victory.

"Both teams were cautious in the first quarter, kicking on first or second down. It was raining and it wasn't long before we were playing in that good old French mud. Finally the first break came our way. We recovered a fumbled kick 40 yards from the goal line and were able to capitalize on this opportunity. Viggo Nelson, who later played plenty of fullback at Michigan, scored the touchdown. He had substituted for Grover Padfield when the latter was injured in the first few minutes of the game. Lindsey kicked the goal.

"The 36th Division came right back and drove down the field in the second quarter. We tried everything but couldn't stop them. Lookabaugh and Clarke picked up most of the yardage, aided by one long pass from Whitney to Frye. They scored on us but missed the goal and we were leading at halftime, 7 to 6.

"With the rain coming down fast and the field getting worse and worse, most of the spectators had come to the conclusion that the game would end with the first half score. But Potsy Clark still had his innings coming up. Starting from the middle of the field, he slipped away from several tacklers and went the whole way to the end zone, clinching the game and the championship for the 89th. The final score was 14 to 6.

"Nearly everybody swarmed on the field when the game ended, but the boys with belts and pistols finally cleared the way for General Pershing and his staff who had come down to congratulate the victors. The General was wearing a fancy uniform and white gloves but this didn't daunt Charlie Gerhardt. He pushed his way to the front, stuck out his hand and said:

"'General, I don't believe I've ever had the pleasure of meeting you.'

"Then, one by one, we added our bit to covering the General with mud. I've often wondered if he appreciated the democracy exhibited by the boys of the 89th.

"When we returned to Coblenz the reception we received at Division Headquarters made us feel as if we were solely responsible for winning the war. The first team rode in Cadillac cars, the substitutes in Dodges. It was dusk as we drove into Milesburg through an archway of trees. Everyone had turned out to meet us. There must have been fifteen bands! After a great banquet we were given two weeks leave and most of us divided our time between Nice and Cannes. On our return to the Army of Occupation we found it necessary to go by way of Paris — just for old times sake."

§ 6 §
All-American Year

ALTHOUGH BOB HIGGINS was away at war during the 1917 and 1918 seasons, college football went on. Georgia Tech and Pop Warner's Pittsburgh dominated play in 1917. Tech was coached by John Heisman, for whom the Heisman Memorial Trophy was named in 1935. Both teams won all nine of their games. Heisman's team outscored its opponents by an amazing 491-17, recording such whopping victories as 41-0 over Penn, 63-0 over Washington & Lee, 83-0 over Vanderbilt, 98-0 over once-powerful Carlisle and 68-7 over traditional Southern powerhouse Auburn. Tech's backfield, regarded as one of the best ever, featured Everett Strupper, Judy Harlan, Albert Hill and Joe Guyon, the latter having run with Jim Thorpe in the Carlisle backfield before transferring to Georgia Tech. Heisman implemented a backfield shift that completely befuddled opposing defenses.

Pitt wasn't as strong offensively as Tech, but shut out six opponents en route to its third consecutive unbeaten season under Warner. Texas A&M, coached by Dana Bible, won all eight of its games without allowing a single point. But lack of respect for the Southwest teams limited Texas A&M's bid for the mythical national title.

Many colleges didn't field teams in 1918, which was the height of America's involvement in the war. Many other teams played abbreviated schedules, such as Pitt, which won four of its five games, including a convincing 32-0 win over Heisman's Georgia Tech.

The most noteworthy football news of 1918, however, was Knute Rockne's debut as head coach at Notre Dame. After graduating Rockne had stayed on at Notre Dame and assisted Jess Harper for four seasons. During the next thirteen seasons as head coach Rockne would take Notre Dame and college football to previously-unimagined heights. Rockne's first Notre Dame team produced a modest 3-1-2 record.

Football went on at Penn State, too, but the Nittany Lions struggled to a 5-4 record in 1917. Head coach Harlow stood on shaky ground even before the season opened, largely because of Penn State's failure to match the powerful program Warner had built at Pittsburgh. To make matters worse, only three Lion regulars returned for the 1917 season, the rest lost to military service or graduation. End Larry Conover served as acting captain in place of the departed Higgins.

The team came together at times, but most of the wins were against weak foes such as Gettysburg and St. Bonaventure. In the more important clashes, Washington & Jefferson, Dartmouth, Lehigh and Pittsburgh all beat Penn State.

One of the highlights of the season was the play of sophomore back Charley Way. His forty-yard punt return for a touchdown in the final seconds beat West Virginia Wesleyan. During one drive in the Dartmouth game Way carried the ball three times for sixty-five yards and scored from the one to tie the contest in the second quarter. Way also played well in the season-ending 28-6 loss to powerful Pitt.

When Harlow departed for military service in the summer of 1918, Penn State needed a new coach to lead the Lions through their four-game schedule. The new coach would also be charged with building up the school's physical education program. Pittsburgh industrialist and Penn State alumnus C.W. Heppenstall suggested Hugo Bezdek for the job. Bezdek was coaching the Pittsburgh Pirates baseball team, but he was better known for his football savvy, having been a Camp third-team All-American fullback in 1905 under Stagg at Chicago and then the head football coach at Arkansas and Oregon. His 1916 Oregon team had gone 7-0-1 and defeated Penn 14-0 in the Rose Bowl on New Year's Day, 1917. Penn State put Bezdek in charge of its physical education department and football team while allowing him to manage the Pirates through the 1919 season.

Bezdek's first Penn State team went 1-2-1 in 1918, beating Lehigh 7-6 and losing to Pitt, 28-6. A young Lion quarterback named Glenn Killinger showed promise. The Penn State squad appeared fundamentally sound and the school eagerly anticipated a return to a full schedule in 1919.

After the 1918 season Bezdek presented his plans to expand the school's recreational facilities, including a new physical education building with a swimming pool, intramural sports fields and a golf course. Bezdek emphasized that a structured physical education and recreational program contributed as much toward a student's intellectual growth as the core curriculum. Support began building for Bezdek.

Penn State's enrollment neared three thousand in the fall of 1919. Among the registered seniors was Bob Higgins, who had been one of 2,200 Penn State students and alumni to serve in World War I. The school had suffered its share of casualties in the war, including two former football players. Guard and wrestling star Levi Lamb, who played at Penn State from 1912-1914, was killed in July 1918 during the allied advance south of Soissons. James (Red) Bebout, a guard from 1911-1913, was killed on the fourth day of the Argonne offensive on September 29, 1918, not far from where Higgins and his men advanced.

The big news in the fall of 1919 was the return of Higgins. His starring role during the 89th Division's march to the A.E.F. championship had identified him as a sure All-American at end. His teammates, many of them also fresh from the service, elected him captain. Harry Robb, captain of the 1918 team, won the starting quarterback position. Way ran at halfback. Larry Conover, the 1917 captain, moved to center. Dick Rauch, Ben Cubbage, Red Henry and Bob Osborn saw action in the line. Hinkey Haines and George Snell played in the backfield. Other lettermen from the 1919 team included left end George Brown and fullback Harold Hess. The 1919 season marked college football's fiftieth anniversary, dating back to the Princeton-Rutgers encounter in 1869.

Former head coach Harlow returned from the service and became an assistant coach. Dutch Hermann, also out of the service, resumed his position as an assistant.

Bezdek became the third head coach for whom Higgins played at Penn State. Bezdek drove his players much harder than the previous coaches and frequently railed at the team for poor play. His scrimmages were not for the meek. At the same time, he knew football strategy on both sides of the ball. He employed the Notre Dame shift on offense but sometimes ran and passed out of the basic formation to keep the defense guessing.

Penn State won its first two games at home, thrashing lowly Gettysburg 33-0 in the opener and stunting Bucknell 9-0. Way scored the lone touchdown in the Bucknell game and Conover kicked a thirty-yard field goal.

But Penn State lost its next encounter on the road against Dartmouth, 19-13. The Nittany Lions led 13-7 after the first quarter when Way ran the opening kickoff ninety yards for a touchdown and then picked up a fumble and ran eighty-five yards for another score. But Dartmouth fullback Jim Robertson, who became a Camp third-team All-American, scored to tie the game at half, 13-13. Dartmouth scored the only points of the second half when it drove sixty yards in the third quarter to go ahead for good.

It was a grim group of Lions that returned to the Track House in State College. Penn State football historian Ridge Riley reported that Higgins and Conover carried grievances to Bezdek. The primary complaint was that Bezdek wasn't playing the right people. Teammates saw Higgins as a coach on the field with his vast football experience. Furthermore, Higgins was no timid youngster: he was a war-toughened veteran about to turn twenty-six. Bezdek agreed to some shuffling in the lineup.

After destroying Ursinus 48-7, Penn State molded into a great football team. It won its last four games against quality opponents by the combined score of 70-7.

The fifth game against rival Penn in Philadelphia was the key game of the season. The day before the game the Penn State players had just come in from a workout on the grounds of the Philadelphia Cricket Club. A fourteen-year-old boy entered the dressing room and stood in front of the big lineman, Dick Rauch.

"Where's Higgins?" the boy wanted to know.

Rauch smiled and said to the boy. "I'm Higgins. What do you want?"

"Well, you're good," the lad said. "I just wanted to tell

you that you're good, you really are. I want to be like you some day."

The boy's sincerity caused Rauch to reveal the truth, and he pointed the boy toward Higgins.

The boy's eyes widened when he met the real Higgins and he repeated, "You're good, Higgins. You're the best. I sure hope your team licks the stuffin' out of Penn tomorrow."

Higgins asked the boy if he intended to go to Franklin Field for the game, but the boy said he didn't have a ticket and didn't have the money to buy one. Higgins found the boy a ticket. The next day before the game Higgins waved to the youth who was sitting in the Penn State section of the stands.

A newspaper story the morning of the game wrote of Higgins: "The peerless player is almost as well known in France, England, Belgium and Germany as he is in Uncle Sam's dominion. He has performed before the eyes of the world's noted military commanders and rulers of nations as well. He is the master of American ends."

Higgins's performance against undefeated Penn, both at end and as the punter, didn't disappoint anyone. The game was billed as a battle of the ends, between Higgins and Penn's Henry Miller, both first team All-Americans following the season. But Higgins was on his game this first day of November and his flawless play was contagious. Penn State looked like the best team in the nation in winning 10-0 before twenty thousand fans.

Higgins's first punt of the game traveled fifty-five yards. He maintained this average the entire game. Penn dropped one of his cannon shots in the second quarter and the Lions recovered deep in Penn territory. Quarterback Robb subsequently scored the only touchdown of the game.

Penn's only threat came in the second quarter when it drove to the Penn State ten-yard line, but Higgins led the defensive attack and the Nittany Lions held.

A fourth-quarter Penn State field goal provided the final margin. A thirty-yard pass completion from Robb to Higgins set up the score.

Newspaper accounts the day after the game heaped praise on the senior right end.

"Never has an end put up a better exhibition on Franklin

Field. Higgins was in every play. His quick brain was working all the time. He coached his men and held them together. His anticipation of Penn plays was amazing. In addition, Higgins did all the punting for State and did it mighty well; caught forward passes like a big league outfielder snares a baseball; broke up every attack aimed at his end and particularly refused to be fooled on trick plays."

After beating Lehigh 20-7 the following week to go 5-1 on the season, Penn State visited Ithaca, New York to tangle with Cornell. It was no contest as the Nittany Lions won 20-0. Penn State threw for more than 100 yards, mostly to Higgins. In the second quarter Higgins caught three passes in Cornell territory to set up a scoring opportunity at the one-yard-line. Fullback Hess crashed over for the score. In the third quarter, following a thirty-yard run by Robb to the Cornell twenty-eight, Robb connected with Higgins on a 27-yard pass play, again to the one-yard-line. Robb ran for the final yard and the score. The third Penn State touchdown came when Cornell fumbled a towering Higgins punt and Penn State's Way picked up the ball and dashed in for the six points.

It had been seven years since Penn State had beaten Pitt when the two teams met on Thanksgiving Day, November 27, 1919 at Forbes Field in Pittsburgh. Warner's squad, after four undefeated seasons in a row, had gone down twice during the season. But with fullback Andy Hastings leading the charge, Pitt was capable of beating anybody on a given day. Approximately 35,000 fans jammed the grandstands, outlying bleachers and temporary seats. Only minutes after they had settled into their seats, the fans witnessed one of the most famous and exciting plays in the history of college football.

The major players in the drama were Penn State fullback Harold Hess and end Bob Higgins. Hess and Higgins had shared punting duties for the Nittany Lions during the season. Assistant coach Dick Harlow had scouted Pittsburgh throughout the year and noticed that when opposing teams punted, the Panthers usually rushed nine or ten players, leaving only the return man back to field the punt. On the first day of practice following the win over Cornell, Harlow gath-

ered the Lion players and said, "If you see Pitt go into a nine-
or ten-man line, try a pass — no matter where you are on the
field."

The scheme excited Higgins, who would be the receiver.
But Hess didn't have much of an arm. Time after time in practice his passes fell far from their intended target.

Coach Bezdek noticed these failed exchanges and asked
what the players were doing. The pair told Bezdek of Harlow's
pass plan. Bezdek replied: "It sounds all right to me, but I'd
appreciate it if you would let me know what's going on around
here in the future."

Hess and Higgins continued to work on the play, but they
rarely connected. Whenever the play worked, the rest of the
squad roared and applauded. Hess asked Harlow if the play
might work better if another player filled in, preferably one
who could throw. Harlow said that for the fake to work, the
punter had best be in the game, and Pop Warner knew that
Higgins and Hess did the punting for Penn State. Higgins
was the obvious candidate to catch the ball and run with it, so
that left Hess to throw the pass. Hess understood, but he had
yet to throw a perfect pass to Higgins.

On a foggy, rainy day, with Forbes Field fast becoming
mud-wrecked, Pitt kicked off and Way returned it to the Penn
State 28-yard line. Two running plays lost two yards and Hess
dropped back to punt. There was no fake this time but Pitt
blocked his punt straight up in the air and recovered on the
Lion twenty-six. Three running plays and an offsides penalty
gave Pitt a first down at the Penn State fifteen. Pitt ran three
times and reached the Penn State six. On fourth down Pitt
lined up to kick a field goal, but then shifted into a running
formation. The rushing attempt lost two yards and Penn State
took over on its own eight.

It was time to make history. Hess immediately dropped
back to punt for Penn State. A first- or second-down punt to
improve field position was a standard play in that era of college football, particularly when the offense took possession of
the ball deep in its own territory. Pitt lined up nine men to go
after the punt, stationed one man just behind the line and
positioned Hastings deep to receive the punt. The linebacker
moved up into the line of scrimmage just before the snap.

Hess took the pass from center and, to the amazement of the crowd, rolled to his right in the end zone and heaved the ball toward Higgins who was in full stride along the right sidelines.

Here's how one Pittsburgh reporter saw it: "Bob never faltered. As the oval spun on this history-making aerial expedition he lifted two cupped hands into the air, and imprisoned the sphere. Pittsburgh was caught flat-footed and outwitted, and before she could recall her scattered wits and bring herself back to the gridiron, the nimble Higgins was racing over chalkmark after chalkmark.

"Hastings alone stood between the fleet end and the goal line, but Andy never had a chance. Two conspirators with Higgins were dashing along in his wake, and they hurled themselves upon the flying Hastings. He hit the ground like a lump of lead dropped into the seas, and when the groaning stands saw him fall they realized that Higgins would score."

Higgins always gave credit to end George Brown for taking out Hastings and allowing him to score.

It may be difficult for modern-day football fans to understand why a forward pass from anywhere near the end zone would seem so spectacular. But in 1919 the forward pass was just becoming a standard part of the offensive arsenal. Even then it was a weapon used primarily beyond the thirty-yard-line, as echoed in another of the next day's game stories: "It was without question a play never known in modern football for a man to throw a forward pass behind his own goal line."

The actual yardage covered by the play changed in each newspaper account. The annual Penn State *Football Yearbook* lists the play as a 92-yard touchdown pass, which is the longest in Penn State history. The *Yearbook* credits Higgins with running seventy-five yards, which would mean that the pass traveled seventeen yards from the line of scrimmage, and that he caught the ball on the 25-yard-line.

Although many observers said the first-down pass play was risky, Higgins declared it quite the opposite. "What if it did fail?" he asked. "There was no chance of a Pitt man intercepting it. Every backfield man was on the line except Hastings, who was fifty yards behind waiting for a kick. Hess would have had to throw the ball fifty yards for Hastings to catch it."

Higgins said the idea of running the fake play at that particular moment hit everybody in the huddle at the same time. "As soon as we saw the Pitt backfield men get on the line we knew the time was ripe. In fact we waited a few seconds to give all the Panther backs, except Hastings, a chance to crawl up close."

Higgins also commented on the throw itself. "The pass made by Hess was a perfect one. It could not be improved upon. It was the first good one he had made. How he made such a remarkable toss I don't know."

Cubbage kicked the extra point to make the score 7-0, and Pitt never got back in the game.

Penn State went to more razzle-dazzle in the second period. The Lions, on a Robb-to-Higgins pass of ten yards and a fifteen-yard Higgins run, drove the ball to the Pitt thirty. Penn State lined up to attempt a field goal with Hess holding, but Hess received the snap and lateraled to Robb who ran right end for twenty yards to the ten. Robb carried three straight times, going over for the touchdown on the third effort.

Penn State's final score came early in the third quarter when Charley Way "passed through the maze of Pitt players with swiftness and dexterity." His touchdown run covered forty-seven yards. The Nittany Lions had finally beaten Pop Warner's Pitt Panthers.

The Penn State performance was the talk of the East the next day. One article stated: "Higgins's work, his touchdown, Robb's generalship, Hess's line-bucking, and Way's sprint for a touchdown were little less than phenomenal. They formed an invincible quartet and with rapid-fire speed they pulled plays that sparkled and shone like the sun on the ocean."

Another article stated: "Coach Bezdek's boys exhibited one of the finest, snappiest and cleanest football contests ever witnessed on a college gridiron. Penn State and Pitt men helped one another to their feet, gave them a friendly pat on the shoulder and then went at it again."

A couple of years later, recalling the 1919 season, Higgins said the State team was at the height of its ability for the Pitt game. "There was no team in the land which could have beaten

State on that day," he said.

The victory ended Penn State's season with seven wins and a single loss, its best record since 1912. Robert "Tiny" Maxwell, sports editor of the *Philadelphia Evening Public Ledger*, put Penn State at the top of his annual rating of Eastern schools. Syracuse, Colgate, Dartmouth and Pitt followed Penn State.

Higgins had completed his college football career but the accolades kept coming. He received his greatest honor when Walter Camp named him first team All-American at end. Other players on Camp's 1919 first unit were D. Belford West, tackle from Colgate; L.A. Alexander, guard from Syracuse; James Weaver, center from Centre; guard A.F. Youngstrom from Dartmouth; tackle Wilbur Henry from Washington & Jefferson; end Henry Miller of Penn; quarterback Alvin McMillin of Centre; halfbacks Edward Casey of Harvard and Charles Harley of Ohio State; and fullback Ira Rodgers of West Virginia.

Many times before his death, Walter Camp described his 1919 team as the most "representative" All-American team of all time.

Higgins became the second Penn State football player to receive first team All-American status, following Mother Dunn's 1906 selection.

The *Philadelphia Record* newspaper wrote of Penn State's curly-haired star: "Bob Higgins is undoubtedly the greatest end that ever wore the blue and white. He has always been classed as a wonderful defensive end, but this year he uncovered two other qualities more sensational. His work in handling forward passes was a revelation and there was not a game in which he did not gain ground in this manner. Another major discovery was his punting ability."

It had been a long and glorious year for Higgins on the gridiron. Including his performance on the A.E.F. team, Higgins had played in an amazing fifteen games, losing only once, and earned All A.E.F. and All-American honors at right end in the same year.

It had been a great year for college football as well. The sports world needed it. As the football season went into full swing, the lid was coming off the conspiracy of the 1919 World

Series and sending shock waves through the baseball world. Cincinnati of the National League had defeated the Chicago White Sox of the American League five games to three. But some questionable plays and performances by the White Sox had ignited rumors that a fix was in. Indeed it was, and in 1920 Judge Kenesaw Mountain Landis banished eight White Sox players from major league baseball for gambling and throwing World Series games. The most popular of the "eight men out" was hitting great Shoeless Joe Jackson, to whom a disillusioned young boy pleaded, "Say it ain't so, Joe."

But college football was going great guns and drawing giant crowds. In 1919 Knute Rockne, in his second season as head coach, guided Notre Dame to a 9-0 record. Running back George Gipp had paced a ferocious comeback that lifted the Irish over Army, 12-9. Harvard went 9-0-1 in 1919 and Dana Bible put together another perfect season at Texas A&M. Cross-state rivals Alabama and Auburn dominated play in the Deep South.

Young boys were anything but disillusioned about college football. They wanted to grow up and become All-American ends. They wanted to be like Bob Higgins.

§ 7 §
A Turn in the West

WORLD WAR I WAS RECENT HISTORY. Lenin was in power in Moscow. And in March 1920 Charles Scribner & Sons published *This Side of Paradise*, a novel by young F. Scott Fitzgerald. In April 1920, Fitzgerald married Southern belle Zelda Sayre and the couple moved from Montgomery to metropolis, residing in the Biltmore Hotel in New York City, enjoying Scott's growing acclaim as a writer and ordering spinach and champagne for midnight snacks.

Between nights on the town, Fitzgerald wrote stories like *Bernice Bobs Her Hair* which helped define the era. The couple embodied, as Fitzgerald wrote, "the arch type of what New York wanted." What New York wanted was the Jazz Age.

As is common in all eras, the Jazz Age spent a lot of time and ink defining its brand of manhood. Fitzgerald had once dreamed of becoming a football star, of being a big man on campus and being a war hero. Ernest Hemingway, like Fitzgerald, was a star of the Scribners literary stable, and both in his life and writing explored the essence of manhood through war, travel, sports and bouts with the bottle.

Bob Higgins was less of a dreamer than his two well-known contemporaries, but was perhaps more of a man. Both Fitzgerald and Hemingway would have envied Bob Higgins had they known him. It is likely the two heard of Higgins when he was a 1919 All-American. Unlike these literary lions, however, Bob Higgins didn't work at his manhood, nor pause long to evaluate it. His manhood came naturally in the fires of battle and on the fields of athletic competition.

Higgins's experiences in the 1920s were far different from the extravagances of New York City, but they were exciting and challenging nevertheless. Between 1920 and 1928 Higgins would serve as head football coach for two colleges, play and coach professional football, marry a West Virgina girl, start a family, and return to Penn State as an assistant coach. The closest Bob Higgins came to Jazz Age debauchery were his annual retreats with the fun-loving though ever-responsible members of the Last Man's Club. And these retreats continued long after the final notes of The Jazz Age had faded.

Bob Higgins generally followed his own direction in life. In this way, he was much like his sculptor-stonecutter father. Higgins graduated from Penn State in January 1920 with a Bachelor of Arts degree in Commerce and Finance. But Higgins liked sports more than business. His teammates and coaches all told him he would be a natural as a coach. He had captained both his high school and college football teams. He had played for Morris Midkiff at Peddie, Bill Hollenback and Dick Harlow at Penn State, Paul Withington on the A.E.F. team and Hugo Bezdek back at Penn State. He had observed the different styles in which these coaches motivated and instructed their teams, from Harlow's accommodating philosophy to Bezdek's hard-line approach. Higgins had seen that the better teams under each man were those that executed on both offense and defense, that blocked and tackled well, that constantly gained field position with the kicking game yet still had enough flair to fake a punt and pass ninety-two yards for a touchdown.

Upon his graduation, Higgins accepted a position as assistant to the Recreational Officer at Fort Leavenworth, Kansas. A few months later, on May 1, he found a head coaching position at West Virginia Wesleyan in Buckhannon. It was the perfect place to get his feet wet because not much was expected of the school's football program, yet it maintained a competitive schedule.

Higgins had learned something else during his years in football: that good football players can help win football games. He went a little overboard in his efforts to attract top talent to tiny Buckhannon, and stepped in hot water during his first year at West Virginia Wesleyan.

It must be understood that college football in the 1920s was still a rather loose organization. Many players bounced around from school to school. Some played on the college gridiron one day and for a pro team the next. Rules governed eligibility, but enforcement wouldn't take hold until the early 1950s when the NCAA began to crack down on violations.

A college team that was a steep underdog going into a game might be inclined to bring in a player from the outside to make the outcome more respectable. Such players rarely provided enough spark to bring victory, and thus their participation was usually forgotten at game's end.

When Higgins arrived at Wesleyan, he supposedly recruited several talented players by paying them each three hundred dollars. But Higgins made these players sign a loan note so charges of professionalism couldn't be brought against him. Higgins also invited to practice several players whose backgrounds were difficult to run down. One such player was a big lineman named Groggins, who said he was from a prep school in New Jersey.

Wesleyan opened the 1920 season against rival West Virginia. It was no secret that Wesleyan planned to play several ringers in the game. The West Virginia coach, not at all surprised by the situation, commented, "I think we can beat them anyway." Indeed, West Virginia spoiled Higgins's head coaching debut by beating Wesleyan 14-0.

In attendance at the game was Alex Stevenson, a scout from Pitt. When he saw the lineman named Groggins he was taken aback, because Groggins was none other than Bob Osborn, who was the starting tackle and Higgins's teammate on Penn State's great 1919 squad. Stevenson reported his observation and school officials called Higgins on the carpet. He confessed to trying to sneak his old teammate into the game and wrote a letter of apology. West Virginia backers were outraged. A newspaper article stated: "Morgantown people feel that such tactics on the part of Wesleyan cannot be tolerated. There was talk among them Saturday night of refusing to play further games with Wesleyan."

Higgins's fate was put on hold until the end of the season. Osborn quietly left town, though he and Higgins would soon meet again.

Wesleyan tied a strong Washington & Jefferson team 7-7 in the next game. Higgins's first win as a head coach came against Grove City, 7-0. Wesleyan also defeated Thiel, Morris Harvey and George Washington. But Wesleyan lost its final three games to Detroit, Marietta and Georgetown, and Higgins completed his first season with a 4-4-1 record. Despite the problems with ineligible players, Higgins became very popular with Wesleyan football fans.

As the Wesleyan season wound down, Higgins received a call from the great Jim Thorpe, now the 33-year-old coach of the Canton Bulldogs professional team in Ohio. Thorpe wanted Higgins to play end for Canton. Higgins wasn't surprised by the offer. Prior to Higgins's last season at Penn State, Thorpe had asked him to sign on with Canton. Higgins initially agreed to the move, but on greater reflection recognized that 1919 was his final shot at Camp's All-American team, and he knew Bezdek was counting on him as squad captain.

This time, however, Higgins accepted Thorpe's offer. He would play for Canton and hopefully return to Wesleyan in the fall. Higgins needed the extra money. He also noticed that in a year's time professional football had done a lot to clean up its act.

Perhaps most importantly, Higgins welcomed the opportunity to play football again. It hadn't been easy for him to open fall practice standing on the sidelines as a coach. The previous year Higgins had played fifteen games in the service and at Penn State. He was in tremendous physical condition, and football was still in his blood.

By 1915 the state of Ohio was the mecca of professional football. Cleveland, Akron and Massillon fielded teams. Canton had organized in 1905, dissolved and then formed again with Thorpe coaching and playing for five hundred dollars a game. But pro football was having trouble shaking its unsavory reputation built on wide-open gambling and blatant use of college stars who changed their names for one-game paid appearances.

In August of 1920 several team owners met in Akron and agreed that something needed to happen if professional football was ever going to receive equal billing with college football and pro baseball. On September 17, 1920, eleven team representatives met in Canton, Ohio at Ralph Hay's automobile agency. Hay owned the Canton team. The representative from the Decatur (Illinois) Staleys was its player-coach, George Halas.

Halas, born in Chicago, had played as a 175-pound end for the University of Illinois. After graduating he became a member of the Great Lakes Naval Training Station team, which defeated the Mare Island Marines 17-0 in the Rose Bowl on January 1, 1919. Halas then played baseball in the New York Yankees organization and had a brief stint in the majors early in 1919, playing outfield and getting two hits in twenty-two at bats. A nagging hip injury steered Halas out of baseball. He returned to Chicago, worked for the Chicago, Burlington & Quincy Railroad and played football for the Hammond Pros on weekends.

In March 1920 A.E. Staley, the owner of Staley Manufacturing Company, asked Halas to organize a pro team in Decatur. Staley Manufacturing produced corn products at its Decatur plant. The members of the new football team, including Halas, would work at the plant while playing football.

In addition to Hay's Canton and Halas's Decatur, the other teams attending the September meeting were Akron, Cleveland, Dayton, Hammond, Massillon, Muncie, Racine (from Chicago's South Side), Rochester and Rock Island. Years later Halas recalled the gathering: "That meeting in Hay's showroom must have been the most informal on record. There were no chairs. We lounged around on fenders and running boards and talked things over."

Informal as the meeting may have been, it certainly had historical consequences: from it came the American Professional Football Association, which in 1922 changed its name to the National Football League. The teams agreed to not sign up collegians before their playing careers were over, and no team would tamper with players on another team. The most popular player in football, Jim Thorpe, who was still coaching, running and kicking for Canton, was named president of the APFA based on his name recognition. Because of this historical gathering, the town of Canton became home to the Pro Football Hall of Fame, which opened in 1963 and inducted seventeen charter members, including Halas and Thorpe.

Teams came and went during the league's first season in 1920. Schedules fell by the wayside and some teams played games against non-league teams. No champion was officially recognized, but Akron claimed the title with an 11-0-2 record.

Higgins joined the Canton squad in early November. His place in the lineup added another great player to an already great roster. Thorpe had two of his old Indian buddies and Carlisle teammates — Pete Calac and Joe Guyon — running with him in the backfield. At tackle was former Washington & Jefferson All-American Wilbur "Fats" Henry.

While most pro football games drew less than ten thousand fans, Higgins quickly found out that the league's biggest draw was Canton because of Thorpe. Canton and Thorpe attracted the season's largest crowd — fifteen thousand — in a game against Buffalo at the Polo Grounds.

Higgins's first game with Canton was against Cleveland in early November, 1920. Thorpe, however, was ill and couldn't play. His story was that he had been out coon hunting all night and caught a cold. Whatever the real reason, Thorpe understood that if his absence was publicized before the game both teams would lose thousands of dollars in gate receipts. Thorpe was also concerned that a minor riot might develop once fans had paid the price of admission and then learned he wasn't in the lineup.

Prior to the game Thorpe gave Higgins a crash course in the team's signals and plays. Thorpe added, "I'm not going to play today so you'll have to do the kicking. Wear my uniform."

"You mean I'm supposed to be you?" Higgins asked.

"Nothing to it," Thorpe said.

Higgins later recalled, "I put on his number 20. They had to practically cover me with tape to keep big Jim's pants up."

No one noticed the ploy the first couple of times Higgins dropped back to punt. But the third time he dropped back a man sitting in one of the lower rows cupped his hands and yelled: "Who's that bum in Thorpe's uniform?"

The crowd caught on and booed the scam. But by game's end the Cleveland fans were comparing Higgins to Thorpe because of his outstanding punting and his performance at left end. Canton whipped Cleveland 18-0.

Higgins's most memorable play with Canton came against the Chicago Tigers. In the second quarter of a scoreless game,

Canton's Guyon punted from midfield to the ten, but Milt Ghee of Chicago misjudged the ball and let it bounce. Ghee then tried to grab it but Higgins on the sprint smashed into Ghee and the ball slipped from the Chicago returner's grasp. It wobbled over the goal line where Higgins jumped on it for the first touchdown of the game.

Another Canton score in the third quarter was set up by a Guyon-to-Higgins pass of twenty-two yards to the Chicago eight. Canton won the game, 21-0.

Thorpe left the Canton team following the season, but Higgins forever marvelled at the big man's skills. "Jim was unquestionably the greatest player who ever lived," Higgins said. "He could do anything. He ran like a streak of lightning. And if he tackled you, you didn't get up for awhile."

Down through the years, whenever fans asked Higgins about Thorpe, he always told the story he and several other coaches heard from Gus Welch as they lounged "with some ice" in Jock Sutherland's hotel room in New York City during a coaches convention. Sutherland was a former Pitt guard and later its great head football coach and still later the head coach of the Pittsburgh Steelers.

One of the coaches in the room, Teg Hawley, asked, "Bob, you played with Jim Thorpe. How good was he?"

Welch, a quarterback who had played with Thorpe at Carlisle, said, "Let me take that one, Bob. We were playing Dartmouth and Pete Calac got hurt and had to be taken out of the game. Pop (Warner) says to me, 'Go in and take Pete's place.' Well, I was really Jim's substitute and knew nothing about the blocking back job. They called an off-tackle play and I said to Jim, 'What do I do?'

"He said, 'Go out and take the end.'

"'Suppose I miss him?' I said. 'What then?'

"'Keep on going,' says Jim.

"So they call the play, snap the ball and out I go to get the end. I missed him and go down to get the halfback. I missed him so I legged it down to the safety man and he sidestepped me and just about that time Jim and I go over for a touchdown. That's how good Thorpe was."

Another coach in the room asked Higgins what kind of guy Thorpe was. Higgins replied, "He was the kind of guy that every time he went out to eat he took along his hunting dog. He would order two steaks, one with onions and one without. The steak with onions was for his dog."

Canton football and a questionable future as Wesleyan's head coach were not the only things on Bob Higgins's mind. On a Saturday afternoon after one of the Wesleyan games, a friend introduced Higgins to a pretty seventeen-year-old girl named Virginia Eleanor Gaylord, one of four children of William and Milicent Gaylord of nearby Clarksburg, West Virginia. Higgins and Virginia chatted on the steps of one of the campus buildings. She attended a country day school and was at Wesleyan visiting a girl friend. Virginia, with a Methodist upbringing, was very proper and well-mannered. Higgins knew she was the kind of girl his sisters would like.

Virginia's father, William, seemed to have an iron in every fire in Clarksburg. One of his ventures was a Buick agency and he employed Higgins as a salesman.

Meanwhile, the Canton Bulldogs were undergoing an off-season facelift, as were many of the teams as the league entered its second season. Coach Thorpe had departed for Cleveland and taken running backs Guyon and Calac with him. Owner Ralph Hay named Eugene "Horse" Edwards to replace Thorpe as coach.

By the spring of 1921 all but a handful of players from the 1920 Canton team had moved elsewhere. Higgins hadn't committed to play for anybody. But owner Hay contacted Higgins and offered him four hundred dollars to co-coach with Edwards and to become team captain while continuing to play end.

Higgins went back to the Wesleyan administrators, who were still considering some form of action against him. The school and Higgins arranged a one-year leave of absence. Higgins then got permission from Virginia's father to loosen up his schedule at the Buick dealership to make time for pro football.

Higgins accepted Hay's offer in July, which moved Hay to comment: "For the life of me I can't see why Canton should not have the greatest professional football combination next fall in Bob Higgins and Horse Edwards."

First, however, Canton had to find some players. Returning with Higgins and Edwards were tackle Henry and center Al Feeney. Higgins then turned to his former teammates at Penn State. Charley Way, a 1920 Walter Camp first team All-American, had considered several pro teams, but he signed on with Canton because of his association with Higgins. Former Penn State center Larry Conover joined the club; so did former Lion quarterback Harry Robb. And to beef up the line Higgins signed guard Bob Osborn, who was of course the notorious "Groggins" of West Virginia Wesleyan fame. Higgins also lured two fellow 1919 first team All-Americans in guard Adolph Youngstrom of Dartmouth and tackle Belford West of Colgate.

Canton finished fifth in the thirteen-team league in 1921. The Bulldogs went 4-3-3. They lost to the eventual league champion, the Chicago Staleys, 10-0 in the next-to-final game of the season. George Halas and halfback Dutch Sternaman had purchased the Decatur Staleys and moved the club to Chicago prior to the season. Ends Halas and Higgins went head-to-head during the Chicago-Canton game. More than sixty years later Halas would tell Higgins's grandson and Bear fullback Matt Suhey that he had gotten the better of Higgins. More likely than not, however, Higgins gave Halas a memorable lesson in endmanship. This was to be The Hig's final year as a pro.

The American Professional Football Association had grown up in 1921. Joe Carr, a former sportswriter who had gone into football and baseball management, replaced Thorpe as league president before the season and began an extremely successful eighteen-year stint. One of the new teams in 1921 was the Green Bay Packers, sponsored by Acme Packing Company in Wisconsin. Curly Lambeau coached the Pack and played tailback. The next year, 1922, the AFPA changed its name to the National Football League. But by then Higgins had hung up his jersey and, just short of his twenty-ninth birthday, returned to Wesleyan as head coach. The move signified his lasting commitment to the college coaching profession.

Upon Higgins's rehiring at Wesleyan, a local paper reported: "The news that he would return here was greeted enthusiastically by the students and townspeople, with whom he is immensely popular."

Wesleyan had suffered through its worst season ever in 1921 while Higgins was with Canton. Several players had transferred or dropped out of school and the team's performance showed it, posting a record of no wins and seven losses. Detroit battered Wesleyan, 55-0, and three Wesleyan players in the game suffered broken bones.

But Higgins quickly rebuilt the team. Wesleyan won eight and lost two in 1922. The losses came against the toughest foes on the schedule. West Virginia beat Wesleyan 20-3. Coached by Clarence Spears, West Virginia went 9-0-1 on the season and was ranked as a top ten team. Washington & Jefferson blanked Wesleyan 14-0, scoring both times on passes.

Higgins had developing talent going into the 1923 season, including Gale Bullman, Everett Brinkmann, Chub Fenton, Chick Weihl, Elwyn Comstock, Brownie Corcoran, Link DeLong, Buck Kraus and Red King. Higgins traveled to Marietta, Ohio to recruit Weihl. He found Weihl digging a ditch for a gas company. Decked out in golf knickers and loud socks, having just played a round, Higgins sat down on the curb and won Weihl over. Weihl became the quarterback. Another Marietta kid Higgins lured was Bullman, who had played a season at Marietta College before breaking a leg. Higgins took Bullman under his wing and turned him into a great end and punter. The young team gained some seasoning and compiled a 3-4-1 record in 1923. Higgins's final season at Wesleyan, 1924, produced a national power and one of the most remembered teams in Wesleyan history. Bullman was its captain and Higgins gave him room to lead, which became a Higgins coaching characteristic. Composed of West Virginia, Pennsylvania and Ohio boys, Wesleyan won nine and lost two. It lost the opener to powerful West Virginia, 21-6, but proceeded to drub Broaddus, Salem and Marietta by the combined score of 97-0. Wesleyan then beat Bethany 19-6 and Davis & Elkins 12-7.

The biggest victory in years for Wesleyan came against Navy, 10-7. Wesleyan scored early, driving ninety-four yards after keeping Navy out of the end zone. Garrity passed to Dietrich for a 58-yard gain and then Garrity scooted thirty-six yards for the score. Bullman's point after made it 7-0.

Navy tied the game 7-7 but the key play of the afternoon came when Corcoran set up to punt for Wesleyan. Corcoran never did the punting and Navy, perhaps remembering Higgins's famous 1919 touchdown against Pitt, thought it was a fake and didn't drop back a returner. Corcoran's boot traveled seventy yards. Navy then fumbled on its twelve-yard-line and Weihl recovered. Bullman's field goal gave Wesleyan the 10-7 victory.

Wesleyan had a let-down after Navy and lost to Waynesburg, but Higgins pulled the team together for the following week's game at perennial eastern power Syracuse. The Orangemen, led by second-team All-American tackle Lynn Waldorf, was 5-0-1, having tied Pitt while beating Penn State 10-6. Syracuse's Archbold Stadium packed in ten thousand fans to watch the clash with surprising Wesleyan.

Syracuse had the ball on the Wesleyan six when Wesleyan tackle John Moore of Connellsville, Pennsylvania caused a fumble with a jarring hit. Bullman picked up the ball and rambled ninety-four yards for the touchdown. He also kicked the extra point to give Wesleyan a 7-0 lead before a stunned Syracuse audience.

All the Orangemen could manage the remainder of the game was a field goal as the Wesleyan defense rose to the occasion time after time. The offense maintained possession with short drives.

One sportswriter described Bullman thusly: "He always made some spectacular play that changed the course of the contest; picking up a fumble and running for a score, catching an impossible pass or kicking the ball sixty yards into coffin corner. He was either a great player or the luckiest one I ever saw, and he did it so many times I don't figure it was luck."

Wesleyan played two games it didn't expect to play after the end of the regular season. The first game, pushed by alumni wanting to see their team in action again, was played December 6 against Kentucky in Charleston. Kentucky had defeated Tennessee 27-6 the week before. Wesleyan won with ease, 24-7, as Kermit Frecka returned two punts for touchdowns on spectacular ninety- and seventy-yard runs. Bullman added a field goal.

91

Wesleyan wasn't through yet. A group of businessmen wanted to host a game on New Year's Day in Dallas, Texas between traditional Southwest power Southern Methodist University, coached by Ray Morrison, and Notre Dame. But Notre Dame and its Four Horsemen had a New Year's date with Ernie Nevers and Stanford in the Rose Bowl. Notre Dame coach Knute Rockne, after graciously declining the Dallas invitation, suggested that the promoters see about inviting Wesleyan which, he said, "has the best line in the East."

Sports historian Kent Kessler wrote: "Most West Virginians don't know it but Wesleyan played in the first bowl game in Dallas. It didn't have a name at that time but later became known as the Cotton Bowl."

After a scoreless first half, SMU scored in the third quarter when a hit on Wesleyan's Garrity forced a fumble which SMU recovered in the end zone for a touchdown. Wesleyan's King kicked a forty-yard field goal in the same quarter to cut the lead to 7-3.

In the final period DeLong substituted for Weihl and threw a long pass intended for Bullman. The ball deflected off the SMU defender's hands into Bullman's grasp and the Wesleyan captain scampered for a seventy-yard touchdown. The score put Wesleyan ahead 9-7, but SMU drove late in the game from its own twenty-nine to the Wesleyan twelve. SMU lined up for what appeared to be a winning field goal, but Wesleyan's line broke through and blocked the kick to preserve the win. SMU threw an uncanny twenty-eight passes on the day, completing only eight.

This was to be the first of two New Year's Day encounters against SMU in Dallas for a Higgins-coached team. Twenty-three years later, on New Year's Day, 1948, Higgins led his undefeated Penn State squad against Doak Walker and SMU in the Cotton Bowl.

Kessler reported that following the Wesleyan victory, Higgins threw a banquet for his players. One of the boys, Elwyn Comstock, apparently had a few drinks and became so noisy that Higgins asked Garrity and Weihl to help Comstock walk it off. Once outside, with Garrity and Weihl on either side of him, Comstock suddenly halted and pointed across the road. "Man, there was another close football game," he said

His teammates looked across and saw a sign in a grocery story window: "Hamburger 20, Liver 19."

While building a strong Wesleyan team, Higgins was putting together a pretty solid unit of his own at home. He had married Virginia Gaylord on December 6, 1922. Their marriage would last more than forty-six years, until Higgins's death in 1969. The first of their three daughters, Mary Ann, was born in the spring of 1924 in Clarksburg. Ginger came along three years later and Nancy in another four years.

Virginia returned to her hometown to give birth to all three children. Her uncle served as her physician.

Nancy recalled of her mother: "She was a Southern lady. She was very proper and really very beautiful; not athletic at all, but more of an artist. She painted plates. She always wore a hat and gloves when she went out. She didn't drive a car and didn't have an occupation. We had a maid until I was about twelve. Nobody else in State College did. But she was used to having one and brought up one from Clarksburg."

Mrs. Higgins did most of the worrying in the family. She was very protective of her husband. She was his greatest fan and attended all of the games.

Between the 1924 and 1925 football seasons, the young family headed West, as Higgins accepted the head coaching post at Washington University in St. Louis. The big city on the Mississippi was thriving in the 1920s and a major reason was its baseball. St. Louis hosted two teams — the Cardinals of the National League and the Browns of the American League. Higgins, who had played baseball at Peddie and also at Penn State his freshman year, spent a good deal of time at Sportsman's Park. In 1925 he saw the great Rogers Hornsby of the Cardinals capture the Triple Crown by leading the league in average (.403), home runs (39) and runs batted in (143). In 1926 Higgins saw the Cardinals, managed by second baseman Hornsby, win the National League pennant and then defeat the New York Yankees four games to three in the World Series. The Yankee team was led by two of the greatest players of all time, Babe Ruth and Lou Gehrig. Ruth hit three homers in the fourth game of the series in St. Louis. Grover Cleveland Alexander, who had pitched the 89th Division to the A.E.F. championship after World War I, got the final outs of the seventh and final game, which included the famous strikeout of Tony Lazzeri with the bases loaded.

The city's other team, the Browns, was led by first baseman and future Hall of Famer George Sisler, who had already hit over .400 twice in his career. Once Higgins took Virginia to a Browns game and when Sisler came to bat he pointed to the star and said, "There's the great George Sisler." Virginia responded, "Oh, I thought he played third base." Higgins rolled his eyes at his wife's lack of understanding.

The Higgins family received the red carpet treatment upon its arrival in St. Louis. The Washington U. newspaper stated: "Alumni appear to be in high glee over the selection of Coach Higgins. Many say they wonder why they did not think of him sooner."

The director of athletics, Dr. W.P. Edmunds, who had signed Higgins to a three-year contract, said, "Higgins struck me at once as the right man for the job. We went over the situation thoroughly and I am sure he is the man who will cooperate with me to build a winning team."

Washington was a member of the Missouri Valley Intercollegiate Association, which had been formed in 1907. The Bears played on Francis Field, which was built in 1904 as part of the Summer Olympics. Along with Washington, The Missouri Valley conference included nationally-recognized programs at Missouri, Oklahoma, Nebraska and Kansas in addition to Kansas State, Iowa State, Drake, Creighton, Grinnell and Oklahoma A&M.

Higgins was well aware of the excellent caliber of football played in the Missouri Valley because his 89th Division team in Europe was composed mainly of Midwesterners, including Adrian Lindsey, Scrubby Laslett, Claude Fletcher and Marshall Wilder of Kansas, and Poge Lewis, the former captain and fullback of the very Washington University Higgins now coached. Washington had won the league title in 1918 and gone 6-0 on the season.

But the pickings were slim when Higgins arrived. He hired his former Wesleyan end and captain, Bullman, as an assistant. They "worked the squad as few ever have been worked, with daily practices two to four hours in rain, shine or hot weather." Still,the Bears suffered through a 2-5-1 season in 1925. Higgins didn't feel the school was providing enough support for his football program. A newspaper article stated: "Higgins does not hesitate to make it perfectly clear that he and the athletic director have not been able to get along."

Virginia Higgins was ready to pack up and head back east. She had been homesick since moving to St. Louis, so much so that her sister Alice came out from West Virginia for an extended stay. In many ways, the Higgins's situation was as bad as the baked turkey Virginia's mother sent them for their first Thanksgiving in St. Louis: the bird hadn't been gutted and spoiled en route to the Higgins home.

St. Louis became forever associated with unpleasant memories when Higgins's oldest sister, Mary, died in 1926. He had confided to her more than any of his other siblings during his youth. She had largely taken the place of his mother and he felt very close to her.

Upon her death, the heartbroken Higgins's jotted down, "Mary B. Higgins — The most heavenly person that ever drew breath. Never was a more wonderful person on the face of this earth. There may have been someone just as good but never never one better and I doubt that ever there was one as good or near as good."

Higgins also lost his father in August 1926. For ten years Michael Higgins had been living at daughter Margaret's cottage at Truro on Cape Cod. Margaret had purchased the cottage from journalist Jack Reed before he traveled to Moscow to report on the Bolshevik uprising. The movie *Reds* was later made about Reed's career and move to Russia.

Higgins last saw his father at Truro a month before he died. He had suffered a cerebral stroke which left his body paralyzed and deprived him of speech. Higgins visited his father with his favorite nephew, Margaret's son Stuart, who had also attended Peddie Institute and been captain of the football team there in 1922.

The only way Michael Higgins could communicate was to blink his eyes. When his son asked him if he'd like something to drink, the father kept blinking in the direction of the kitchen cupboard where he had stored a jug of local dandelion wine. Higgins assisted his father with a small drink of the wine and the son and nephew drank a toast to the 82-year-old man.

Michael Higgins had asked to be buried in Corning beside his wife. It was a simple burial that served as one of the last occasions for all of his children to be together.

Things didn't get any better for Higgins on the football field in 1926. His Bears plummeted to a 1-7 season and a last place finish in the conference. But, as would become a pattern in Higgins's head coaching career, he overcame the adversity and turned the team around. Several recruits came into their own and the Bears improved to a 5-2-2 record in 1927. Washington tied Kansas 21-21, and lost a tough one to league champ Missouri, 13-0, after Missouri had stopped the Bears on the one-yard-line in the opening quarter.

A movement in the conference swelled for several of the better teams to split off and form another league, including 1927 conference winner Missouri. But Washington wasn't one of this group. Following the season Nebraska, Missouri, Oklahoma, Kansas, Kansas State and Iowa State split from the pack and formed what was known as the Big Six and later became the Big Eight. Washington, Drake, Creighton, Grinnell and Oklahoma A&M formed the new Missouri Valley Conference.

Higgins didn't like the writing on the wall for the Washington football program. Furthermore, he and his wife still pined to move back east. He contacted head coach Bezdek at Penn State to let Bezdek know he wanted to return to his alma mater. Bezdek wasn't long in responding. Penn State needed an ends coach. What better man to fill the position than the greatest end in Penn State history?

The Higgins family, now including a second daughter, Ginger, born in the summer of 1927, packed up and headed for the only real home Higgins had ever known: State College, Pennsylvania.

§ 8 §
Home To State College

AS HIGGINS MADE HIS MARK as a head coach at West Virginia Wesleyan and Washington University, college football embarked on its Golden Decade. The Rockne legend began taking shape when Notre Dame went undefeated in 1919, and emerged even stronger when Notre Dame again went undefeated in 1920 with All-American half-back George Gipp leading the way. Gipp ran and passed for 332 yards in a memorable 27-17 win over Army. Two weeks later he cracked his collarbone and dislocated a shoulder against Indiana, but rallied the Irish from a ten-point deficit to win 13-10. The Gipper would be dead of pneumonia a few months later.

The most consistent team from 1920 to 1924 was California, coached by Andy Smith. Cal's "Wonder Teams" didn't lose a game for five seasons: they won forty-four and tied four. They outscored opponents 1,578 to 139 in that period. Led by end Brick Muller, California romped Ohio State in the Rose Bowl on New Year's Day 1921.

Cornell, coached by Gil Dobie and led by Eddie Kaw and George Pfann, went 8-0 three consecutive years — 1921, 1922 and 1923.

In 1923 Bob Zuppke's Illinois went 8-0, thanks largely to sophomore running back Red Grange, better known as "The Galloping Ghost." Grange ran seventy yards for a touchdown and scored three times in his first varsity game, a 24-7 win over Nebraska. He ran ninety-two yards for a score in the win over Northwestern and streaked sixty yards to score the only points in Illinois's 7-0 shutout of Amos Alonzo Stagg's Chicago.

Illinois fell to 6-1-1 in 1924, but Grange continued to put up his amazing numbers. He had touchdown runs of ninety-five, sixty-seven, fifty-six and forty-four yards against Michigan, ninety-four and eighty yards against Chicago and ninety-four yards against Iowa.

Fielding "Hurry Up" Yost's Michigan went 6-0-1 in 1922 and 8-0 in 1923. All-American Harry Kipke became recognized as one of the game's greatest punters.

Notre Dame's "Four Horsemen" backfield of Harry Stuhldreher, Jim Crowley, Elmer Layden and Don Miller paced Rockne's Irish to a 9-0 record in 1924. Notre Dame followed up the regular season with a 27-10 win over Stanford in the Rose Bowl. Pop Warner's Stanford team was led by running back Ernie "The Tank" Nevers.

Alabama, coached by Wallace Wade, rose to the top in 1925, sweeping undefeated through its nine regular season games and then edging Washington 20-19 in the Rose Bowl. The Tide defense yielded only one touchdown during the regular season, while Grant Gillis, Pooley Hubert and Johnny Mack Brown spearheaded the offense.

Alabama returned to the Rose Bowl in 1926 with a 9-0 mark. Warner's Stanford reached Pasadena with a 10-0 record. The two teams fought to a 7-7 tie.

Jess Hawley's Dartmouth, with All-American back Swede Oberlander, went 7-0-1 in 1924 and 8-0 in 1925.

Navy, coached by Bill Ingram, sailed through its first nine games in 1926, and Army had lost but once (to Notre Dame) when the two met at Soldier Field in Chicago before the largest crowd ever to witness an American football game — 110,000. Navy jumped out to a 14-0 lead, but Army rallied and went ahead 21-14 late in the game. Navy halfback Alan Shapley then intercepted a pass, and the Midshipmen drove to Army's eight before Shapley scored on a double reverse. Tom Hamilton's third drop-kick point after conversion accounted for the final 21-21 score.

No team was perfect in 1927, but Zuppke's Illinois went 7-0-1. Minnesota came in at 6-0-2 behind the running of Bronko Nagurski. Dana Bible's Texas A&M went 8-0-1 and Bob Neyland, in his second year as head coach, guided Tennessee to an 8-0-1 season.

The decade had started out golden for Penn State as well. Bezdek's 1920 team went 7-0-2, including wins over Dartmouth, Penn and Nebraska. Season ending ties came against Lehigh and Pitt. First-team All-American Charley Way was joined by Glenn Killinger and Hinkey Haines in one of the country's finest backfields.

The 1921 Lions went 8-0-2, beating Georgia Tech before thirty thousand fans at the Polo Grounds in New York and also whipping Navy and Washington, while tying Harvard and Pitt. Killinger made Camp's All-American first team. A new name in the backfield was sophomore Harry "Light Horse" Wilson. Following the season Penn State increased seating capacity at New Beaver Field to twelve thousand.

Penn State under Bezdek would never be as good, though there were many bright moments and great players. The 1922 team — because of an awkward delayed-recognition of the 1921 performance — had dibs on the Rose Bowl. After Penn State started out 5-0 it received the invitation from the Pacific Coast Conference, then proceeded to win one, lose three and tie one in its final five games. The losses came against Navy, 14-0, at Penn, 7-6 and at Pitt, 14-0. Penn State lost to Southern Cal 14-3 in the Rose Bowl on January 1, 1923. The matchup caused the Tournament of Roses Association and the Pacific Coast Conference to bicker over invitation jurisdiction.

The highlight of Penn State's 1923 6-2-1 season was Light Horse Wilson's performance in the Lion's 21-3 homecoming win over Rose Bowl-bound Navy. It was Navy's first visit to State College. Fifteen thousand fans jammed Beaver Field for the tilt. Wilson intercepted a pass and ran fifty-five yards for one touchdown, returned a kickoff ninety-five yards for another touchdown, and on a fake reverse sprinted seventy-two yards for his and Penn State's third touchdown of the afternoon. It was Navy's only loss of the season.

Including the Navy game, Wilson scored all of Penn State's touchdowns in its final six games in 1923. He scored twice in a 13-13 tie against West Virginia at Yankee Stadium before fifty thousand fans; scored the lone touchdown in a 7-0 win over Georgia Tech; and crossed the goal line three more times in a big 21-0 win at Penn in front of 56,000 fans at

Franklin Field.

In an unusual twist on today's eligibility regulations, Wilson entered West Point after the 1923 season and was able to play four more seasons for Army.

Another highlight of Penn State's 1923 season was the play of senior captain and guard Joe Bedenk, who made first team All-American and would have a long-standing position in Penn State athletic history.

Bezdek's squads went 6-3-1, 4-4-1, 5-4 and 6-2-1 from 1924 to 1927. One of the biggest home games was a scoreless tie against Rockne's Notre Dame in 1925. Twenty-thousand partisan fans crammed in and around Beaver Field for the game. Big victories during those years came against Navy, Michigan State and Penn, but the thorn in Bezdek's side remained rival Pittsburgh. Bezdek hadn't defeated Pitt since 1919, when Higgins broke open the game with his 92-yard reception and run for a touchdown on the faked punt. Even Bezdek's undefeated teams in 1920 and 1921 settled for scoreless ties with Pitt, and the 1922-1927 teams not only lost six straight to Pitt, but were outscored in those games 135-19.

Bezdek had been able to draw the likes of Notre Dame, Navy and Michigan State into State College and place road games at the Polo Grounds and Yankee Stadium, but Penn State's performance against Pitt put Bezdek's job on the line. At the same time, with a new college president who opposed athletic subsidies, the Penn State football program took a strange turn.

By the time Higgins arrived in State College for the 1928 season, Penn State had adopted a strict amateurism program, meaning it no longer gave scholarships to athletes. This program was generally known as The Purist Policy.

Penn State was one of many schools around the country to question its athletic policies. The Golden Age of college football had peaked in 1927. Penn State, like many schools, was profiting from the college football frenzy. But while these schools raked in the money, they did so with some guilt over the inordinate emphasis placed on sports without similar compensation for academics.

In January 1926 the Carnegie Foundation for the Ad

vancement of Teaching began studying the role of athletics on college campuses. At the annual Penn State alumni association meeting in June, a faction of the alumni felt the school had been over-emphasizing football and neglecting the development of physical education for all students. They said Bezdek had neglected intramural sports and pointed to the recent construction of Varsity Hall to house athletes. Mike Sullivan, since 1919 the executive director of the association, shared this point of view, as did incoming alumni president James Milholland.

The alumni association created a committee chaired by engineer and businessman John Beaver White to survey the school's athletic policies. The committee began its work in the summer of 1926 and reported its findings in March 1927 to the alumni board of directors. The committee made four recommendations, the most drastic being that the school award no more athletic scholarships. The committee also recommended that physical education and intercollegiate athletics be separated, with the latter being supervised by a new board of athletic control. Intramurals and general PE would fall under the department of physical education, whose director could not be a coach of any sport. Bezdek reportedly spoke in favor of the recommendations, expecting to resign as head coach and carry on as director of physical education.

The new board met for the first time in August 1927 and immediately discontinued the awarding of any new athletic scholarships. The board also banned any scouting of upcoming opponents.

Officially putting intercollegiate athletics under board control was delayed, however. New Penn State president Dr. Ralph Hetzel felt that the college administration should control intercollegiate athletics instead of the board, which included five alumni and three students among its thirteen members. Hetzel had strongly endorsed the no-scholarship rule. He had become president of Penn State in December 1926 after a similar post at the University of New Hampshire, where he had also opposed athletic subsidies in New England intercollegiate athletics.

It is wrong, however, to suggest that Penn State had suddenly lost interest in its football team. Many alumni, particularly those from the Pittsburgh area, still held Bezdek on the hot seat because he couldn't beat Pitt. No one fully understood the ramifications of a no-scholarship policy, and many alumni simply jumped on the reform bandwagon then sweeping the nation.

Higgins may have sensed similar reform in the wind at Washington, but when he rolled into State College in 1928 it hit him between the eyes. The Hig couldn't have known then that the purist policy would burden him for the rest of his coaching career.

Aside from the politics, the 34-year-old Higgins was glad to be back at Penn State. He had been unsettled since he left Corning for grade school in Ontario. He had been happiest when he attended Penn State before and after the war, and something about State College never let go of him during his years in West Virginia and St. Louis. His wife was much closer to her home and her spirits brightened. The small community was a wonderful setting in which to raise their daughters.

The business at hand for Higgins was coaching the ends. But he saw that the football program was unsound. Recruiting had obviously fallen off even before implementation of the no-scholarship policy. The 1928 team fell to 3-5-1, losing most of the big games, including a 26-0 bashing from Pitt.

Penn State improved its record to 6-3 in 1929, but another season-ending drubbing by Pitt left a bad taste. Talk of Bezdek's ouster as head coach prevailed throughout the season.

During the 1929 season the Carnegie Foundation finally released the study it had begun in 1926. The report said intercollegiate athletics carried such tremendous material value that administrations — and particularly alumni — often resorted to unethical practices. The report said that an emphasis on intramurals would improve the situation, but schools would have to "wrest" control of athletics from alumni to move in that direction.

The report criticized Penn State for awarding seventy-five football scholarships and tutoring varsity athletes without doing the same for other students. It also criticized Penn State's housing of athletes in Varsity Hall, depriving them of interaction with other students.

Penn State had of course already taken action on scholarships, but the Carnegie report supported President Hetzel's position that athletics come under administrative control. As a result, in early 1930, intercollegiate athletics became part of a new School of Physical Education, in which all staff would have academic rank under a non-coaching director. Once again Bezdek supported the measure, which meant he was out as head football coach, but would continue as director of the new School of Physical Education. Influential alumni had stepped up their action to remove Bezdek as head coach and this latest development appeased them.

Higgins's playing record at Penn State, his seven years of head coaching experience, and the fact that he was already on campus made him the only serious candidate for head football coach. It became official on May 27, 1930. Higgins thus joined an elite fraternity which in 1930 included Rockne at Notre Dame, Warner at Stanford, Sutherland at Pitt, Stagg at Chicago, Alexander at Georgia Tech, Neyland at Tennessee and Kerr at Colgate.

Purist policy or not, Higgins was only too happy to take the post. The stock market crash of October 29, 1929 had sent shivers throughout the nation, and the economic situation was worsening with each year.

The appointment of Higgins, one newspaper stated, "will serve to arouse dormant enthusiasm among local Penn State men and will cause the flickering flame of victory hope to take on added fire in the breasts of Penn State men who have been too long awaiting a State victory over the (Pittsburgh) Panthers."

Higgins's first staff included line coach Joe Bedenk, who had come back to assist Bezdek in 1929. Dutch Hermann moved up from the freshman team, and Larry Conover, Higgins's former teammate at both Penn State and Canton, came in to replace Hermann as freshman coach.

Higgins promptly received a letter from Dick Harlow, the former Penn State coach who was chiefly responsible for bringing Higgins to Penn State as a player in 1914. The tone of the letter had to be reassuring to the young head coach.

Dear Bob:

I just wanted to drop you a line to wish you all the luck in the world. Please be sure to make the boys realize that the opportunity which they have all prayed for is here and that it is up to them to show the world that we were all right in our belief as to what was wrong up there.

I know every Penn State man is solidly behind you, Bob, and I have every faith that you will have just as good a team as any coach could have with the material at your disposal.

Don't let them worry you and give my best to the two Dutches (Bedenk and Hermann) and Larry (Conover). I have full faith in every one of them.

Always,
Dick

Since the no-scholarship rule had taken effect in 1928, ten seniors on the 1930 team possessed the last scholarships handed out in 1927.

Jack Livezey was a halfback on Higgins's first team in 1930. He had walked on and made the freshman team in 1927, lettered in 1929 under Bezdek and would letter again in 1930 under Higgins. Livezey recalled that the players were aware of the pressure Bezdek was under from the alumni association. Therefore, news of the coaching change was not a surprise to the team. Neither did it surprise the players that Higgins got the job.

"Bob Higgins was so well qualified in so many ways, from his days as a player, his years in coaching and his excellent military record," Livezey said. "Bob had done a great job coaching our ends the previous two years. He worked a lot with Earle Edwards. We had a great amount of respect for Bob and he showed respect for us boys."

Livezey recalled that on the first day of pre-season practice the players did a double-take at the coaching style Higgins brought to the field. "Bez was a terrific guy, but he was a taskmaster," Livezey said. "Bob had a more lenient attitude toward the training program and scrimmaging. Bez had some high notes and would chase you off the field. But Bob never lost his cool."

Livezey was captain of the baseball team in the spring of

1931, which was Joe Bedenk's first of thirty-two years as Penn State head baseball coach.

Higgins inherited some talented senior personnel such as Edwards at end, halfback Cooper French and halfback and team captain Frank Diedrich. But the simple fact was that since 1928 Penn State had attempted to lure football players without being able to offer scholarships.

The ranks had thinned.

§ 9 §
Penn State's Purist Policy

PRIOR TO THE OPENING GAME kickoff at home against Niagara, Higgins sized up his 1930 squad this way: "I've got some smart boys. They can fight, too. We'll lick more teams than will lick us."

Higgins's first Penn State team numbered fifty-seven players, eleven of them returning lettermen. His boys brought him a 31-14 victory over Niagara before four thousand fans. French returned a punt sixty-five yards for a touchdown and scored again out of Higgins's single wing offense on a fifty-yard run.

Penn State followed up as expected with easy home wins over Lebanon Valley and Marshall, but no more victories were forthcoming for the 1930 team. The following week's 0-0 tie at Lafayette was nothing to be ashamed of. Lafayette had maintained a strong program during the 1920s, going undefeated with Jock Sutherland as head coach in 1921 and going unbeaten again in 1926 under G. Herbert McCracken.

The next foe, Colgate, was the toughest game on the schedule. Andy Kerr's first year as Colgate head coach in 1929 had resulted in an 8-1 record, the only loss a close one to Wisconsin, while seven Colgate opponents failed to score. Colgate was led by Len Macaulso, Johnny Orsi and Les Hart.

A homecoming crowd of eight thousand turned out to see if Penn State's unbeaten record could last. It couldn't. Colgate blasted the Lions 40-0.

On October 28, 1930, three days after the game, Kerr wrote Higgins.

Dear Bob:
I am taking the liberty of writing to you about our game

last Saturday. I am writing this note in a friendly spirit with the hope that from it you may be able to arouse the men on your squad for their remaining games on your schedule. In many respects I hesitate to do this, but as you told me some time ago, you realize that I am an older fellow and because of that fact I am taking the liberty of writing to you as I am.

Since the game last Saturday I have spent a lot of time in analyzing it and I must confess it is very hard for me to figure out how we scored forty points against a team as strong as Penn State. As I told you on Saturday, things broke very well for us and we had a very fair share of good luck. It takes breaks and luck to beat a team as strong as your team is. I am thoroughly convinced that we are not forty points better than Penn State.

In talking with our players I find that the Penn State boys were hitting hard and fighting throughout the entire sixty minutes of the game. In fact our fellows said that there was no let-up in the game and that it was just as strenuous and rugged in the last five minutes as it was in the first five. In spite of the size of the score, I am convinced that your players never let up for a minute. I always admired the fighting qualities of the Penn State teams and I feel that this team, even in its defeat, carried out the fighting traditions of your school. I feel that at Penn State you have a lot of high spirited boys and I believe that in the games to come they will rise to the occasion and turn in for you some wonderful performances.

I am going to give you an instance from my own coaching career that may be of service to you. In 1928 at Washington & Jefferson we had very scant material and a very weak team. The boys were keyed up to the highest pitch for Carnegie Tech and gave them a terrible battle. We were beaten the next week by Fordham. I made no effort to key up the team and as a result received the worst defeat of my coaching career. The next Saturday we played Lafayette and the Fordham game had added some more to our list of cripples. I felt that the Lafayette team was at least four or five touchdowns better than we were. In doing this I forgot to count on the splendid spirit of the W & J boys. Crippled as they were, they went into that game with the finest spirit and put up one of the greatest fights that I have ever seen a team display. Instead of losing by four or five touchdowns, the score ended in a 13 to 13 tie and at the end of the game the ball was in our possession on the Lafayette four yard line — as a matter of fact we should have won the game.

I am citing this instance to you in the hope that you may be able to arouse your boys to the highest pitch for their game with Bucknell next Saturday. I really believe that you are good enough to beat Bucknell and I am convinced that no team on the rest of your schedule will beat you by anything like the one-sided defeat you suffered last Saturday.

To be perfectly frank, I have written this letter with a great deal of hesitancy because I was afraid that you possibly might not understand my attitude. As I said before, my only motive is that of friendliness with the hope that you may be able to pull together the Penn State squad and finish the season with a good record.

With kind personal regards and with best wishes for your success in the remaining games of your schedule, I am

Most sincerely yours,

Andy

The sportsmanship exhibited in the letter to Higgins was typical of Kerr. He and Higgins remained close friends. Kerr retired after eighteen years as Colgate mentor following the 1946 season. Higgins was head coach at Penn State for nineteen years, retiring after the 1948 season. The two coaches squared off nine times and broke even with each having four wins, four losses and a tie.

Penn State played much better football the remainder of the season than it did in the Colgate game, but fell to Bucknell, 19-7, tied Syracuse 0-0, lost at Iowa 19-0 and dropped a tight one at Pitt, 19-12.

Penn State's effort against Pitt was its best since the early 1920s. End Earle Edwards, starting his last game for Penn State, scored a touchdown off a blocked kick. Penn State supporters would hear again from Edwards in several years.

In 1931 the Penn State football program caved in under the weight of the no-scholarship rule, which was compounded by the nation's Great Depression. Very few scholarship-quality football players could afford to pass up scholarships at competing schools to come to Penn State. The record fell to one win and eight losses in regular season play. Opponents outscored the Lions 167-38. It was bad enough losing big to traditional strongholds Pitt, Colgate, Lafayette and West Virginia, but Penn State also lost at home to the likes of Waynesburg and Dickinson. Pitt coach Jock Sutherland started his second team and played his third and fourth teams much of the game. After the game ended, Sutherland had his first team warm up for fifteen minutes in preparation for the following week's game.

The highlight of the year was a 31-0 post-season victory over Lehigh. Philadelphia community leaders put on the game at Franklin Field to raise funds for the city's unemployed. Lehigh had also de-emphasized intercollegiate sports.

Early in the dreadful season Higgins received a letter from Dick Rauch, his teammate on the 1919 squad.

Dear Bob,

I want to express my opinion in a short way about football up there. I realize a great many changes have taken place and under present conditions you are faced with difficulties beyond the ken of the average big institution mentor. I'm not offering a solution for these burdens but rather casting a vote of confidence and allegiance to the present regime.

Bob, I'm for you and the fellows helping. I know that even the weakest member of your squad is given some consideration and is treated as an American youth of the present century.

How much better it is that you have the respect and admiration of those who have known you as a man, than the recollections of an undefeated season which are forgotten in a short time.

I hope things break so that some time soon you may achieve the peak. But win or lose, I've been prouder of being a Penn Stater in the past two years.

Best regards to all.
Sincerely,
Dick Rauch

Higgins hung on in spite of his modest record. During

these hard economic times he was glad to be back at Penn State and glad to have a job. He was also very careful about expressing his views on the purist policy. For example, he tried to be diplomatic about the football program in a speech he delivered following the season:

Football at Penn State is no longer just a game to be played and to be won. It is a part of the college curriculum; in fact it is a department in the School of Physical Education and Athletics. The coaches are regular members of the College Faculty and there are no football scholarships given to prep-school stars.

The department is divided into three groups: Varsity football, Freshman football, and Intramural football. In the season just passed 1,098 boys were out for the sport at some time during the season. Sixty-five boys reported for Varsity, 147 reported for Freshman, and 896 reported for Intramural football. Many of these boys, however, were out for the sport only a short time. It was necessary to eliminate a team in Intramural football after it had been defeated once due to the fact that there were not enough playing fields. Other boys on the Freshman and Varsity squad felt that they were getting little or no attention from the coaches and became discouraged and dropped out. Next year with the additional playing fields and coaches that have been requested, it will be possible to keep many more boys playing football throughout the season.

Last year's football season was more interesting than any I can recall, due to the fact that there was no team of any caliber that went through its schedule undefeated or untied. This shows clearly that no section of the country dominates the game.

Many followers of Penn State believe that our past season was very unsuccessful due to the number of defeats that occurred during the season. Now I claim that we had, and our records show that we had, the best amateur team in the East. The only other strictly amateur teams that I know of were the University of Princeton and the University of Lehigh. Lehigh defeated Princeton in the middle of the season by a rather large score and in our post season game with Lehigh we won with a score of 31 to 0, giving Penn State the championship of the three pioneers.

Asked if he thought more colleges would go the path of Penn State and Lehigh with regard to strict amateurism, Higgins responded, "That seems to be the tendency, especially throughout the East. Lehigh started it years ago; Penn State was the second to follow; Pennsylvania is falling in line; both Columbia and N.Y.U. are discontinuing scholarships and in a year or two Syracuse is expected to do the same thing.

"I believe that we will see more and more colleges discontinue scholarships each year. I also believe that in a very short time the colleges who have cleaned up their athletics will have nothing to do with the colleges who are giving scholarships. It would not surprise me if, within the next four years, a conference was formed by colleges who are not subsidizing athletics."

Higgins was also asked about his upcoming 1932 football team. "I had hoped that you would not ask me that question because it is extremely difficult for me or for anyone else to tell what is going to happen in the future. I am, however, inclined to believe that next year's team will be an improvement over last year's team. We lose a great many regulars but there are some boys who will make good football players still in college. They would have been better this year had they had experience. I look for next year's team to be fair. Our schedule of course is difficult and any reasonable person does not expect us to beat Pittsburgh, Colgate, Temple and teams of that kind."

By the beginning of the 1932 season, Penn State's declining status in the college football ranks had caused administrators to drop Pitt and Lafayette from the schedule. Penn State that year played only seven games and lost all but two of those, including a loss to Waynesburg for the second year in a row.

Higgins received some criticism from alumni for the poor results, but the prevailing view was that the administration had tied his hands. Letters poured in to the student newspaper, the *Collegian*. An example of these letters follows:

Dear Sir:

Certain propaganda, which to my mind is insidious, has been put out lately by various people who are at the moment occupying rather prominent positions on the faculty, to the effect that the football material at Penn State at the present time is the best assembled here in ten years. To one who has followed the fortunes of Penn State in athletics for over twenty years, any such statement, to be very frank, and with due respect to the clean-cut young men who are battling against odds for the glory of Old State, is very far from the truth and it is an injustice to the coaching staff to allow such propaganda to remain unchallenged.

Before trying to refute the statement, let me say that I heartily disagree with the present policy of non-scholarship athletics. I see no difference between granting a scholarship for proficiency in athletics and proficiency in scholarship, since they both give to some youth an education and both scholarships are dependent on maintaining a good average in the classroom. Let us look at our coaching staff as well as the Director of the school and I think you will find that all of them who can be classed as "big-league coaches" went to school because of an athletic scholarship and one can hardly say that they are the worse for it. I believe if any alumnus desires to send a boy to school, that is his just right and why should the authorities here question that boy as to how or why he is sent to school. As long as they are not supplying aid to athletes under the name of Penn State, it seems to me that their responsibility ends there and alumni should be encouraged to take an interest in Penn State instead of discouraged, but that is probably explained by the fact that the athletic policies of Penn State are not dictated by Penn State members of the faculty.

As one looks over the present Varsity squad, let us compare it with some of those in the past. Where is there an end (and I admire the ability and fight of [current end] Tom Slusser) to compare with Higgins, Brown, McCollum, Frank or Weston? Where is the tackle equal to Cubbage, Henry, Black, Baer or Michalske? Where is the guard to compete with Osborn, Rauch, Griffith, Bedenk or Greenshields? Where the sterling center to battle with Conover, Bentz or Gray? Where the feared backs such as Robb, Killinger, Haines, Lightner, Wilson, Way, Roepke, Shell and Lungreen? Everyone gives the present squad their just due credit for playing for the love of the game and for competing with schools which subsidize athletics, but one cannot lose sight of the fact that the athletes of outstanding ability are attending schools where scholarships are maintained openly and above-board and most of the cream has been skimmed off before we receive any athletes.

"I think any thinking person will agree with me when I say that it is utterly impossible to expect to obtain as good as football or any other athletic material here under the present system, as it was under the previous regime which spent around $40,000 each year in bringing athletes to Penn State. It is not fair to expect the high school and prep school stars to enroll here when they can go to other schools which are spending that amount each year, and it is more unfair for any person in a position of authority and with a knowledge of the true facts to disseminate the report that our material is the best in ten years and in this way endeavor to put the coaches on the spot and blame them for the loss of football games. How many coaches in the country, and especially those in institutions of this size, are working under the same restrictions and conditions as here?

I know that our head coach is well-liked and respected by his brother coaches as a teacher of clean, hard football, and one who is at all times solicitous of the health of his boys. These same coaches have said publicly that if he were given the material on a par with other schools that he would put us back on the map as we were in 1919, 1920, 1921, when we had so many lettermen who returned from the war and who were classed as the finest football players in the country.

Sincerely,
An alumnus.

This letter cut to the heart of Higgins's coaching dilemma. The situation discouraged him. His personality had evolved through competition on the field of play. To watch his counterparts in the coaching community manhandle his teams was frustrating, no matter how high the odds were stacked against him. In a letter to his buddies in The Last Man's Club, Higgins revealed a rare moment of downtrodden spirit when he wrote, "The prospects for a team next year are better, but not great. With our Simon-pure and lily-white policy, it is impossible for us to ever be up there, unless the good Lord so wills it."

But Higgins was in no position to attack the situation at Penn State. Most importantly, he valued his job and the security it gave him and his family. A third daughter, Nancy, had come along in 1931; the Depression hit its grisly depth in 1933, and publicly criticizing his employer's football policy didn't seem wise. The few times he spoke publicly of it he put it in a positive light, but his statements seemed contrived.

It wasn't Higgins's style to focus on the negative or to make excuses. The purist policy was in place and a man could grow old in a hurry trying to change it. Higgins intended to grow old enjoying other things in life. He simply considered his situation a challenge and he worked hard to place competitive teams on the gridiron.

He had his work cut out for him.

§ 10 §
The Turnaround Begins

HIGGINS NEVER FORGOT the players who worked so hard for Penn State during the lean years of the Purist Policy. One of the players who rode the "no-scholarship train" to Penn State in the midst of the Great Depression became one of the best-known and best-loved men in the school's history.

Jim O'Hora, a small center, had never been to State College before the day he enrolled in the fall of 1932.

"I didn't even know where State College was," O'Hora recalled sixty-two years later. "Jack Harding was the coach at St. Thomas College in Scranton and he came up to our school in Dunmore and offered scholarships to each one of us he talked to that day. My mother said, 'No, I don't think that's a good idea because you'll be hanging around with your old buddies. You won't do much schoolwork that way.'

"We had a superintendent of schools, Jim Gilligan, who was a Penn State alumnus, and he thought some of the boys like myself would make a good addition to the squad. Jim Gilligan said, 'You fill out your applications and I'll take care of them.' He put us on a train in Wilkes-Barre and we got down to Bellefonte and took the bus over to the main campus. We were saying, 'I wonder where the college is.' We walked up to what is now Schlow Library, the old post office, because that looked like the biggest building we could see. Some kid who looked like a fraternity boy said, 'Hey, where are you guys going?' We said, 'We're going up to the Old Main,' and he told us we were going the wrong way. We turned around and went back down."

In an hour O'Hora found himself checked into Varsity

Hall. "When I came in 1932 there was one more scholarship person left on the squad, and that was Spike Collins," O'Hora said.

O'Hora recalled his initial impression of Higgins. "He was the kind of person that when you met him, you liked him. He was very honest, very helpful with people. You could tell that he loved life."

O'Hora lettered from 1933-1935. He graduated in 1936 and Higgins asked him to stay on as an assistant freshman coach. O'Hora completed his master's degree in the meanwhile and became a high school coach at Roaring Spring and Mahanoy Township in Mahanoy City. After he got out of the service he returned to Higgins's staff assisting line coach Bedenk in 1946. O'Hora served under four head coaches — Higgins, Bedenk, Engle and Paterno — before retiring after the 1976 season. Paterno named O'Hora assistant head coach in 1974.

The won-loss record of Higgins's teams from 1933 to 1938 does not reflect the transformation the Penn State football program was undergoing. Higgins and his closest friends and alumni made heroic efforts to pull in football players. As this recruiting push gained structure and momentum, the talent level of Penn State's teams grew. With quality players finally in his service, Higgins assembled a small but extremely diverse and talented coaching staff, and instilled in them his philosophy of basic, fundamental football. Beginning in 1939 until Higgins's final year in 1948, Penn State was an Eastern power and barely missed a national championship, despite competing against schools with long-established scholarship programs.

One alumnus who stepped forward was Casey Jones, Higgins's close friend, former teammate and World War I comrade. An executive at West Penn Power Company, Jones devoted his spare time to bringing football players to Penn State. Prior to the 1934 season Higgins and Jones devised a plan that Higgins took to the Athletic Board and President Hetzel. Higgins wanted an arrangement in which freshman players could be guaranteed part-time jobs for a year. The college would employ the players in cleanup positions in restaurants and fraternities. After their first year, the players would have made enough contacts to find work on their own.

Higgins also asked that during the football season a training table serving one meal a day be re-established. The college approved both of these requests effective in the fall of 1934. The player-job arrangement generally remained the status quo until 1949, the year Higgins retired, when the college reinstated athletic scholarships.

One of Jones's early recruits was lineman Sever "Tor" Toretti from Monongahela in western Pennsylvania. Toretti lettered from 1936-1938 and completed his master's degree while assisting with the freshman team in 1939. He coached high school ball at Steelton and Williamsport before joining head coach Joe Bedenk's staff in 1949. He left coaching in 1963 but remained with Penn State as a recruiter and fund raiser until his retirement in 1979.

Toretti recalled his first years on campus: "I came here in the fall of 1935. Casey Jones helped me. He and a few other people grew tired of getting beat so they wanted to help Bob and began raising a little bit of money here and there. They would raffle off an automobile after the Pittsburgh game. It was down to that, having to do that kind of financial endeavor.

"Casey Jones was a great person, a good athlete himself in his days. I learned from him how to recruit. A number of us were scheduled to go other places because Penn State didn't have the reputation. Pitt had taken us down there for a visit. They had a great program. But Casey Jones worked over my mom and she said, 'I don't know much about colleges, but you go where Mister Jones is.'

"They gave me a job in Watts Hall making beds. Doggie Alexander also gave me a job as a greeter at the Rathskeller (restaurant). That's where I got most of my meals."

In 1935 Higgins spoke at an alumni meeting about the momentum he sensed in recruiting. He had traveled statewide to visit with alumni about the football program.

"The fact was brought out that a certain situation existed here at the College and that it was up to us as Penn State people to make the best of it," Higgins said. "In almost every section one or two members of the alumni went into a huddle with me, and in a general way this has been the outcome. They have looked up one or two promising boys in their section. They have interviewed the high school principal and examined the boys' scholastic records. They have made personal contact with the boys and have interested them in Penn State. Later these alumni have taken the time and trouble to bring these boys to visit the campus. We have shown them over the campus and have had them meet heads of departments of the courses in which they are interested. Finally, we have turned them over to a fraternity. We find that undergraduates can do more to 'sell' high school boys Penn State than we alumni can. And with only one or two exceptions, every boy that has visited the campus has gone away 'sold' on Penn State.

"We have no athletic scholarships, but we have been able to get employment for a few deserving boys. This whole procedure not only helps our athletic teams, but helps our alumni as well. It gets them in closer touch with the student body. In three or four years, athletically, we will be right back at the top where we once were."

From 1933 to 1938 Higgins's teams went 22-23-2. The first sign of a turnaround came in a 6-6 tie against Penn in 1933, with captain Tom Slusser scoring the touchdown.

The 1934 squad had big victories over Lehigh and Lafayette, but its best game was a 14-7 losing effort at Columbia. Columbia, coached by Lou Little, had defeated Stanford in the Rose Bowl the previous season and was led by backs Bill Nevel, Ed Brominski and Al Barabas. Penn State fullback Tommy Silvano, another Dunmore product, scored to put the Lions ahead. Quarterback Al Michaels passed to Frank Smith to set up the touchdown. Michaels also kicked the point after. But Columbia came from behind in the second half.

"When we went to New York that was big because we'd go by train," O'Hora recalled. "After the game we'd eat dinner and then try to decide what to do that night. We decided to go up to Broadway and 42nd to the burlesque. Well a bunch of us are in there and who's up front but the coaching staff — Higgins, Bedenk, Ritenour (physician) and Charlie Speidel (trainer and wrestling coach). We ducked our heads and stayed in the back."

Prior to the Penn game in 1934, a reporter asked Higgins why Penn State always seemed to play "beyond themselves" on Franklin Field and come through with one of its best performances of the season.

"This situation has existed as long as I have had any contact with Penn State football," Higgins said. "I don't believe we make any special preparation for the Quaker encounter, but there is always a feeling among the players and among the student body that success or failure of the season is dependent on the result of the Penn game. As a result the players are naturally keyed up for the contest and play good, hard football in Philadelphia. Of course, the fact that we have had moderate success here in recent years serves to develop a feeling of confidence on the squad."

Higgins also commented on the positive development of the 1934 team. "It is very evident that the spirit among the players has changed considerably. They are young and tough and they don't seem to mind body contact. They love to play football. As a result they have learned fundamentals, and it has been this improvement in blocking and tackling that has been largely responsible for our better showing this year."

In a typical bruising contest before 35,000 fans, Penn edged the Lions 3-0.

The 1935 squad broke even as had the 1933 and 1934 teams. Pitt returned to the schedule and Penn State put up a proud defensive effort, but Pitt won 9-0, its tenth consecutive victory over the Lions. Penn State's best game was a 27-13 win over Villanova.

Missing from Penn State as the 1936 season began was Hugo Bezdek. The college administration and alumni had again formed committees to study athletics at Penn State. While they loosened the noose somewhat around intercollegiate sports, they tightened the rope around Director Bezdek's neck, citing his lack of leadership. The athletic program's struggle for definition and the accompanying unrest throughout the School of Physical Education had settled on Bezdek's shoulders. The college and Bezdek parted company. Carl Schott became Dean of the School of Physical Education in 1937.

Bezdek had compiled a 65-30-11 record as head football

coach from 1918 to 1929 at Penn State. Had he moved on to another coaching job instead of becoming an administrator, Bezdek might have been remembered as one of the more successful college football coaches. He became head coach of the professional Cleveland Rams in 1937, but the Rams won only one game that season and had lost their first three games of 1938 when Bezdek was dismissed. Bezdek was elected to the National Football Foundation College Football Hall of Fame in 1954, two years after his death.

Only Penn State grads served on the coaching staff going into the 1936 season. Higgins and Bedenk were joined by Earle Edwards and Al Michaels, while Marty McAndrews coached the freshmen. Remarkably, the varsity staff remained intact for Higgins's thirteen remaining seasons as head coach. Bedenk coached the line, Edwards coached the ends and Michaels coached the backs.

Bedenk was a rugged, traditional hard-liner from the old school. Edwards was intense, possessed a good football mind, and was an innovator. Michaels was a stickler for detail.

Higgins was hands-on with the kicking game. He provided his expertise to the other phases when he deemed it necessary to step in. He oriented his practices toward fundamentals and execution. He controlled the starting lineups and game substitutions. Higgins also kept his players loose, telling a funny story or making light of an error. When a problem arose off the field Higgins didn't seek counseling from his assistants. He handled it himself.

"I enjoyed his philosophy and his approach to the game," said Wendell "Rabbit" Wear, a great halfback on the 1935-1937 teams. "He never spoke in harsh terms. He just told us to get out there and do the best you can do and let the ball fall where it falls. He was not one to bite his lip or fire at will. He never lost his temper, never got worked up physically or mentally. He made the players see the way he looked at it. He either put you in or left you to sit there. He was in command."

One thing Higgins wouldn't put up with, from coaches or players, was profanity. When he heard a foul word he threatened to wash out the guilty party's mouth with soap, or invited the culprit to do it himself. Joe Bedenk, whom one player said cussed more in a day than Higgins did in a lifetime, was regularly scolded by Higgins.

The no-cussing policy complemented Higgins's desire that his boys leave Penn State as class acts. He frequently corrected them for improper grammar. When a punt returner shouted "I got it! I got it!" Higgins met him after the play and reminded him, "For goodness sakes, say 'I have it! I have it!'"

Those players who wore hats received lessons on when to remove or tip their hats in the presence of ladies.

Table manners was another Higgins pet peeve. Jim O'Hora remembered: "We had some players who were like pigs at the training table down in the Old Main. They would serve family style and there was a lady there who took real good care of the squad, Hazel Fall. They served a big platter of turkey or steaks and there'd be one on this end and one on that end, and then one of these big bowls of mashed potatoes, and there would be this player and he'd take one scoop and there was no more left for the rest of the guys. Bob would get on him and say, 'You don't even know where your fork is. You know you have a fork and a knife and a spoon, and you have a napkin there. Now put the napkin on your leg. And don't try to eat it all at once. Now slowly, slowly.' That epitomized more the type person Bob was. I think his strong point was in his ability to get the kids to be better people, to grow up, a morale type of thing for the better."

Speedster halfback Wear, only 140 pounds, was the center of Higgins's single wing offense and the primary punter from 1935-1937. Wear had played high school ball in Huntingdon, Pennsylvania and was heavily recruited by several schools, including Southern Cal. Wear attracted Pitt as well, but head coach Jock Sutherland didn't favor running backs who weighed less than 165 pounds.

Higgins visited Wear in Huntingdon and the head coach was surprised at Wear's size. "When I came in the room I thought I'd see a bigger player," Higgins said.

Wear remembers pumping gas on Sundays in State College for five dollars. He received an academic scholarship beginning his sophomore year, with the provision that if his grades suffered he'd lose the scholarship the next semester. Wear never did lose the scholarship and it saved him a few precious dollars as the Depression played itself out. Still Wear played summer baseball for a company team to make a few more dollars to put toward college. In his junior year he washed dishes and served meals for his room and board at a fraternity.

Wear played second base and shortstop for Bedenk on the Penn State varsity team each spring and later became a great player on a famous pre-flight baseball team in North Carolina. The squad included Hall-of-Fame outfielder Ted Williams and shortstop Johnny Pesky, both of the Boston Red Sox.

Wear received the best punting instruction available from Higgins and Herman Everhardus, who joined Higgins's staff for the 1934 and 1935 seasons. Everhardus played on the unbeaten Michigan teams of 1932 and 1933.

"After practice Everhardus would put on an exhibition," Wear said. "He'd stand on the goal line and roll them out the other end. He had tremendous snap in his leg."

Wear called the offensive plays during the game. He would meet with Higgins and assistant coach Michaels and they devised seven or eight plays to take into a game and made adjustments as the game progressed.

"He never second-guessed me," Wear said of Higgins. "The plays were sometimes conservative, sometimes not. He let me do the things I wanted to do. I loved the single wing, the traps and all the fakes."

Indeed the single wing could be an exciting offense. It included four backs and an unbalanced line, meaning more linemen were on one side of the center than the other side. The fullback, stationed in the backfield, usually received the snap, with the tailback (or halfback) set not far behind him and to the side, while the quarterback (or blocking back) was forward and closer to the heavy side of the line, and the wingback was positioned straight out from the blocking back and beyond the end.

The basic play from the formation was the snap to the fullback who would half-spin or full-spin, perhaps fake a pass or fake a handoff to the tailback, and plow off tackle (called line-bucking). He might also hand off to the tailback, or fake to the tailback and hand off to the wingback coming around. He could fake to the tailback and throw to the wingback or to the end on a crossing pattern. Higgins also ran the flea flicker, in which the fullback faked to the tailback and passed to the end who handed off to the wingback coming across.

In the buck-lateral series the fullback received the snap and handed off to the quarterback, who could lateral wide to the tailback or fake the pitch and throw, or the quarterback could pitch to the tailback who threw to the fullback.

The single wing also included a series of plays in which the center snapped the ball to the tailback who could run or pull up and pass, or hand off to the wingback on the reverse.

Penn State fell to 3-5 in 1936, its biggest win coming against Syracuse, 18-0. But Higgins enjoyed his first winning season as Penn State's mentor in 1937 with a 5-3 mark. A contributing factor was that Higgins and his staff were now reviewing game films during the week, which was not a common practice at the time.

Higgins assigned the responsibility of shooting the opening game of the 1937 season to two students. The head coach bubbled with enthusiasm when the film came back a couple of days later, until he turned on the projector and discovered the students hadn't filmed Penn State's return for a touchdown of the opening kickoff. The students said they didn't film it because nothing ever happened on the kickoff.

Higgins shook his head in disbelief and walked into the dressing room where several students and coaches were chewing the fat between classes. "Anybody here interested in movies?" the disgruntled Higgins asked.

Someone said, "I showed movies at Carleton College."

Ray Conger was an instructor in zoology and a part-time track coach. He had starred as a miler at Iowa State in the 1920s (with a best time of 4:13) and reached the finals of the 1500 meter run in the 1928 Olympics in Amsterdam.

While working at Carleton College in Northfield, Minnesota, Conger ordered films and showed them to the students on Saturday nights. But Higgins thought Conger meant he had shot the films himself, which wasn't the case.

"You're it," Higgins said. "You're going to take the movies of the games."

Alternating between two cameras on top of or inside the press box, Conger, who wasn't all that interested in football, became Higgins's movie man. For the first couple of years Conger ran the film to Rochester to be processed and picked it up on Wednesday. Then he took the footage to an Eastman plant in Washington, D.C. and had it back to Higgins on Sunday nights. Conger shot the games for thirty-nine years during his Penn State career.

Cornell beat the Lions in the 1937 opener, 26-19, despite Wear's bootleg for a sixty-yard touchdown. But the biggest win in several years was Penn State's shut out of Penn, 7-0. The Lions hadn't defeated Penn since 1929. In front of fifty thousand fans at Philadelphia's Franklin Field, Wear completed a 21-yard pass to Harry Harrison at the Penn seventeen, and then Harrison connected with Wear for the winning touchdown pass.

Wear commented on his lack of size and his injury free career, "My high school coach told me if you really hit it and put out 100 percent you'll never get hurt. I was tough, but I didn't run at the other team's big guys. I liked having my big guys in front of me."

A 21-14 win over Maryland gave Penn State a 5-2 record, but once again the Pitt Panthers prevailed in the final game of the season, 28-7, before twenty thousand fans in Pittsburgh. The victory gave Jock Sutherland's team the 1937 national championship — bestowed by the Associated Press, which had begun its ranking system the previous season.

Higgins asked Wear to stay on as a graduate assistant coach in 1938. Wear taught the single wing to incoming freshmen such as Pepper Petrella, Bill Smaltz and Lenny Krouse. Wear also spotted and telephoned plays from the press box to the field during the games. "Higgins chose me over some of his veteran coaches," Wear said of his responsibility. "He must have had confidence in me to do that."

Wear went on to coach high school ball at Altoona, Pennsylvania and West Orange, New Jersey.

Though Wear and a growing number of talented athletes had slowly turned the program in the proper direction, Higgins continued to received his share of "fan" mail, such as this letter from a follower in Reading, Pennsylvania, dated October 18, 1936.

Bob:

Saw the Lehigh and Villanova games (won by Lehigh, 7-6, and Villanova, 13-0) and to say that all the alumni were thoroughly disgusted is putting it mildly.

I have always claimed you should not be too harshly criticized, due to the Bezdek influence and that you should have a chance. However after the poorly coached teams you have placed on the field the last two games, my efforts, small as they may be, are going to be towards a complete renovation of the football department. Opinions of disinterested football authorities seem to be that State has the poorest coached teams we have had in years, and I am with many others convinced of that too.

We all know you are not getting the pick of the field in the freshman players but we do feel that State needs an exceptional coach to overcome this condition and that's what we are going after. I believe if you had exceptional players, no doubt you could have successful teams, but that you are not the coach for the difficult job of having a good team with the material you are getting. To keep you in charge of our football department seems to me to be unfair to the School, the Alumni, the boys on the team and even to yourself. My own opinion was that after the Lehigh game was lost that you would resign and I believe it is the right move for you to make, for the good of everybody connected with Penn State.

A crowd of us are having this appeal printed and sent to all Alumni clubs, Members of the Board of Trustees, and College Authorities and are requesting it be printed in the *Collegian* within the next month and the Alumni News. In other words it is an open letter to you appealing for your resignation.

Yours for Penn State
H.K.

However, the same writer experienced a change of heart by season's end.

Friend Bob:

Well I can admit when I make a mistake, and I've made one. First, let me congratulate you on the splendidly coached team you put on the field against Penn. It was fine and you can well feel pleased and satisfied.

It isn't pleasant to apologize but I certainly do to you and hope you will forget the former letter I wrote you.

But Bob, what happened in the Villanova game and particularly in the Lehigh game? I saw State play everybody but Pitt and they were certainly off in the above two games. How do things look for next year? Do you have any good freshmen?

Incidentally, there is a good big back on Mt. Carmel Township High who is a bearcat. If you have time, look him up as he will be worked on plenty.

Let me hear from you.

Again, apologies,

H.K.

Higgins also put the following letter, dated November 7, 1938, in his file for safe-keeping.

Dear Bob:

I suppose that like most people you will not heed any advice from grandstand coaches, but there are a few remarks that I must make because I love football and would like to see Penn State play the brand of football that they are capable of playing.

I know that you do not have championship material to work with, but your team is capable of a much better brand of football than they have been playing. And so I want to point out a few glaring errors in fundamentals that occur time after time in every game. If you will study the movies of the games, you will note that the following blunders have been made so often that your players must regard them as part of the Penn State system.

1. You do not have an accurate passer. Why then do you allow long passes? Short passes do not demand one tenth as much accuracy and can be used as a real weapon. But here again there is danger in throwing them straight over the line of scrimmage for if they are too high for the receiver they will be right in the hands of the secondary defense. Therefore you should concentrate on short passes which are thrown to the receiver as he is running laterally and slightly forward. Long passes should be allowed only when you are within throwing

distance of the opponent's ten yard line where an interception is usually not too dangerous. Can't you develop a short
pass that is thrown as the passer runs laterally along the
field? When your passer fades back before making a short
pass he has practically ruined the play at that point.

2. Can't you plead with the boys to get up after being
knocked down? Time after time they are taken out of a play
too early and would have plenty of time to get up and make
the tackle but they make no attempt to do so. Why?

3. Tell the boys that when they see a player lying on the
ground they are not required to fall over him. Explain to them
that it requires little effort to jump over a man who is lying
on the ground.

4. When it is your opponent's last down with ten yards to
go and they are in their own territory so that a punt is practically a sure thing why does not your secondary defense drop
back to help the receivers? They never do it. To be specific
look at the pictures of Saturday's game and count the number of times that the ends were even delayed as they came
down under the punts. If they (your backs) must stay up close
on most occasions then they should dash back with the punt
and take out the tacklers at the right time rather than too
early as they always do.

Here is hoping for improvement,
A loyal fan

By the 1938 season, thanks to the recruiting efforts of
Casey Jones and other alumni, Penn State had a wealth of
sophomore talent that with a few games under its belt had
the potential to develop into something special.

Even some recruits who had gotten away suddenly
wanted to come to Penn State, as indicated by the following
(heavily edited) letter written to Higgins by a player who had
gone to the University of Alabama in Tuscaloosa.

Hi Coach:
Remember me? Well I made a mistake. I wish I would
have taken your advice. I suppose it is too late now to come to
Penn State. Hope there is still a chance for me to come there
to school this semester. I made the first team and started the

first game. I am doing o.k. but this place is no good for me. I belong up North.

The reason I want to leave is this:

1. The food is lousy
2. Too far from home
3. Failed to keep promise
4. Too hot

I would accept an offer from you if it still holds.

Joe Pascarella

P.S. answer soon as possible

Higgins played a big role in the recruiting turnaround at Penn State. He turned many sons of coal miners away from Notre Dame with the warning that Notre Dame had a big wall around its campus. "You can't get out!" Higgins would emphasize. "You're in there for four years!"

Higgins didn't feel too badly pulling one over on his fellow Irishmen.

§ 11 §
The Last Man's Club

HIGGINS HAD ALWAYS BEEN ABLE to leave the pressures of coaching at the practice field. He had little choice. His wife and three daughters didn't want to hear about the daily grunts and groans on the gridiron, which was fine with Higgins.

By 1938 Higgins's daughters had turned thirteen, ten and six. Sometimes Higgins couldn't keep from turning around on the sidelines during the games to look for them and their mother sitting in the stands, all dressed in their Sunday best with nice coats and hats.

"He was a very happy person, and he made you happy," eldest daughter Mary Ann Lyford recalled.

Mary Ann remembered summer family trips to their Aunt Margaret's cottage at Truro on Cape Cod. With few friends around, the girls turned to their father for companionship. He didn't disappoint them.

"He was our playmate," Mary Ann said. "Daddy was fun. He loved jokes and loved talking to people. He was fun to go to the grocery store with. I think of him and I have to smile."

The middle daughter, Ginger Suhey, said her father's outlook remained positive. "He wasn't an up-and-down person," Ginger said. "He was always up. There aren't too many people like that."

Outside of football, when not tending to his family or playing golf with some local buddies, Higgins spent a good deal of time corresponding with fellow members of The Last Man's Club and making arrangements for the next annual retreat. The members of the club, all very successful in their career endeavors, looked upon the rendezvous as a chance to get away and let down their guard. Their families were glad to see them have a chance to escape the pressures of the home front, but at the same time a few stories inevitably trickled back which made the family wonder if dad was ever going to grow up.

One such story had the members eating a late snack at a diner following a full day of fun in the sun. The men became a little unruly and started admiring each other's clothes. "I like that tie," one of them said, pointing at another member's tie. "Why don't you give it to me?" The other members joined in, "Go ahead, give it to him." The one wearing the tie removed it and handed it over. The men applauded and hooted their approval. Then the one who had removed his tie pointed to another member's shirt. "I like that shirt," he said. The member stood and took off his shirt in the middle of the diner, drawing another ovation. Soon pieces of clothing littered the table and floor. When pairs of pants became part of the exchange the diner manager called the local authorities, who arrived just before the scene became even more unsightly. The police escorted the rowdy crowd to jail where they had to telephone someone to chaperone them back to their rooms.

One of the gritty veterans of the Western Front, Earl Shively, with a drink or two under his belt had a knack for speaking his mind too loudly and stepping on the toes of some of the locals. But "Shive," as he was called, always made sure that the muscular Higgins was nearby in case the opposition reared up. One time Shively, having assumed Higgins was present, started something with several local boys. But Higgins had drifted off with the other members. A clothes-tattered, beaten-up Shively later returned to the group. "What happened to you?" one of the members asked. "Higgins wasn't standing behind me," Shively grumbled.

As the years passed, the original ten members who survived the war invited a few others into the club, including Higgins's friend Claude Aikens, who was publisher of the *Centre Daily Times* newspaper in State College, and Vincent Smith's friend, Heister Painter, who ran a hardware operation in Greensburg, Pennsylvania. The club's excursions during the 1930s and 1940s took them to Huntington, West Virginia; Pittsburgh (Conneaut Lake Park); Wheeling, West Virginia (Hotel Windsor); Richmond, Virginia; Greensburg, Pennsylvania (Old Stone House); Uniontown, Pennsylvania (The Summit Hotel); Bluefield, West Virginia; State College, Pennsylvania (Spruce Creek); Philadelphia; and Charlottesville, Virginia (Farmington Country Club).

Higgins corresponded the most with attorneys Smith of Greensburg and Shively of Columbus, Ohio. The subject of football usually came up at some point in the letters. Following are excerpts from several letters written during the late 1930s.

July 23, 1935
Dear Bob:
There is a boy named Montgomery from this vicinity who weighs around 210 pounds and played on the freshman team at Temple last year. I am advised by reliable authority that he can make any first class football team in the country. He has been dropped from Temple by reason of failure in one or more subjects. He would have to have all expenses paid. Please advise if you are interested.
Sincerely yours,
Vincent R. Smith

July 26, 1935
Dear Vince:
In regard to Montgomery from Temple, he would not have a chance getting into Penn State. Never in the history of Temple University has a football player, who is a good player, flunked out. I have known many of them go to the movies three times a day and pass all of their subjects with a 95% grade.
Sincerely yours,
R.A. Higgins

April 7, 1938
Dear Vince:
A copy of your letter to Hammitt received and I think it is quite an imposition for you to have the gang back again so I am going to suggest that Shively, Crane, Hammitt, McWane and Higgins chip in on the party.

I am sure we would be able to furnish all refreshments and food and make you responsible only for our quarters.

After I received your letter I wrote Shively and told him that I was not going to be attending the reunion this year and I think the big lunkhead believes me.

I have been especially busy this year with my spring practice, but it will wind up on May 1 and I intend to take a few days to fish with Aikens. After that I am going to run out and see you and Mary.

Best wishes.

Sincerely yours,

R.A. Higgins

Football Coach

December 20, 1938

TO MEMBERS OF THE LAST MAN'S CLUB:

Gentlemen:

An in-and-out, up-and-down, good-and-bad football season for yours truly has just come to an end. I am now roaming around the State on the circuit of high school football banquets, eating cold mashed potatoes and turkey. These country churches are full of drafts, and if your feet are not cold, it will hit you on the back of the neck. If it had not been that I have fallen off the wagon, I could not make it.

We are going to have a big Christmas at our house. The children's grandmother came in the other day, loaded with Christmas presents. I have promised Virginia to keep away from Aikens on Christmas Eve so we can all get up early on Christmas morning and open our gifts together. I am going to try to keep my promise. I won't stay away from him altogether because I have to go out and help him trim his tree, but I will be good.

It has been twenty years since the War and they have gone mighty fast for me. They tell me the next twenty years will go faster, and by that time, we will all be on the shelf — all except Higgins.

I just want to wish each and every one of you a Merry Christmas and a Happy New Year.

Sincerely,

R.A. Higgins

May 11, 1939
Gentlemen:

A new sport swept the college campuses last month — swallowing live goldfish. And by the way Joe College is going at it, gulping goldfish may soon become a major sport. The athletic fathers should be for it. Here is a diversion that requires no stadium, little equipment and no high priced coaches. All the contestants need would be a weak mind and a strong stomach.

R.A.H.

June 22, 1939
Gentlemen:

Aikens and I went down to see Smith; drove over to Monessen to get a 220-pound fullback for our freshman team next fall. Smith, being the solicitor for the City and being able to understand Polish, Slovish, and German in addition to his fluent French, was of great help to me with the boy's father. However, after spending three-quarters of an hour with the "old gent," we discovered the boy had gone the previous week to Durham, North Carolina, to cut grass on the Duke University campus for $150 a month.

From there we went to Uniontown where we engaged rooms number 57, 58, 59, 60 and 62 — all large double rooms on the second floor of The Summit Hotel (shut off from the hotel by double doors). Room 60 will be headquarters. Aikens is paying for the rooms.

I think the set-up is great. With the exception, of course, of the Stone House, I think the set-up is as good as any. There is a swimming pool at the Hotel, a good golf course with a Club House where one can see Pennsylvania, Maryland and West Virginia. It is five degrees cooler at Mount Summit than at Uniontown, and the distance is only four miles. There is a highboard there for Shively.

The manager of The Summit Hotel is Leo Heyn. I told him we were all fat, forty, and fairly harmless, and that we might sing for him, we might have a cocktail or two, but we wouldn't get "pushy." He assured me that "anything goes."

I hope that each and every one of you fellows will be on hand, and that we can all have a great time together once more.

As ever,

R.A.H.

July 5, 1939

To all members:

Higgins' description of the set-up for the reunion at Uniontown was very modest. The suite engaged at the Summit Hotel is, without question, the finest quarters that we have ever had. In addition to the hotel having beautiful surroundings, swimming pool, night club, there is a private club on the knob behind the hotel. This club will be available for those who desire to play golf and for those who do not like to drink in public places.

All members will be in their seats at the Old Stone House, Lincoln Highway East, Greensburg, Pa., Thursday, August 3rd, 1939, at 6 P.M.

Respectfully submitted,

Vince

October 19, 1939

Dear Bob:

Today, your sister's autobiography was returned to me from New York, with an inscription dated October 15, 1939, as follows:

"To E.C. Shively—a pal of my brother's (Bob Higgins) and to whom I send my best wishes and kindest regards."

Margaret Sanger

If I knew your sister's New York address, I would personally write her and express the appreciation of Marg and me for this fine inscription. If you do not send me the address, I want you to pass along my sincere thanks.

Many thanks to you for the help.

As ever,

Shive

As Higgins's popularity blossomed throughout the college football ranks, his sister Margaret Sanger had become a famous international figure for her leadership in the birth control movement.

In the summer of 1912, Higgins and a friend took jobs as lifesavers at a hotel pool in New York. Even as a teen Higgins displayed an athlete's physique. Higgins was called "tramp" by his classmates at Peddie Institute because, unlike the other boys, he didn't have a regular home or family he could visit between school terms.

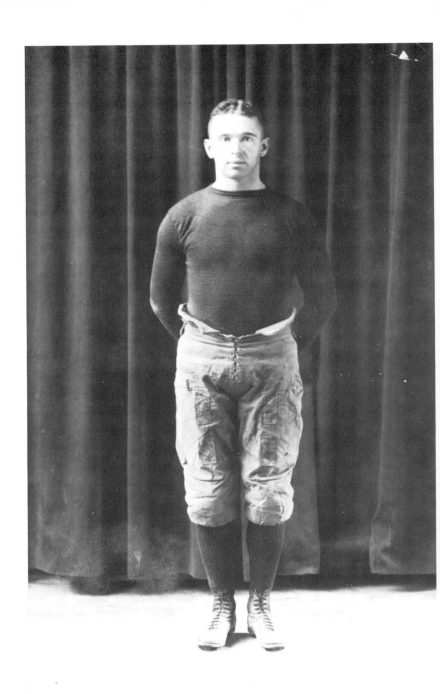

Higgins had never played "American football" when he arrived at Peddie. By the end of the year, Coach Morris Midkiff was calling him "one of the best schoolboy ends in the East."

Captain Robert Higgins served the Infantry's 80th Division with honor and heroism on the Western Front in World War I. It was in a French cafe during a brief respite from the trenches that The Last Man's Club was formed. The group remained steadfast friends for the rest of their lives.

Carroll, W & J star No. 12 on ground at left. Higgins swinging into position to stop play. Kellison, former Wesleyan tackle facing front with "C" on jersey.

Following his All-American career at Penn State, Higgins played and coached for the professional Canton Bulldogs. His teammate at Canton was Jim Thorpe. Higgins is shown here in the center of the photo, swinging into position to stop an opposing runner. Chicago Bears' player/owner George Halas described end Higgins as "tough and quick."

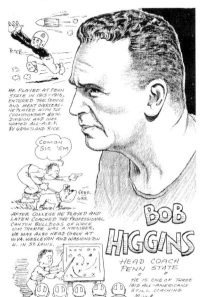

This "historical cartoon," which ran in the early 1940s, summarized Higgins's career up to that point and illustrates his popularity as both a player and a coach. Note that Higgins is shown catching a "bomb," which references not only his military career, but also his famous 1919 touchdown catch to defeat Pitt.

X's and O's. No coach can win without them. The Pittsburgh paper open in front of Higgins announces that Penn State's Red Moore and John Jaffurs have been named to the All-Pennsylvania Eleven. When not in athletic garb, Higgins was always a careful dresser. He once told a player, "If you're going to wear a hat, you need to learn the responsibilities of wearing a hat."

While Higgins built his reputation on the athletic field, his sister Margaret Sanger was making international waves as the founder of Planned Parenthood International and as America's earliest advocate of birth control, a term she coined. Sanger lectured with Albert Einstein and H.G. Wells, and met with such international notables as Mahatma Ghandi. Here, she and brother Bob pause for a photograph with the movie actor Barry Sullivan.

In 1958, Higgins relived great memories when his undefeated 1947 Cotton Bowl team held its ten-year reunion. The Hig is shown here with son-in-law Steve Suhey and Ed Czekaj. Higgins holds the Cotton Bowl trophy.

Life to Higgins was much more than football. He is shown here at a 1940s reunion of the Last Man's Club at the Old Stone House. Pictured (l-r) are Jim Douglas, The Hig, Earl Shively, Vince Smith, Claude Aikens, Guy Dirom, Henry McWane, and Jack Hammitt.

Part of Higgins's great legacy was his daughter Ginger, who married one Penn State star and was the mother of several more. She is shown here in a familiar position— feeding hungry people on South Sparks Street.

Like his father-in-law before him, Steve Suhey interrupted his Penn State football career to serve his country in World War II. Steve is shown here with a war buddy somewhere in the South Pacific about 1945. He never talked about his military service.

"A strong guard with halfback speed." Although Steve Suhey was most famous as a blocker and tackler, he knew what to do with a loose football.

When Steve was named All-American at Penn State, he only wanted to know "if any of the other boys made the team." When he was honored in his hometown of Cazenovia, New York, Steve was so surprised and embarrassed at the attention that he didn't have a speech prepared. The townspeople thought so much of the poor farm boy, however, that they presented him with a new automobile. He smiled and stated that, after his parents, Ginger Higgins of State College would be his first passenger.

The Cotton Bowl. Steve Suhey and Penn State vs. SMU and Doak Walker.

CERTIFICATE OF MERIT

This is to Certify that

𝕾𝖙𝖊𝖛𝖊𝖓 𝕵. 𝕾𝖚𝖍𝖊𝖞

A MEMBER OF THE

PENNSYLVANIA STATE COLLEGE FOOTBALL TEAM

PARTICIPATED IN THE

1948 COTTON BOWL CLASSIC

Given under our seal and hand at Dallas, Texas, January 1st, 1948

COTTON BOWL ATHLETIC ASSOCIATION

ATTEST: _____ *Secretary.*

SIGNED: _____ *President.*

Equal in skill though differing in style, All-American guard Steve Suhey visits with SMU All-American halfback Doak Walker prior to the Cotton Bowl on New Year's Day, 1948. Suffering from a mental lapse as a result of poor accommodations in Dallas, it took Penn State until the second half to wake up and get in the game. The contest ended in a 13-13 tie, giving Bob Higgins his only undefeated season as a head coach. Suhey went on to a professional career the next season. Walker, just a sophomore, made All-America teams for the next two years and took home the Heisman Trophy.

Although Steve Suhey accomplished a lot in life, he never forgot where he came fro[m] thought he was better than anyone else. Here he is shown visiting with Joe Costello, a fo[rmer] classmate at Cazenovia Central High School.

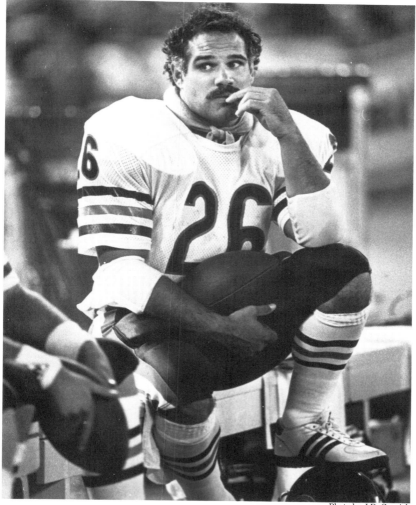

Photo by J.D. Cavrich

Photo by Bob Sharpe

Whether with Chicago or Penn State, Matt Suhey played hard and remembered what he learned in school: "Nice and clean. Not a lot of big talking, always humble, always playing hard. It's going to be a long day if you want to beat Penn State."

Above, Larry's struggle to regain his former athleticism after repeated knee injuries made the going tough, but he and his brothers Paul and Matt (below) were rewarded in the 1976 Gator Bowl, when they all played against Notre Dame with their parents in the stands. Little did they know Steve Suhey would be dead two weeks later.

Paul, Larry and Matt Suhey with their mother, Ginger, during their playing days at Penn State. Below, all nine Suheys gather for a Christmas portrait in 1960. Several years later, Larry dropped in on his mother and sister Betsy — both avid fishermen — and found they had teamed up with another famous angler: former President Jimmy Carter.

Sanger's early writings and activism culminated with her and her sister Ethel opening the first birth control clinic in Brooklyn in 1916. Both were arrested and convicted for disseminating information on contraception and both served time in jail. The 1918 State Court of Appeals decision, though it upheld Margaret's conviction, provided momentum for the birth control movement by giving physicians the right to give advice for "cure and prevention of disease."

In 1921 Margaret organized the first American Birth Control Conference in New York City in spite of strenuous protests from the Catholic Church. The subsequent publicity drew international attention to Sanger and her cause.

The following year Margaret made her first world tour and spoke on population control in Japan and China. On the same lecture circuit in Japan were intellectual giants Albert Einstein, Bertrand Russell and H.G. Wells.

In 1925 Margaret organized the International Birth Control Conference in New York City and received more than ten thousand letters from physicians asking for birth control information.

Two years later Margaret spearheaded The First World Population Conference in Geneva, Switzerland.

She resigned in 1928 as president of the American Birth Control League to form the National Commission for Federal Legislation for Birth Control. Higgins frequently wrote "Last Man" buddies Smith and Shively asking them to use their influence in the legal field on their Congressmen to help push his sister's birth control bill. Sanger served as president of the Commission until 1937, but it would be the courts, not Congress, that eventually endorsed birth control.

In 1930 Margaret became president of Birth Control International Information Centers in London, a position she held until 1936.

In 1931 a New York Academy of Medicine resolution was passed supporting birth control. Countless educational, civic and religious groups came out in support of family planning.

In 1935-1936 Margaret visited India and China. She met with Mahatma Ghandi and attempted to persuade him to endorse contraception, but Ghandi refused.

In 1936 the courts affirmed the legality of importing contraceptives from abroad, making it possible for physicians to mail whatever was needed for the purpose of saving life or promoting the well-being of their patients. In 1937, the American Medical Association endorsed birth control.

The following year, *Margaret Sanger, An Autobiography,* was published, which was the book Higgins had Margaret sign for Earl Shively.

While his sister became much sought-after as a speaker around the world, Higgins became a headliner in gridiron circles. He had served as a head coach for seventeen seasons going into 1938 and his insights helped develop the game of football and gave it structure. Following is part of a speech he made while serving on the Committee on Ethics for intercollegiate football. It sheds considerable light on the status of college football during the pre-World War II years.

All the practices which occur in the coaching of football may be divided, with respect to the ethics of these practices, into three classes. First is that group of practices and procedures that are universally considered clearly unethical. There is, for this group, no diversity of opinion among those who are connected with the game of football. A partial list of this particular type would include the following statements. It is unethical for a coach:

1. To play a boy who has a serious injury, no matter what the provocation.

2. To use cocaine or any other preparation which would make an otherwise seriously injured boy available.

3. To inspire his team through the element of hate for the opponents. Also to be decried is the practice of attributing to opposing coaches untrue and vicious statements, hoping to arouse your players by this obviously unfair method.

4. To be guilty, or allow his team to be guilty, of heckling and intimidating the officials.

5. To accept the opposing team's signals, no matter what the source.

6. To flash the signals from the bench, acting throughout the game as the quarterback. It follows naturally that he should not permit anyone else to flash the signals for him.

7. To give his team any play, shift, or formation designed with the prime purpose of drawing the opponents off-side.

8. To teach his players any practices which violate the rules to any degree.

9. To use ineligible players or players about whose eligibility he has the least doubt.

10. To permit a player to wear any equipment which may be dangerous to the opponents.

11. To allow his team or to encourage his team to direct particular efforts to the star of the opposition, to an injured opponent, or, as is too often done, to a racial opponent.

12. To humiliate the opposing coach by running up a large score.

13. To alibi a defeat or to boast of a victory.

The second class might be termed the one that includes all those practices which are clearly ethical. There is no necessity to list them as the nature of this report is to point out unethical practices.

The third class is the most interesting one from a discussion standpoint. In this group are those practices which may be considered ethical or unethical, the classification depending upon the interpretation given by the individuals or the particular group. In this case what is sauce for the goose is not always sauce for the gander.

Is it unethical for a coach:

1. To teach his players to steal the ball? The rules say no.

2. To predict the scores of impending games, thus lending himself indirectly to the nefarious practice of gambling, which is fast becoming a major problem of the game?

3. To use moving pictures in scouting?

4. To use trickery, such as the sleeper play, the shoestring play, the fake squabble and quick snap, the old substitute play, and many of the other old favorites?

5. To use a changing starting signal?

6. To talk from the bench to any players of the team, or to admonish a player verbally or by sign to back up, play wider, look for a pass, etc?

7. To take advantage of any loophole in the rules?

We suggest that some effort be made to standardize ethical procedure for practices such as these.

Talking to your opponents is not prohibited by the rules, but there are no rules that can make a gentleman out of a "mucker" and no good sportsman is ever guilty of cheap talk to his opponent.

Joining Higgins on the committee on ethics were Dana Bible of Nebraska, L.C. Boles of Wooster, Fred Brice of Maine, Jack Chevegny of Texas, and Tom Lieb of Loyola.

§ 12 §
Gajecki Joins The Fight

FROM THE DAY LEON GAJECKI set foot on campus in 1937, the Penn State football program never looked back. Gajecki, from the coal mining town of Colver, Pennsylvania, had played high school ball at nearby Ebensburg for Earle Edwards before Edwards joined Higgins in 1936. Gajecki didn't attend Penn State right out of high school, but attended St. Francis College in Loretto. Gajecki, however, couldn't shake the football bug or the inspiration Edwards had given him to become a good athlete, and he transferred to Penn State in mid-semester. Gajecki would start three years at center and linebacker for Penn State and become, in 1940, Higgins's first All-American. In 1939 and 1940 Gajecki spearheaded a ferocious defense that led Penn State to heights not reached since the early 1920s, including the first victory over Pittsburgh in twenty years. Gajecki was captain of the 1940 team his senior season.

"I worked in the coal mines with my father in the summer and came to Penn State with about 350 dollars in my pocket, which paid my fees," Gajecki recalled of his Penn State years. "I was able to join a fraternity my junior and senior years and work for my room and board there in the kitchen. On top of that I was in fuel technology in the school of mineral industries with courses like chemistry and physics. Between studying and practicing football I was meant to be fatigued."

Gajecki recalled receiving only one football meal per day at dinnertime during the season at the Old Main restaurant. "After the football season we were on our own," he said. "It made us scramble and made us enjoy what we did earn."

Gajecki added, "You get a kid like myself coming out of the coal mines, I was a little estranged. But Bob Higgins was like another father to me. He was the father of our team and we played hard for him. He always managed to keep us motivated. He wanted us to stay together, to know each other. I was a little boy when I came to Penn State. They made a man out of me."

Higgins and Penn State made a big man out of Gajecki, as he jumped from 190 pounds his sophomore year to 225 for his senior year. And as Gajecki got bigger, Penn State got better.

The 1938 season only hinted at the success that was just ahead. Penn State went 3-4-1, losing close ones to Bucknell (14-0) and Lafayette (7-0), while also falling to Cornell and Pitt, the latter a 26-0 whipping. But even in defeat, line coach Bedenk was implementing some innovative maneuvers for his defense that would pay off down the road. For now, however, sometimes they worked and sometimes they didn't.

Lineman Toretti was a senior leader on the 1938 squad and he recalled when one of Bedenk's strategies backfired. "We were just beginning to experiment with the looping (shifting) lines and the blitz," Toretti said. "Penn State was one of the pioneers in this technique. Joe Bedenk was always working with this thing."

Going into the Bucknell game Bedenk told Toretti that a good time to loop or shift the defense would be when Penn Sate had Bucknell backed up.

"We punted the ball deep, down to about Bucknell's six-yard-line," Toretti said. "I called sixty-two (six man line, two linebackers) loop to the wingback. In those days with the single wing you usually ran off tackle with the halfback or ran inside tackle with the fullback. We looped to the left to the wingback and filled those two holes. I was thinking, 'Boy, we're going to mash these babies.' The trouble was Bucknell gave the ball to King Funair and he ran a deep reverse ninety-four yards for a touchdown. After they kicked the extra point we come back for the kickoff, and rule or no rule I can hear Mr. Higgins yelling, and he got my attention and said, 'Hey Tor, no more of that loop!' But that didn't dampen our enthusiasm for the looping lines. That was the kind of defense they were using when they set the national records in 1947."

Gajecki felt that the young team began to come together the latter half of the 1938 season, following a 21-6 loss to Cornell. The defense allowed only one touchdown in each of the next three games — a 33-6 spanking of Syracuse, a 7-0 loss to Lafayette and a 7-7 tie with Penn in front of fifty thousand fans at Franklin Field. Despite the lopsided season-ending loss to Pitt, the Lions set an NCAA record for fewest passing yards allowed per game, 13.1 (105 yards in eight games). That record continued to stand fifty-six years later in 1994.

Another sophomore letterman on the 1938 team was tackle Carl Stravinski. He had been recruited out of Plymouth, Pennsylvania by freshman coach McAndrews and alumnus Gilligan.

Stravinski waited his share of tables and washed dishes for his meals and room. But he also put in between twenty to forty hours a month for thirty-five cents an hour doing tabulation and statistical work for the horticulture school. He also cleaned apartments owned by an English professor who paid him one dollar for each afternoon of work.

Stravinski played freshman football in 1936, broke an ankle and was redshirted in 1937, and began his first of three years as a varsity starter in 1938, playing at close to 220 pounds. Stravinski recalled the daily workouts:

"It was a tough session in eighty and ninety degree weather. We never drank water. We practiced and practiced our blocking until we got it perfect. We beat the machines and beat the bags and it meant a lot as to what happened in the ballgame. We beat each other up, too. The name of the game was to get out there in an alley fight with one of the bigger boys and whip 'em. Higgins and Bedenk were right in there with us. Higgins would get upset, but he wouldn't be boisterous. He was controlled. Higgins was a knowledgeable coach as far as covering all aspects of the game."

Stravinski recalled playing most of every game his junior and senior seasons. "We went the whole damn game, sucked it up and played hard. If you didn't play hard you were going to get hurt. You didn't take any guff from anybody. At the end of the game you felt like you could play another game, if you won. When you win you never get tired. If you're losing you're the sorriest looking old crud. If you won you went out that night and got your two hamburgers and your two milkshakes and you were happy."

In addition to Gajecki and Stravinski, several other experienced linemen returned for the 1939 season. Tom Vargo, whom Stravinski said was one of the best ends in the country, had a complete varsity season under his belt. Spike Alter returned for his senior season at end and was the team's captain. Higgins expected good things from tackles Frank Platt and Walt Kniaz, guards Mike Garbinski and Wade Mori, and senior end Grover Washabaugh. Higgins also looked for assistance from the successful 1938 freshman team. Backs Bill Smaltz and 140-pounder Pepper Petrella looked as if they could help right away. Another promising youngster was wingback Lenny Krouse. Tackle Leonard Frketich was a young but imposing figure at three-hundred pounds. Meanwhile senior spinback Lloyd Ickes, junior tailback Chuck Peters and wingback Craig White anchored the single wing.

Prior to the beginning of the season, Higgins wrote Last Man Shively.

My dear Shive:
This Saturday I open with Bucknell and while we should take them without any trouble, I am getting the jitters. We should have licked them last year, but we didn't. However, I believe we will this year. Lehigh doesn't have anything, and I am counting on taking Cornell. Syracuse will be tough. Maryland shouldn't be too tough. We always do well at Philadelphia against Pennsylvania, and while they are going to be the choice of the Ivy League, I think we will be in there. Army had a difficult time beating Furman College last week, so unless they improve a lot, we will beat them. Then we have Pitt. We have them on our own field this year, and it has been twenty years since we beat them. So, we are going to try and give them a pasting. I see by the papers they did pretty well against Washington out there, but all those coast teams are bums.

If I have a rotten football team this year, I am going to join the French Foreign Legion if those frogs over there will promise to give me a horse. I did enough walking in the last war.

Sincerely,

R.A. Higgins

Going into 1939, Higgins had coached Penn State to only one winning season since his arrival nine years earlier. His teams had won twenty-nine, lost forty and tied four. But now his coaching staff had been together three seasons, and the recruiting efforts of the staff and alumni had lessened the effects of the no-scholarship policy. Solid high school players were coming to the program.

As veteran assistant coach Jim O'Hora said, "It all comes down to football players. If you don't have football players you can be the greatest coach in the world and you're not going to win."

From 1939 to 1948 Higgins won big. In his final ten years as head coach of Penn State, the Nittany Lions won sixty-two, lost seventeen and tied seven. Throw out the records of the 1943-1945 teams, when World War II caused considerable shuffling of the rosters, and Higgins's record for the other seven years was a spectacular 46-8-6. Few head coaches in the land could match it. Penn State put together impressive unbeaten strings of twelve games in 1939-1940, ten games in 1941-1942 and seventeen games in 1947-1948, which included the perfect 9-0 regular season mark in 1947, followed by a tie with SMU in the Cotton Bowl. Perhaps the most remarkable statistic is that in the seven non-war years, Higgins's defenses shut out twenty-four opponents.

Many years later O'Hora praised the impact Higgins made on the football program: "The success of Penn State football began back in the Bob Higgins era because Bob Higgins started with nothing, absolutely nothing, and brought it up through a successful undefeated season."

All Higgins knew going into 1939 was that it was going to get better and — with a break here and there — maybe a lot better. Penn State won its opener 13-3 over Bucknell before eleven thousand at Beaver Field, which now seated sixteen thousand. The victory came despite six lost fumbles and two interceptions. Sophomore Smaltz showed his passing and punting talents, completing seven of twelve passes and booming one punt sixty-nine yards. The defense completely shut down Bucknell, allowing just twenty-one total yards.

The following week's 49-7 homecoming win over Lehigh, in which the Lions racked up 547 total yards, set up a big confrontation with Cornell in New York. Line coach Bedenk, who was also the chief scout, reported to Higgins on the Sunday after the Lehigh game that this Cornell team was stronger than the 1938 team that beat the Lions. Cornell, like Penn State, was 2-0 on the young season with wins over Syracuse and Princeton.

Penn State's optimism met cold reality as Cornell shut down the Lions with an embarrassing 47-0 score. The game started off bad and got worse. Cornell scored early when the Penn State punt returner was hit and fumbled and a Cornell player caught the ball in mid-air and raced thirty yards for a touchdown. Almost the same thing happened again in the next minute. On Penn State's next possession it had the ball on its own forty-one when the Lion running back was hit and the ball popped into the hands of a Cornell player who ran for the second touchdown of the game. Penn State never recovered, having to go to the air and losing four interceptions. On the miserable day Cornell had 302 total yards to Penn State's fifty-two, and eight first downs to Penn State's one.

Following the game Higgins allowed Cornell head coach Carl Snavely to speak to the Penn State squad. Snavely told them that the lopsided score was no indication of their ability and that if the two freaky touchdowns hadn't occurred it would have been a close tilt all the way.

A report of the game stated, "A bewildered Nittany Lion football eleven, caught with their mouths wide open, swallowed one of the bitterest pills ever taken by a Penn State team."

Higgins wrote Shively of the Last Man's Club a few days after the game.

My dear Shive:

We certainly got a fine pasting from Cornell. They had two touchdowns in four minutes, and we only had the ball twice — two fumbles hopped out of the air into their hands and each time up jumped the devil. After that it was pretty much of a hopeless job. The breaks came their way all afternoon. It is quite an experience to go into a dressing room between halves with the idea in mind to get the team ready for the second half with the score against you 34-0. The peculiar part about the whole thing is that I am sure that if we played them again, the game would be nip-and-tuck.

We are going on to Syracuse this Saturday and we are all hoping for better things. Perhaps we don't have it, but we are certainly giving the boys the works this week.

Sincerely,
R.A. Higgins
Football Coach

During the week after the disappointing Cornell debacle, in a column in the *Collegian* newspaper entitled "Between The Lions," sports editor Bob Wilson viciously attacked Higgins in the form of an open letter.

Dear Mr. Higgins:

I have just summoned the Society for Prevention of Cruelty to Good Athletes to an emergency meeting here tomorrow.

I took the liberty of wiring them because I feel, like all of the undergraduates here at school and the alumni abroad, that drastic steps should be taken at once to aid your bewildered football Lions—especially in the face of what happened to them at Cornell last Saturday.

As if I need to remind you, Saturday's defeat was the worst any Penn State football team has suffered in the past ten years. And yet, this was supposed to have been the best Lion outfit to stalk the Nittany Valley for a good many seasons.

Now don't get me wrong, Mr. Higgins, your team isn't bad. It's the way they're taught to play!

Your system might have been great back in the days when Penn State teams used to pack 'em in. I say "might have been great" simply because I can't find figures that prove you ever did coach a really great team.

In fact, a quick glance at your record shows exactly the

opposite. In nine seasons (not counting the current one) as head Lion mentor your teams have won only 28 games against 40 defeats. Four games were deadlocks. The books also show that while your team managed to defeat Lebanon Valley and Lehigh rather consistently and maybe pull one upset a season, they were drubbed often and easily by teams from inferior schools. Pitiful, isn't it?

There must be some reason, then, for Penn State's perennially poor showing on the gridiron. I for one (and I am not alone) believe that the answer lies in State's inbred coaching system.

Eminent physicians claim that inbreeding weakens families. Eminent sportswriters claim that inbreeding also weakens football systems. And yours, Mr. Higgins, is certainly an inbred system. Penn State coaching staffs for years have been composed of Penn State men only—men who know no other system than the Penn State system.

Oh, I won't say your system is the worst in the country. But I can think what I damn please, and boy, am I thinking!!!

Well, as I was saying, I am meeting with the boys from the Cruelty Prevention Society tomorrow.

What shall I tell them?

Should I say that Bob Higgins has 45 good athletes, the majority of whom would be stars at any other college?

Should I point out that at Penn State they are not stars: that their talents are being abused?

Should I tell them that Bob Higgins is making sows ears out of silk purses?

What would you tell them, Mr. Higgins?

The column touched a deep enough chord in Higgins that he kept it in his files until his death. Mrs. Higgins thought it was in poor taste and would vent her rage on editor Wilson later in the year.

Higgins, despite the growing criticism, knew he had a young team on his hands and went about restoring their confidence. He suspected that Cornell was one of the better teams in the country — which they were, winning all eight of their games and finishing the season ranked fourth in the nation. As for Penn State, they didn't lose the remainder of the 1939 season, and into 1940 season they maintained a twelve game unbeaten streak, shutting out eight opponents.

In the next two games Penn State tied Syracuse 6-6 and beat Maryland 12-0. Then before forty thousand at Franklin Field in Philadelphia they blanked rival Penn, 10-0. Petrella's seventeen-yard touchdown run capped a 73-yard drive in the first quarter. In the second quarter, after an Ickes punt pushed Penn back to its eight yard line, Gajecki recovered a Penn fumble on the fourteen. Three plays moved the ball to the eight and John Patrick kicked the field goal for the Lions to provide the final margin. Penn didn't mount a serious scoring threat the entire game.

A report of the game addressed rumors of Higgins's dismissal if Penn State had failed to beat Penn. "That was their answer to the rumors...that coach Bob Higgins's future employment at State College would depend on the score of this 38th meeting with the haughty host. If there was any fragment of truth in the reports, then Lieutenant Higgins has a job for life."

A 14-14 tie against Army the following week gave Penn State a 4-1-2 record, guaranteeing Higgins his best record yet as Lion head coach.

For only the second time in thirty-seven years Penn State would play host to Pittsburgh to close the season. Penn State had not beaten Pitt since 1919 in the famous Hess-to-Higgins fake-punt from the end zone game.

Twenty-thousand fans packed New Beaver Field on November 25 and saw the Lion defense totally dominate the contest, never allowing Pittsburgh closer than the 25-yard line. Linebacker Gajecki, who had one of his greatest games, made two sensational defensive plays in the first quarter, the latter setting up the only touchdown of the afternoon.

Both of Gajecki's defensive gems were at the expense of Pitt running back Dick Cassiano. The first was when Cassiano broke into open field and after scampering thirty-three yards was nailed from behind by Gajecki. The second play came after Penn State had driven and missed a field goal, with Pitt taking over on its own twenty. On the first play from scrimmage Gajecki's tackle caused Cassiano to fumble and Gajecki recovered the loose ball on the Pitt twenty-two. Penn State needed just three plays to score — a three-yard run by Peters, an eighteen-yard reverse by White, and Smaltz's one-yard plunge off tackle for the touchdown. Ben Pollock's extra point made it 7-0. The only other scoring came in the final period when Penn State, behind the running of Peters and Ickes, moved to the Panther sixteen. Patrick's field goal from the twenty-four iced the contest, 10-0, and broke the twenty-year drought against Pitt.

The *Collegian* reported, "Thousands poured out on New Beaver Field after the referee's whistle. Goal posts were lifted intact from the ground and paraded down to Co-op corner."

Peters had led all runners with 102 yards on twenty attempts.

Gajecki recalled the game many years later: "I tried to do my best and I especially wanted to beat Pittsburgh for them trouncing us all those other years. They had some great ballplayers. I had to be at my best to do anything at all to have our team win. It was an inspiration for me to play tough against Pittsburgh."

In the post-game dressing room a reflective Higgins said, "We've waited twenty years for this moment, and naturally when it has arrived it's hard for me to express my real feeling. We told our kids before the game that if they outfought Pitt, man for man, we could win, and that's exactly what they did. Their spirit and determination was the deciding factor."

The victory so aroused the campus that President Hetzel declared the Monday following the game to be a student holiday.

Telegrams poured in to Higgins:

"Congratulations on your win over Pittsburgh." Harold Hess (hero along with Higgins of the 1919 win over Pitt).

"Congratulations on your game today, also on a splendid season. I've watched with enthusiasm each victory. It's time you had a break and you got it. Love to all." Margaret (Higgins's sister Margaret Sanger).

But the high note of the big win over Pitt was sung by Mrs. Higgins. She didn't forget the scathing attack on her husband by the *Collegian* sportswriter following the loss to Cornell. *Pittsburgh Press* sports editor Chester Smith wrote about her revenge following the Pitt game.

"When the whistle blew to end the contest, a swirl of slightly screwy alumni and students descended on the coach to pound him on the back, shake him by the hand, muss his hair and tell him what a grand old geezer he was. In the excitement, no one thought of his wife.

"She was sitting far up in the press box, having a perfectly good cry. After all, a woman's nerves can stand only so much.

"How long she cried there before the school's publicity man came along and found her she didn't know, but he was as solicitious as he could be. He brought her a drink of water, and loaned his handkerchief because her's was a perfect mess from dabbing at her eyes.

"'Isn't there something else I can do for you?' he asked.

"'Yes, there is,' she sobbed. 'You can get that student editor and bring him here so I can give him a good kick — I'm so happy I'm mad.'

"So the publicity man disappeared and, sure enough, a little while later he was back. And the student editor was with him.

"'Here I am,' the student editor said.

"So the coach's wife, the most dignified person you could imagine, got up and very deftly booted the young gentleman in the right place. She hadn't listened to her husband talk to his punters all these years for nothing."

The 5-1-2 winning season in 1939 was the first of a staggering forty-nine consecutive winning seasons for Penn State, lasting until the 1988 season.

Of the eleven players who started against Pitt in 1939, only the end and captain, Spike Alter, was lost to graduation. Several other players who saw considerable field time, including Lloyd Ickes, were also gone for the 1940 season, but it was no secret that Penn State was loaded going into the season.

By season's end the nearly impenetrable line of left end

Lloyd Parsons, left tackle Stravinski, left guard Mike Garbinski, center Gajecki, right guard Wade Mori, right tackle Frank Platt, right end Tom Vargo, and their backups, were known nationwide as "The Seven Mountains," a reference to their strength and the geography southeast of campus.

The backfield was also deep, with Petrella and Peters sharing time at tailback, Krouse and White at wingback, Smaltz at fullback and Patrick at blocking back. As a defensive unit they shut out five of eight opponents. As an offense they mixed the passing and running game and methodically controlled the ball.

"All of us on the line were sixty-minute men," Gajecki said. "I would have felt disappointed if Higgins had taken me out of the ballgame. Most of the fellas felt the same way. We had been together three years and by our senior season we had an outstanding line. We just seemed to know where to be at the right time."

Stravinski echoed Gajecki's comments.

"The guys we had worked hard and we were well drilled in the fundamentals of blocking and tackling," he said. "That was our whole secret those last two years. Our defense was set up where each man was responsible for a certain area. We had a bunch of zip games. When I get together with the guys from the 1947 team, we almost get in a fight when we talk about whose defense was better."

Veteran players or not, Higgins and his staff drove the 1940 squad hard in practice. "We scrimmaged quite often during the week," Gajecki said. "It would get so doggone hot. We always tried to dig for the water buckets and they used to put any kind of junk in there to prevent us from drinking it. Sometimes they'd take the buckets away."

Higgins had to chuckle every time he glanced at some of the names in his lineup — Gajecki, Stravinski, Garbinski. "I can't pronounce these names," he'd squall. "You guys have got to change them to something I can say and read."

"Bob Higgins was a nice man to play for," Gajecki said. "He was a guy who was really very instrumental in us playing very hard."

Higgins had his eye on the season finale at Pitt early on in the season. On September 19 he wrote "Last Man" Shively.

Dear Shive:

Pittsburgh plays Ohio State at Columbus on October 28. I would like to have someone from Ohio that knows something about football scout them for me. I will send two press box tickets to you, and I would appreciate it if you could get two fellows, not necessarily Ohio State fellows, to scout for me. If you get Ohio State fellows who are interested in Ohio State, naturally they will watch Ohio State and I don't care about Ohio State—all I want to know about is Pittsburgh.

I wish these scouts would watch the pass lanes particularly. In English to you that means the lanes in which the receivers travel. I would like to see if there is any give-away when either Jones, left halfback, Thurbon, right halfback, or Dutton, Thurbon's substitute, are going to receive the ball. Cassiano had a habit of wetting his fingers every time he was to take the ball. I would like to get something especially on Jones.

I would like to know as a second important thing whether or not the center comes out and takes the weak-side to protect on pass protection.

Pittsburgh has one of the best first teams in the East. They are not as deep as they were last year, and if they don't get anybody hurt, they are going to be tough.

Sincerely,
R.A. Higgins
Football Coach

Higgins's concern for Pitt would be justified at season's end.

Penn State's season opening win over Bucknell set the tone for the season. Petrella, his darting runs dazzling the crowd, rushed for ninety-six yards. The defense, which lined up in the 6-2-2-1 formation, held Bucknell to eighty-four total yards.

Petrella rushed for 119 more in a 17-13 win over West Virginia, which was held to minus six yards rushing. The story of the game, however, was sophomore backup fullback Sparky Brown. An ankle injury to Smaltz forced Brown into service and he delivered with several key runs and passes for first downs, and intercepted a pass late in the game to clinch the victory.

Peters returned to form and ran for 105 yards in a 34-0 win over Lehigh, which managed only thirty-six total yards on offense. Again fullback Brown ran and punted well for the Lions.

The unbeaten streak, carrying over from 1939, stretched to twelve games with dominating wins over Temple, South Carolina, a 13-13 tie with Syracuse and a 25-0 romp over New York University.

Against a good Temple team, the Lions racked up almost three hundred yards on the ground with Krouse, Petrella, White and Peters all gaining more than fifty yards. Petrella scored twice and Peters ran for one touchdown. A report of the game stated, "Higgins was substituting players with his usual keeness. The way he maneuvered Petrella and Peters back and forth so that Pepper was always present when yardage was particularly needed, and Chuck was in there for pass defense, was pretty to watch."

Following the Temple game, Higgins wrote Last Man Jim Douglas.

My dear Jim:

I am sorry that I didn't get down to see you after the game on Saturday. I got out to this cocktail party and found they were giving it in my honor and there were people dropping around until 9:30 or 10:00.

Our victory over Temple seems to give us a better rating now. News services, agencies, et cetera are wiring us for stories, pictures, and they are beginning to recognize us more and more each Saturday. I don't know how long we can keep going without getting licked, but I am going to do my best to see if we can't get through, although I believe a person has to have Lady Luck with him or just one whale of a football team.

Sincerely,
R.A. Higgins
Football Coach

Penn State overcame a late 13-6 deficit at Syracuse when Krouse made a sensational leaping catch at the five of a long Smaltz pass and sidestepped two Syracuse defenders en route to the end zone. The play covered fifty-three yards. Smaltz completed twelve consecutive passes in the game, which fifty-four years later in 1994 remained a Penn State record. He accounted for most of Penn State's 193 yards passing against Syracuse. A Smaltz-to-Krouse pass also accounted for the Lions' first touchdown. On the day, Krouse caught eight passes from Smaltz for 150 yards.

Smaltz and Krouse had competed against each other in high school before arriving at Penn State in 1938 — Krouse at Rochester and Smaltz at Aliquippa.

Krouse, who played at six feet, 180 pounds, remembered those confrontations: "Bill would run three times and punt, and I'd go back to receive it. Then I'd run three times and punt, and he'd go back to receive it. We banged heads a lot. When we came to Penn State it just seemed natural that he looked to throw to me first.

"Bill had a great arm. He threw a soft pass, but he could throw hard and long when he needed to. I don't remember dropping a pass because they were so easy to catch."

Krouse had played for Ernie Meyers at Rochester, which was just northwest of Pittsburgh. Krouse chose Penn State over Pitt and Alabama. State College was close enough to home so that his parents could travel to the games.

A high national ranking and a bowl bid were assured if Penn State had been able to add to the 6-0-1 record and twelve-game unbeaten streak it carried into Pittsburgh in the final game of the season. But 31,000 fans watched Pitt upset the Lions, 20-7. The key play of the game was a naked reverse in which Pitt's George Kracum ran forty-four yards and, upon being hit at the five-yard-line, pitched the ball to Ralph Fife who carried it in for the score. Kracum also intercepted a pass late in the game and ran thirty-five yards for a touchdown to put it out of reach. Krouse accounted for the Lions' only score on a pass from Smaltz.

Following the game Higgins shook his head over the naked reverse touchdown that shaped the contest early. "We use the same play and I can't figure out how it tricked us," he said.

Ridge Riley wrote, "Within the grimness of the Pitt Stadium, Penn State's visions of an undefeated season went up in the murky Pittsburgh sky and heavy Penn State hearts finished out a weekend in the Smokey City with forced gaiety and dreams of what might have been...Say goodbye to the twelve seniors who have been largely responsible for bringing Penn State out of the football doldrums—Chuck Peters, Craig White, Johnny Patrick, Tom Vargo, Lloyd Parsons, Wade Mori, Frank Platt, Carl Stravinski, Jim Woodward, Walt Kniaz, Ben Pollock—and last, but greatest of them all—Captain Leon Gajecki."

Gajecki made first team All-American following the season.

"I didn't know too much about it until I started reading the papers and seeing my name as an All-American," Gajecki said. "It made me feel good. It flattered me. I think I deserved something like that. I played very hard."

In retrospect, Gajecki took great pride in being one of the players who helped put Penn State football back on the map. "We had a lot of heart," he said. "With Bob Higgins's guidance, we turned the program around."

§ 13 §
From Cazenovia To College

THE SEVEN MOUNTAINS HAD GRADUATED, which meant Higgins and line coach Bedenk had to do some fast work to get the team ready for the 1941 season. Higgins didn't have to worry about his backfield. Smaltz, Petrella and Captain Krouse all returned for their senior seasons. Smaltz and Krouse also shared punting duties and Smaltz kicked extra points. Manny Weaver, a substitute blocking back on the 1940 team, was ready to step into a starting role.

The Smaltz-to-Krouse passing combination had become nationally recognized. Krouse had been one of the top receivers in the country in 1940 with six touchdown catches. Prior to the season Ridge Riley wrote about the new football captain in his newsletter.

"We hope you get a chance to meet this boy Krouse. He is all the football captain you would want Penn State to have. He combines the exceptional qualities of intelligence, leadership and ability. He is the president of the senior class, an excellent student in the difficult mechanical engineering department, and a very fine football player."

Krouse recalled that school always came first and Higgins never put pressure on him to adjust his class schedule to accommodate football practice.

Krouse enjoyed his relationship with Higgins, whom he compared to an Army drill sergeant as Higgins constantly emphasized conditioning. Krouse said that Higgins was always fair and that he put a lot of responsibility on the shoulders of his assistant coaches and captains.

Higgins would rely on Krouse to call the plays in the huddle during the 1941 season. There were plenty of exciting single wing plays available, but the line had lost a lot of its strength from the previous season. Senior Bob Wear had the edge on the center position vacated by Gajecki. The remainder of the line would have to be built with underclassmen, including sophomore end John Potsklan who had played high school ball at Brownsville. Potsklan was recruited by alumni Judge Vance Cottom and Casey Jones. Potsklan was the first of several Brownsville players to attend Penn State during the decade. Other sophomores going into 1941 included end Bob Davis, Bernie Brosky at tackle, and John Jaffurs and Ted Kratzke at the guards. Junior trenchmen included tackle Ken Schoonover, end Van Lenten and tackle Mike Kerns.

Higgins suspected that his line's inexperience might lead to a slow start, but he also knew that the team had enough potential to finish strong if the coaching staff did its job. His observation was right on target.

The offense never got started in a tough 7-0 opening loss to Colgate in Buffalo. But the Penn State linemen, none having ever started in a varsity game, played excellent defense to keep Penn State in the game. A Buffalo sportswriter wrote of the contest, "Buffalo gridiron fans yesterday saw the best college football game staged here in many, many years. Gallant gridders from Colgate and Penn State put on a spectacle that was a treasure and a treat. No college or university ever turned out more inspired, intelligent, determined or aggressive human machines than we saw engage in 60 minutes of pulsating action on the Civic Stadium turf."

In the week prior to the home opener against Bucknell, Higgins drilled his team on blocking punts after hearing Bedenk's scouting report. It paid off. Penn State fell behind 13-0 in the first quarter, but then Schoonover blocked a punt on the Bucknell eighteen that was returned to the one-yard-line. Petrella pushed it across for the score.

Early in the second quarter Penn State's Van Lenten blocked a punt on the Bucknell six and the Lions recovered on the three. Petrella scored again and Smaltz's extra point put the Lions ahead 14-13. Set up by a Smaltz-to-Krouse pass, Petrella scored his third touchdown late in the first half, and ran for a remarkable fourth touchdown in the third quarter as Penn State won 27-13.

The team fell to 1-2 on the season after losing in Philadelphia to Temple, 14-0. An injury forced Smaltz out of the game in the first quarter and Penn State never rebounded.

But from there on it was gravy, with Penn State winning the remaining six games on its schedule. It whipped Lehigh and New York University, and thrashed Syracuse 34-19 before sixteen thousand partisans at New Beaver Field. The night before the Syracuse game Higgins and Captain Krouse decided Penn State would throw on its first offensive play, which it did for fourteen yards. The offense promptly drove sixty-five yards for a score and never looked back, taking a 27-0 lead into halftime. The last play of the half was a Smaltz-to-Krouse touchdown that broke the Orangemen's spirits.

The record improved to 5-2 as the defense totally stymied West Virginia. The only score of the 7-0 Penn State victory came on a fourth-and-long Smaltz-to-Krouse pass of twenty-eight yards in the second quarter. A report of the play said, "The next play had to be a pass and West Virginia knew it. Everybody in the grand stands knew it. What's more they all knew it would be a pass to Krouse. It was. Seemingly well covered by two defenders, Krouse darted to the one yard line, took a high pass by leaping in the air, and fell into the touchdown zone."

Going into the November 22 clash at Pittsburgh, it had been twenty-two years since Penn State had defeated Pitt on the road. That was the 1919 game in which Higgins scored on the famous 92-yard fake-punt formation.

Pitt jumped out 7-0 this time, but it was all Lions after that. Petrella scored three touchdowns and rushed for ninety yards in the 34-7 victory. The defense held Pitt to seventy-four yards rushing.

Krouse felt great satisfaction in competing on the winning side in two of the three Pitt clashes during his varsity career. "Being from the Pittsburgh area, it was an important game to me as a lot of my friends watched my progress at Penn State," Krouse said. "I had a lot of boosters, the biggest one being my father."

Penn State defeated South Carolina 19-12 to finish the season with a 7-2 record. Smaltz, Krouse and Petrella completed their college careers in excellent fashion. Petrella rushed for 110 yards and scored two touchdowns. And fans got a final look at the Smaltz-to-Krouse passing combination, as they hooked up on eight passes. One of their connections, a 42-yarder, set up Penn State's second score of the game.

Ridge Riley wrote of Higgins's coaching efforts in 1941:

"No coach in the country had any more obstacles in the way of a successful season. Ten of eleven starters were missing. Four lettermen returned. But these obstacles were overcome, and they were overcome with a vengeance. Let's doff our lids to Bob Higgins. He's our nomination for Coach of the Year."

Higgins later reflected on the season, "That 1941 team has to be one of my most satisfying. We had the fewest men back I ever had, and it wasn't as good as some of the others, but that team did more with the talent it had than any other."

The senior leadership on the team from Krouse, Smaltz and Petrella had much to do with the success. Their confidence spread to their younger teammates. "We thought we were good," Krouse said. "We thought we could beat anybody. We played hard. We got along well together."

Krouse and Smaltz played in the East-West all-star game in San Francisco following the season.

As Higgins drove his 1941 team beyond everybody's expectations, he couldn't help but keep one eye on the freshman squad. Great athletes seemed to be coming out of the woodwork for preseason practice. The college's first black football players, Dave and Harry Alston of Midland, Pennsylvania, so excited Higgins that he had frosh coach McAndrews call a special scrimmage in order for the varsity staff to get a closeup view.

Dave, a speedster at 6-1, 198 pounds, was a triple threat back in high school and the more talented of the two. Harry, at 202 pounds, blocked for his brother and caught his passes. Alumnus Casey Jones had convinced the boys' father that Penn State was their kind of place, much to the disappointment of a dozen other schools.

In the scrimmage Dave threw fifty- and sixty-yard bullets to his brother and showed excellent ball handling skills. Higgins noticed, however, that when Dave ran the ball his brother Harry tended to slack up on his blocking. When Higgins asked him about it, Harry replied, "Dave runs so slick, I like to see him go on his own."

Another freshman player caused Higgins to wish it was already 1942. A 5-11, 205-pound guard named Steve Suhey combined more speed and power than any lineman Higgins had ever seen. The thought of Dave Alston passing and running behind Suhey for the next three years had Higgins and his assistants giddy by the end of the scrimmage.

Little did Higgins know that the rock-solid guard would become his son-in-law, marrying his middle daughter Ginger in 1949. The Higgins-Suhey family tie was destined to become the most famous in Penn State football history.

Steven Joseph Suhey was born in Syracuse, New York on January 8, 1922 to Mr. and Mrs. Michael Suhey, who had immigrated separately from the Ukraine and met in Syracuse. The parents spoke broken English, but preferred to speak Ukrainian Slavic. As a result, Steve didn't speak English until he entered grade school.

The family escaped their cramped quarters and unruly urban streets when Steve was in eighth grade, moving to a small farm near the rural crossroads town of Nelson, four miles east of Cazenovia, New York. When Steve told his parents he wanted to play football for Cazenovia Central High School, his father reminded him that farm chores were more important. Steve argued that he could manage the chores before and after school and still play football. Mrs. Suhey agreed with her boy and volunteered to help him. The discussion was over. Steve Suhey was going to play football.

The family lived off the land and its own labor to a large degree, maintaining a few cows and growing corn and other vegetables. Going to or from school or practice, Steve usually had little choice but to cover the four miles from Nelson to Cazenovia in a dead sprint. He was up early milking cows before school, would return home during the day to do quick maintenance on equipment or tend to the crops and was back at it again after football practice.

While his parents were very taciturn people and shied away from the community, Steve longed for the moment each day he could escape his grim existence at home. Sports, and football in particular, would always be more than a game to him. Discarding his tattered work clothes for the football uniform was like taking a breath of fresh air. Football was his freedom.

This poor farm boy became one of the greatest guards ever to play college football. In high school Suhey played tackle, guard, and occasionally ran the ball at fullback. His first coach was Max Buckley of the Cazenovia Central Cornhuskers.

"Buckley had a lot of power in his voice," recalled Ed Ammann, who played left guard when Suhey, a sophomore, was playing left tackle for Cazenovia in 1937. "Nobody fooled around. You played football and that was it. He would tell you something and you would do it."

Buckley fielded the greatest team in Cazenovia history in 1937.

"Two-hundred thirty-two points scored, no points allowed," recalled Earl "Sparky" Brown of Cazenovia's perfect season in 1937. Brown played halfback on the team. He said that only one opponent moved the ball inside the Cazenovia twenty-yard line the entire season, and that lasted for just one play as Suhey broke through and tackled the ballcarrier for a loss on the ensuing play.

Ammann and Brown agreed that the muscular Suhey never met his match in line action, which was why school officials delayed the start of one home game until Suhey arrived. "Here it comes time to go out on the field and he wasn't there," Brown said. "So the principal, Doc Lowe, gets in his car and goes over there to see where Steve is, and here's Steve on the run coming toward the high school. Doc Lowe picked him up, brought him in and he got dressed and played. Steve had had to go home and draw corn after lunch."

Suhey nearly missed another game his senior year because of farm duty, but the team bus detoured by his house and picked him up.

Teammates remember Suhey as a very well-liked, hardworking person. "He was one great guy," Ammann said. "Football meant everything to him. He was dedicated to it."

Steve was the favorite of many of the town's youngsters, including Dallas Trammell, who was the water boy for the

1938 team. "Steve was very much my idol," Trammell said. "I was a lot younger and very small. He was huge and had these giant, thick hands. He was a very mild tempered guy. He knew how strong he was and he didn't have to prove anything to anybody or try to be a bully."

Trammell recalled the time Suhey broke both of his wrists during the 1938 season and had to wear a cast on each arm. But that didn't stop him from playing. "He used those casts as semi-lethal weapons," Trammell said.

After every game, Suhey hoisted the knicker-clad Trammell onto his shoulders and carried him off the field. "We called him 'Chopper,'" Trammell said.

While playing four years of football and serving as co-captain in both his junior and senior seasons, Suhey also competed in track and field three years, played baseball two years and wrestled his senior season.

He graduated on June 24, 1940 in a class of forty-nine students. The class motto was: "Less than our best is failure." Suhey applied the motto to his life both on and off the field. He preached the message to his large family in later years.

Suhey didn't attend college his first year following graduation because he felt obligated to help his father on the farm. His father doubted the value of a college education even if alumni support of Steve's football efforts could cut costs. Suhey took some post-graduate courses at Cazenovia, which was not unusual in that period, and also played some more high school football in the fall of 1940.

Cazenovia principal Wayne (Doc) Lowe knew Suhey was thirsting to play college football. Lowe, a Penn State man, had helped Cazenovia halfback Sparky Brown enter Penn State in 1939. Lowe suggested to Suhey that he talk with Brown about the school and the football team. Brown invited Suhey to join him on his next trip to State College and offered to introduce Suhey to the coaching staff. Again the matter came up for family discussion and again Steve's mother prevailed. She wasn't an educated woman, but she supported schooling for her son.

"We hitchhiked," Brown recalled. "That's the way I always went. I went back for practice the last of August and

Steve went with me. He wasn't enrolled yet. He had a few dollars in his pocket; I'm sure it was all the money he had."

Higgins had gotten wind of Suhey from both principal Lowe and Cazenovia coach Buckley. Suhey was talking to one of the assistant coaches when Higgins walked up. Brown nodded toward the big guard.

"That's Suhey," Brown said.

"Do you think he can make the team?" Higgins asked.

"I think so," Brown replied with a grin.

When Brown introduced the two, Higgins blurted, "Boy you have big hands!"

Higgins proceeded to introduce Suhey and show off his hands to many of the players. One of them was Bill "Red" Moore, a freshman tackle from Rochester, Pennsylvania, who would not only play alongside Suhey at the college and pro levels, but become one of Suhey's lifelong friends.

Moore, another Casey Jones recruit, recalled his initial meeting with Suhey. "Higgins brought him to the training table that day and introduced him to me. The Hig was overwrought with the size of Steve's hands. He couldn't get over them. He showed them to the guys. Steve was just embarrassed. But Steve's hands *were* like meat cleavers."

Doc Lowe's brother and fellow Penn Stater, Dick Lowe of Williamsport, picked up Suhey's tuition fee, for which Suhey was always grateful. Several years later, when Suhey returned to Penn State after World War II, he attempted to repay Lowe, but Lowe waved him off and said, "Steve, you take care of young people when the time comes." Steve took the advice to heart and for years and years his and Ginger's home on Sparks Street in State College was a revolving door for their children's friends. Many budding Penn State athletes benefited not only from Steve's coaching guidance but from his compassion and wisdom concerning character and family values.

Higgins invited the incoming freshman Suhey to live at the three-story Higgins household on McKee Street. Higgins typically put up two athletes on the top floor, which had two bedrooms and a bathroom. The boys would perform various chores around the house.

Sparky Brown shared the third floor with Suhey. "I did all the work and he goofed off," Brown kidded. "We used to take care of the furnace and shovel the sidewalks."

Mrs. Higgins kept a copy of their class schedules in the kitchen so she'd know when they were supposed to be available for home duty. She didn't have to feed these growing boys as they continued to eat one meal a day at the training table and work on campus for their other meals. Suhey worked in a fraternity kitchen.

It was on McKee Street that Suhey met the Higgins's three daughters for the first time, including Ginger, who was a sophomore in high school and an excellent athlete in her own right.

The freshman team lived up to its billing and swept through the 1941 season with five wins and no defeats. Three linemen on the team — Suhey, Moore and Leo Nobile — would become professional teammates on the Pittsburgh Steelers in 1948 and 1949. Jeff Durkota, a back from Ebensburg, played with the Los Angeles Rams in 1948. Center and linebacker John Wolosky played a year with the New York Giants. Wolosky had followed his friend Potsklan from Brownsville to Penn State, though several schools wanted him. Finally, it seemed, scholarship-caliber players were coming to Penn State in spite of the no-scholarship rule.

At 5-10 and 195 pounds, Wolosky had played for three consecutive undefeated teams at Brownsville for head coach Carl Aschman, who was assisted by future Penn State freshman coach Earl Bruce. One high school coach who had noticed Wolosky was Paul Brown at Massillon, Ohio. Brown, after nine years at Massillon, had accepted the head coaching position at Ohio State prior to the 1941 season. High on his recruiting list was Wolosky. Wolosky visited Columbus along with Nobile and several other players. Olympic gold medalist sprinter Jesse Owens, who had attended Ohio State, hosted the recruits.

The University of Alabama also wanted Wolosky. While sitting in class one afternoon at Brownsville, Coach Aschman motioned Wolosky out into the hallway and took him to his office. An Alabama assistant coach was waiting and asked Wolosky to turn around and drop his trousers in order to inspect Wolosky's legs and backside build. "I'll take him," the

Alabama coach said.

But neither Alabama nor Ohio State got him. Judge Cottom, who had persuaded Potsklan to attend Penn State, did likewise with Wolosky.

The young Lions beat Bucknell 19-0 in the first game with Dave Alston running for two touchdowns and throwing a pass to brother Harry for the third score. They beat Colgate 21-0 with Dave scoring two more touchdowns and drop-kicking an extra point. He was one of the few kickers who still used the traditional method. In the third game of the season Dave scored all three touchdowns in a 20-12 win over Syracuse.

Midway through the season as cold weather came in, freshman coach McAndrews called the squad together on the field and told them additional clothing was available at one of the assistant's houses.

Wolosky recalled that most of the players wore their ROTC uniforms beyond the call of duty because they couldn't afford other clothes. Wolosky couldn't get to the assistant's house right away, but encountered Nobile, who had already been there. "What'd you leave me?" Wolosky asked. "Some neckties," Nobile said with a smile.

The freshmen went to 4-0 with a 20-6 victory over Cornell. Dave Alston ran fifty yards for one of the scores. The season-closing win over Army gave the frosh a perfect mark and gave Higgins reason to look ahead. While he was losing veterans Smaltz, Petrella and Krouse, he had the bigger and faster Alston brothers ready for their first varsity year, a solid line returning with a year of varsity experience under its belt, and several talented linemen moving up from the freshman team.

Then, only eight days after the varsity team's season-ending win over South Carolina, the Japanese bombed Pearl Harbor on December 7, 1941. Priorities changed and so did football rosters.

But it wasn't the war that struck one player from Higgins's lineup, as Higgins so informed Last Man member Vince Smith:

August 17, 1942
Dear Vince:
This is to say many thanks for the fine time at the reunion. I think it was our best one.
I had a terrible misfortune over the past weekend. My best halfback, Dave Alston, 20 years old, six feet tall, 200 pounds, in perfect health, passed away after a tonsillectomy.
Sincerely yours,
R.A. Higgins

Dave Alston had died tragically on August 15 at nearby Bellefonte Hospital of complications following surgery. Fifty-two years later Wolosky remembered Dave Alston. "He was the greatest ballplayer I ever saw, better than Tom Harmon, Bill Dudley or Doak Walker," Wolosky said. "He was a nice fella, too, and a good student. He came from a good family. It was really a shock for all of us."

Dave's brother Harry, stricken with grief, dropped out of school. Judging from Dave's phenomenal freshman performance as a virtual scoring machine, it is difficult to project how great a player he may have become, and how such talent would have affected Higgins's overall record as a coach. But all who knew Dave Alston said he was among the best athletes they'd ever seen. Higgins called Alston "half a team in himself."

Shortly before the opening game of the 1942 season, Higgins wrote Earl Shively.

September 25, 1942
Dear Shive:
I don't want to get out the crying towel with you, but it might be well for you to be informed on certain things that have taken place since I last saw you. At that time, you perhaps noticed I was quite optimistic relative to the coming football season this fall. Since then we have lost exactly twenty boys to the Service — lost three as late as last week. Now before losing these boys I had a backfield that was well over 200 pounds and could do everything. Besides being over 200, they were all over six feet. Every last one of them have gone. I am not crying the blues, because I think they should be in

the Service. This, however, was to be my year. Then I lost Dave Alston, who was half a team in himself. This, however, gives your friend, Sparky Brown, a chance to get his name in the lineup. He'll be my regular tailback, and he'll do pretty well. I have about fourteen good men, and if I am lucky as I was last year and don't have too many injuries, I might win 50% of my games. We should be able to take Pittsburgh.

Sincerely yours,

R.A. Higgins

Six starters from the 1941 team, including Potsklan, had joined the service. Nine players from the 1941 freshman team had entered the war. However, experienced talent returned in the line with Schoonover, Jaffurs, Kerns and Davis. Sophomores Suhey, Wolosky, Moore and Nobile were anticipating plenty of action in backup roles. Center Lou Palazzi was tapped as captain.

The war had opened the door for freshmen to play on the varsity, and yearling Joe Colone and high school sprint champion Larry Joe looked like early contributors in the backfield.

When it was all said and done, Higgins had matched his best record as head coach at Penn State. The 1942 team went 6-1-1, losing only to West Virginia while defeating Pitt for the third time in four years.

John Watkins was a student manager for the 1942 team. He recalled that the players suited up in the old water tower behind the Nittany Lion Hotel. He remembered the laughter and friendship on the team, a family spirit to which Higgins was father.

"The Hig was such a jovial guy, always in a good frame of mind," Watkins said. "On the field he was a disciplinarian without being an ogre. He was like a teacher. He'd tell you something once; he didn't want to have to tell you twice. If he corrected you he would do it in such a nice way you would want to please him and do it the right way.

"One thing I always admired about Bob and line coach Bedenk was that nothing they did was unnecessary. It was so fundamental. They wanted you to be indoctrinated with things that were going to win ballgames."

Watkins recalled a humorous incident involving Higgins

and sophomore fullback Bob Weitzel. Weitzel had checked into the infirmary the day before a game and Higgins called Watkins the next morning and told him to look in on Weitzel. "Bob thought that Weitzel may have been dogging it a little bit cause Hig was trying to change his throwing position," Watkins said. "Weitzel was getting a little disgusted. He had been a great all-state fullback."

Watkins went to the infirmary and asked where Weitzel's room was. The nurse informed him that Weitzel had left. "What do you mean he's left?" Watkins inquired. "He went hunting," she said. Watkins realized it was the first day of hunting season.

Watkins went to the stadium and Higgins confronted him. "Is he going to make it?" Higgins asked.

"I don't think so," Watkins replied.

"I didn't lie to him," Watkins later said. "But I never did tell him that Weitzel went hunting."

Penn State defeated Bucknell in the opener. Brown ran seventy-nine yards for a touchdown. Freshman Joe also scored in the game as he did in the following week's victory over Lehigh.

The Lions fought Cornell to a scoreless tie in the mud and rain at Ithaca. Penn State punted a mind-boggling twenty-seven times to Cornell's twenty-four punts. Freshman Colone averaged over forty yards with his fourteen punts. The teams combined for a meager six first downs and 112 total yards.

A newcomer to the starting lineup for the upcoming Colgate game was sophomore Red Moore. Moore, who became a great college and pro lineman, remembered Coach Higgins:

"Bob commanded respect of the players. I think he expected his players to conduct themselves as gentlemen and he demanded that we always look right. We all loved him.

"We had very spirited practices. Bob would blow the whistle and we ran from one drill to the next. There was no wasted time. Bob wasn't one who believed in staying out there until the lights were out. After practice we had to get down to the training table and then hit the books. There was no time to fool around.

"Bob was a student of the game. He was an innovator with some of the plays we ran out of the single wing, like where Bucky Walters would go down and hook it about ten and he'd catch the ball and turn to the outside where the wingback had looped around and he'd either hand or toss him the ball. We scored touchdowns that won football games on that play."

Such was the case in the 13-10 homecoming win over Colgate. The Thursday before the game Higgins had decided to insert a play that had been in the book for several years but never used in a game. In the second quarter Colone threw a thirteen-yard pass to left end Walters at the Colgate forty, and Walters handed the ball to wingback Cliff St. Clair who raced in for the score.

"It worked just like I planned it in bed," Higgins said proudly the morning after the game. "I had a homecoming hunch."

The record improved to 3-0-1 and extended Penn State's unbeaten string, stretching from 1941, to ten games. Prior to the next clash against West Virginia in Morgantown, Higgins wrote Last Man Jim Douglas.

October 26, 1942
Dear Jim:
I am delighted to know that you are thinking about gathering the clan in Philadelphia for our Penn game. I like that. I will, of course, provide the tickets on the fifty-yard line — two for you, one for Smith and one for Shively, or in case the two court jesters would like to bring their wives, I'll be glad to furnish tickets for Marg and Mary. Virginia is coming down and if you boys would like to be separated a short distance from your wives so that you can really get the feel of the game and help with the coaching, I'll arrange for that. I have found that sometimes women and football do not mix.

My old friend, Bill Kern, from West Virginia is hanging back waiting to give me a pasting. Our game with Colgate was tough and rugged and we were perhaps fortunate to win. The problem of keeping a team up for each succeeding Saturday may seem simple to some of you sincere good wishers, but it is quite a job.
Sincerely yours,
R.A. Higgins

West Virginia indeed pasted Penn State, 24-0. The Mountaineers accumulated 266 total yards to Penn State's eighty. Backup right guard Suhey never forgot it. "I was beaten to a pulp, physically and mentally, and I never thought I'd amount to much after that."

Fellow lineman Moore knew better. "Steve was quiet and unassuming, but strong-willed and an excellent football player. He had all the necessary makings of an All-American, which he later became."

Fellow lineman Wolosky also knew Suhey had better days ahead of him. "Steve was the fastest lineman I ever played with. He could run down halfbacks. Larry Joe was the fastest back we had, a state track record holder in high school, and Steve at 220 pounds would keep up with him in the hundred wearing their football uniforms."

Penn State beat Syracuse 18-13 in its next game, with Sparky Brown rushing for 108 yards and Colone gaining eighty-one. Colone also punted superbly, with four of his boots traveling over fifty yards.

Yet another game went down to the wire as the Lions beat Penn 13-7 at Franklin Field in Philadelphia before fifty thousand. Penn had more than three-hundred total yards to Penn State's 131. Penn State never attempted a pass. But the break of the game came in the opening period. Student manager Watkins remembered it.

"Joe Bedenk was the chief scout as well as the line coach. He was a master at that. He had scouted Penn three times. He mentioned that part of our strategy should be in shaking up the Penn center, Don Bitler, on every play. Joe described Bitler as a fine athlete, which he was, but was sometimes shaky on the snap for punts. Our guards were to pummel Bitler on every play and hope that a bad snap and a blocked punt would result. It was a blocked kick by Ken Schoonover that was the key play of the game. It stood out so strongly, that I'll never forget it."

Penn State's Bob Davis picked up the blocked punt at the Penn twenty-four and ran the ball to the two-yard-line. Brown plunged over for the touchdown. Joe also scored in the final period.

Penn State continued its domination of Pitt by winning

the final game of the season at New Beaver Field, 14-6, before twelve thousand. It marked Penn State's sixteenth win in a row on the home front, from 1939-1942. Again Higgins played it conservatively and the Lions threw only six passes. Joe returned the second half kickoff ninety yards for a touchdown for the first score of the game. Another freshman back, Bobby Williams, threw to Aldo Cenci for a touchdown to put the game on ice in the final period.

Amazingly, Penn State never scored more than nineteen points in any of its games in 1942, yet pulled off a 6-1-1 record. The Associated Press ranked Penn State nineteenth in the nation. Ohio State won the AP title, followed by Georgia and Wisconsin. Georgia halfback Frank Sinkwich won the Heisman Trophy.

Though the war had riddled the roster prior to the 1942 season, Higgins had been able to count on the same boys from game to game. But for the next three years, 1943-1945, so many players came and went that Higgins often didn't know until game day what names he could pencil in.

§ 14 §
The War Years

MANY COLLEGES DROPPED FOOTBALL for a year or two during World War II, but Higgins pointed out that because Penn State hosted several military programs an abundance of players would be shuffling through. He emphasized that a football team would be good for the morale of the soldiers, the student body and the community. As a result Penn State fielded teams from 1943-1945, putting up 5-3-1, 6-3 and 5-3 records. Higgins's challenge was not so much winning football games as keeping up with what players would be available for the upcoming contest. He put these thoughts into a June 7, 1943 letter to Last Man Henry McWane.

Dear Henry:

I hereby accept your kind invitation to be with you and the other old soldiers the first weekend in August. I am hoping I can pick up Smith somewhere en route and he and I can go together.

I notice what you said about liquid refreshments and I am now aware of the fact that the State of Virginia is dry. I will promise to start off with one pint. I am not guaranteeing that Smith and I will arrive with more than half the amount we started off with. This is one of the reasons why I refuse to contact Shively in Washington. If we would fall in with him, we might arrive without any.

We are having 600 Pre-Flight kids to train in physical education besides about 600 engineers. I have lost ten pounds and I am in pretty good shape. We run the golf course, three miles, twice a day. This is a terrible lot besides the obstacle course. The obstacle course, at first, was rather difficult for me but I have leveled that seven foot scaling wall down to the place where I can almost hurdle it.

It doesn't look too good for football this year at Penn State. I have three seventeen-year-olds and two 4-F's in. We are getting about 600 Navy V-12 boys who are eligible to play if they have the time, but the schedule the Navy has given them takes every minute of the day.

Best wishes.

Sincerely,

Bob

As of early fall 1943, to back up what Higgins wrote in his letter, no players from the 1942 varsity were on the roster. But shortly before the first game several players who were in the ROTC program returned to campus because officer's candidate schools were temporarily filled. These players included Aldo Cenci and Johnny Jaffurs, who would play at quarterback and guard, respectively, the entire season. Fullback Sparky Brown was also among them, but shipped out after a few games.

A couple of familiar faces in the Navy V-12 party of six hundred returned to campus before the season began: tackle Red Moore and back Bobby Williams.

Two of the more promising freshmen to enter school were tackle Marino Marchi and center Mike Slobodnjak.

The five returning varsity players started the opening game against Bucknell, along with six Navy V-12 men, including end and kicker Ed Czekaj from George Washington University. Marines from Dayton, Cincinnati, Pittsburgh, Toledo and Ohio State rounded out the first two teams.

Higgins commented: "We coaches who were fortunate enough to have the V-12 program at our colleges got a break and while we appreciated it and while the experience of coaching boys who had been on teams in other colleges was pleasant, it was impossible for the boys to give us 100 percent effort because of their schedules. One day they couldn't come out because of a strength test. Another day they couldn't come out because they were on watch. Another day they couldn't make it because it was pay day. It also depended very much on the Commanding Officer's attitude. If he were athletically minded, you got a good break—if he was not, your V-12 players were not much help to you."

An example of the coaching obstacles Higgins encountered occurred prior to the Cornell game near the end of the 1943 season. Navy on-call requirements scratched Williams and Moore from the lineup at the last moment. Another player was suddenly transferred to Penn.

But the 1943 season had its moments. Penn State, 1-1-1 at the time, almost pulled off the upset of the year, losing a close one to Navy, 14-6, in Annapolis. Navy finished in the top five in the nation in 1943, 1944 and 1945. The 1943 Navy team was led by back Bill Hamburg, who made a run at the Heisman Trophy.

While Navy rushed in wave after wave of replacements, Higgins's thin ranks held firm. Higgins went to a seven man line for much of the game to stop Navy's vaunted running attack. It worked, as Navy managed only six first downs. Unfortunately, that was two more than Penn State could muster.

"We might have won," a dejected Higgins said. "I thought so before the game, and I told the boys. And there was hardly a time on the field when I didn't think we had a good chance to come out ahead. Why, except for a few mistakes, our defenses worked out exactly as we had planned it.

"I don't want to take a bit of credit away from our boys who played a grand game. Most of them felt pretty good after it was over, too. They'd been reading the papers. Navy has a fine team, with enough players warming the bench to make up a first class eleven. But we had enough to upset them, and frankly I can't help feeling that we didn't take advantage of our opportunities."

Following a Williams-to-Jack Castignola pass for twenty-eight yards to the five-yard-line, Williams in four tries scored Penn State's lone touchdown of the day to cut the score to 7-6. Navy clinched the game with a fourth quarter score. The contest was heard worldwide on CBS.

The defense continued its excellent play, holding Maryland to just two first downs in a 45-0 win. The following week, despite the departure of several players to active duty, the Nittany Lions blitzed West Virginia 32-7. At the Quarterback

Club meeting the Monday before the game, Higgins had predicted Penn State would block a punt.

Penn State jumped ahead 7-0 as wingback Cass Sisler, whose Uncle George was one of the greatest batters of all time, ran and passed Penn State to its first score. A few plays later the Penn State line broke through and blocked a Mountaineer punt with Czekaj recovering on the Mountaineer thirty-six. Following two penalties against Penn State, fullback Allen Richards rambled forty-nine yards for the touchdown that broke the game open.

The season ended on a high note with a 14-0 whipping of Pittsburgh. Clark Shaughnessy, who had brought the T-formation to the attention of the college world while coaching at Stanford in 1940, had come to Pittsburgh and implemented the T there as well. Higgins countered with a 5-3-2-1 defense. The Penn State line played head up and put on a strong pass rush. Middle linebacker Jaffurs had a "field day" as one report of the game stated. The Nittany Lions held Pitt to minus twenty-six yards rushing and just ninety-seven yards passing on four completions in eighteen attempts.

Shaughnessy, who followed Stagg at the University of Chicago, had observed the T-formation run by the Chicago Bears and had worked with the Bears' George Halas and Ralph Jones in further developing it. His 1940 Stanford team went undefeated running the T and beat Nebraska in the 1941 Rose Bowl. Overnight, many head coaches switched to the T. Notre Dame's Frank Leahy even junked the Notre Dame box and shift in 1942. The quick timing of the center's snap to the quarterback — in contrast to the single wing center having to throw the ball back to the fullback or the tailback — was the fundamental factor that caused most coaches to change their basic offense. Defenses would no longer have the jump on the offense that the single wing allowed as the ball was in flight to the backfield.

Some coaches, however, didn't change their basic formation. General Bob Neyland stuck with the single wing and won a national championship at Tennessee in 1951, the year before he retired. Higgins, who retired after the 1948 season, never strayed from the single wing either. In 1944 he addressed the commotion over the T and the growing opinion that the single wing had become outdated:

"The T-formation was considered a revelation in football because the Chicago Bears and Stanford University were champions respectively in their league in the same year. It might be well for us to consider the material along with the formation. I have no quarrel to pick with the T-formation and if I am convinced that the T-formation is the best formation, I will put it in. I would hate, however, to change to the T for a year or so and have to go back to the single wing. That would be embarrassing. The T-formation has done one thing. It has made we single wing guys use some variations, such as the man in motion, flankers and split lines."

Higgins's best seasons as head coach at Penn State, 1947 and 1948, hinged on the single wing.

Going into the 1944 season Higgins had far more to worry about than changing his offense as most of the 1943 team disappeared into the war. In the opening game against Muhlenberg in 1944, the starting lineup had ten new names. Only Richards returned at fullback. Higgins also knew that Richards and the seven other Marines who were to start the opening game in 1944 would be shipped out by the middle of the season. This meant that Higgins would field primarily a freshman team for the last four games.

Brownsville High School sent two more freshmen to Penn State in guards Joe Drazenovich and John Simon. Brownsville had continued to be a high school powerhouse under head coach Earl Bruce, who had succeeded Carl Aschman in 1941.

Freshman Elwood Petchel, a 140-pound tailback from Easton, would start in his first game at Penn State, as would freshman left end Bob Hicks of Lancaster.

Freshmen Negley Norton at tackle, Johnny Chuckran at tailback and Larry Cooney at wingback had promise. Cooney was only sixteen years old when the season opened. Four games into the season these seven freshmen had seen considerable action that would pay spectacular dividends a couple of years down the road.

For the fifth game of the season against West Virginia, Higgins started only freshmen, including Hicks and John Stoken at the ends, Norton and Howard Caskey at the tackles, Simon and Jim Matthews at the guards, Bronco

Kosanovich at center, Drazenovich at quarterback (having moved from guard), Chuckran at tailback, Cooney at wing-back and Al Bellas at fullback. It was the first time in Penn State history that only freshmen started a varsity game. West Virginia started nine freshmen.

Youngsters on both sides of the ball played their hearts out. Penn State lost a thriller, 28-27, which dropped its record to 3-2 on the season. Chuckran scored three touchdowns and threw to Hicks for another. He rushed for 157 yards. The loss was Penn State's first at home since dropping one to Lafayette in 1938.

Penn State's yearlings rebounded with a vengeance with a 41-0 whitewashing of Syracuse, marking Penn State's first win on Syracuse turf since 1929, the year before Higgins came in as head coach. Penn State racked up 402 total yards with Petchel and Cooney's running and Chuckran's passing accounting for most of it. Traveling up to the game in carloads Friday afternoon, the team came upon a barn fire near Homer, New York. The buoyant freshmen jumped out and joined the bucket brigade to help quash the blaze.

Higgins, who had always presented himself as a father-like figure to his players, worked overtime at it now.

"The war has made me positive that the freshman rule in college (the pre-war, no-freshmen-on-the-varsity rule) is a blessing, and my respect for all freshman coaches the country over has increased tremendously. At Syracuse last week, after a big meal of steak, Idaho baked potato, spinach, cauliflower, hard rolls, ice cream and milk, we assembled in the lobby to go to the movies. We were scheduled to leave the hotel fifteen minutes after we finished the meal. Some were down there in two minutes and others didn't come for a half-hour. There was a dinner dance at the Hotel Syracuse and these freshmen crowded around the door, looking at the dancers so no one else could get in the dining room. Another group was over at the jewelry counter, putting the talk on the girl whose husband was probably in the Army. When we decided to leave the hotel together, the first six got a running start at the revolving doors. Fortunately, at that time, no elderly people were trying to come into the hotel through those doors.

"Our tickets for the movies had been arranged for and as

we filed in, this pack of wolves saw a candy counter with three attractive girls behind it. They bought candy bars, peanuts and popcorn. They yelled back and forth in the theater to each other and bothered people until I became ashamed of them. I caught two of them smoking but due to the small squad I made believe I never saw them. After this football season is over, win or lose, I know I am going to look back on it with a great deal of pleasure."

Penn State won two of its final three games, losing only the closer to Pitt, 14-0, despite a great passing-running-punting exhibition by Petchel. The season ended with a 6-3 record.

The lineups continued to fluctuate in 1945 as several of the 1944 freshmen entered the service, several war veterans returned and some newcomers arrived on the scene. Among the newcomers was tackle John Nolan, who had been in the Navy V-12 program first at Holy Cross and then at Penn State and who opted to remain at Penn State following his discharge. Nolan, from Glens Falls, New York, was also an excellent lacrosse player. Other fresh faces included yet another Brownsville product, center Chuck Drazenovich (Joe's brother), who would be starting at quarterback by the fourth game of the season. Freshman end Sam Tamburo from New Kensington started every game. Tailback Wally Triplett from Philadelphia saw more playing time as the season progressed and he started against Michigan State. Joe Tepsic, who had sustained a shoulder wound at Guadalcanal, ran much of the season at tailback. Back Ralph Ventresco (age twenty-six), guard Mike Garbinski (age twenty-seven) and guard Ted Kratzke (age twenty-five) — war veterans all — had not played since the 1940-1941 seasons when they returned to the gridiron in mid-season.

Penn State won five of its first six games, losing only to Navy. A few days before the Navy game Higgins took home honors for the best reply to a reporter's question. A writer asked Higgins if he had devised a special defense for the potent Navy running attack. "Well, I had a special defense all worked out," Higgins quipped. "But when Earle Edwards checked it he found I was using a 5-4-3."

Higgins could have used the twelfth man as Navy beat Penn State 28-0.

Tepsic scored twice in a 27-7 win over Colgate. In a rout of Bucknell, Cooney rushed for 144 yards, including a 65-yard dash for a touchdown. Tepsic rushed for 139 yards in a 26-0 blitz of Syracuse.

The season soured with closing losses to Michigan State and Pitt. Guard Bob Rutkowski and tackles Marino Marchi and Nolan played sixty minutes in the 7-0 loss to the Panthers.

Earl Blaik's Army continued its domination of college football in 1945. Led by backs Glenn Davis and Heisman Trophy winner Felix "Doc" Blanchard, Army beat everybody on its schedule. Navy, coached by Oscar Hagberg, lost only to Army.

Higgins had a busy off-season. In February 1946 nearly three-dozen old acquaintances in St. Louis gave him a surprise luncheon at the Missouri Athletic Club during a national coaches convention. One of the men attending was Poge Lewis, the former Washington University star who had played with Higgins on the championship A.E.F. team following World War I. Assistants Edwards and Bedenk also attended.

Higgins recalled to the group the toughest game his Washington team played during his three years as head coach. Washington lost to rival Missouri 13-0 in Columbia. The bloodletting throughout the contest carried past the final horn when one of the Missouri players slashed Washington player Al Hayes across the face with his helmet. The ensuing free-for-all lasted an hour. Hayes was also in attendance at the luncheon.

One by one attendees praised Higgins not just for shaping football teams but for molding men. The final tribute of the luncheon came from an attorney, whom a newspaper report of the event purposefully left unidentified.

"I didn't get my education from the law school," the attorney said. "I got 80 percent of my education from Bob Higgins out on the football field and 20 percent from the law professors." Turning to Higgins the attorney said, "Do you know, Bob, that in my classes today, I still quote you and the things you taught me?"

Tears filled Higgins's eyes at the close of the luncheon.

Early in February, in the role of athletic advisor for the

U.S. Eighth Army, Higgins departed for Tokyo along with several other coaches, including Jock Sutherland of the Pittsburgh Steelers. The coaches held clinics on a number of sports with the aim of boosting GI morale. They also traveled to Yokohama.

"McArthur is a big fellow," Higgins observed. "All his MPs are big, too. All his aides are big and the Japanese are so small. It makes a big impression on the Japanese people. He is a great showman and has done very well. He comes out four times a day and he lets the people know he is coming. His word is law. He tells them every day if they are doing anything wrong.

"The Japanese are very industrious, always working from early in the morning until late at night. If there is any hope for the Japanese people, it is because they are industrious.

"The Japanese are very honest, too. There were about 20 Japanese in the hotel. A bar of candy or piece of chewing gum could be left on the desk and even though they wanted it very badly they would not take it. If that same bar of candy were put in the waste basket, it would disappear almost instantly — that was a different story — that was theirs. They are poor. They always have a baby on their back. They were barefooted in the snow.

"I saw only one one-legged Jap while over there. Never saw any crippled people. I asked a general about this. He said they all died. There was no medicine to treat the people so they all passed out of the picture.

"I wanted to go over the area that the atomic bombs hit. It was really flattened out. It was about 10 miles long and about four miles wide."

Shortly after his return to State College Higgins wrote Shively.

April 19, 1946
Dear Shive:
Of all the places I have been in this large world, I like Hawaii best. The climate is good and the country is beautiful.

After a few days in Japan I got to hobnob with the big shots. General Robert Eichelberger had me up to dinner and gave me his plane on two different days. This happened after

I had been with the Eighth Army for about five days. His first statement was, "Where in the world have you been? Why didn't you come to see me? I've been looking for you." Being a civilian I could tell him off, and I told him that if he had wanted to find me it would have been easy for him to do so, but that I was over there in the interest of GI's who were homesick and having trouble. He said, "Trouble, Hell! I've got more trouble than all of them put together." They had just had a census report and the report was there would be 14,000 Japanese babies born to American GI's before Christmas. He said that was his trouble and wanted to know what to do about it. I told him that wasn't my line—I was in athletics. I told him I had a couple of friends in the states that had Master's Degrees in that field. I was thinking of Smith and Douglas.

Sincerely yours,
R.A. Higgins

While Higgins's popularity in the coaching ranks was at its zenith, he was also a favorite of the Penn State faculty. He and President Hetzel may have differed over the non-scholarship situation, but Hetzel liked Higgins. Higgins's impeccable manners and proper speech, which distinguished him from many other coaches, made him welcome at trustee and faculty functions. He was frequently the main speaker at such events.

One of Higgins's best friends on the faculty was George Harvey, who served on the physical education staff for almost forty years. Harvey taught the first angling course at Penn State and became internationally famous as a pioneer of fly tying and fly fishing techniques. He lived next door to assistant coach Earle Edwards and became close with Higgins and the staff. Harvey had roomed with Al Michaels as a freshman. Michaels of course played for Higgins and became a mainstay on Higgins's staff.

Harvey often took Higgins fishing. "We fished mostly in Spring Creek, a limestone spring that runs along the edge of the campus," Harvey recalled. "Then we fished over in some of the mountain streams, over on Stone Creek. We'd catch enough fish (trout) to have a fish fry. Chet Smith, sports editor of the *Pittsburgh Press*, would come up and a few other fellas would come around. We'd have a party. We used to sing some, but we weren't much at singing."

Harvey was in charge of the PE program for the Navy V-12 students during the war. Higgins helped him with some of the organization.

"There's no way I can explain what a great man Bob was," Harvey said. "I never heard him get in an argument or bad mouth anybody. He was one of the nicest men that I ever knew. He was very much interested in all students and their welfare."

By the fall of 1946 two familiar names had joined Higgins's staff. One was Earl Bruce, who had served as an assistant coach at Brownsville High School beginning in 1937 and then become head coach in 1941. Four Brownsville players — Potsklan, Wolosky and the Drazenovich brothers — would start for the 1947 Cotton Bowl team, while another Brownsville product, John Simon, saw backup action.

With the return of war veterans to campus, dormitory space became a problem. Penn State arranged with several state teachers' colleges to plant incoming freshmen at their campuses. Higgins was concerned about the status of his freshman football team. Earle Edwards is credited with working with his friend, Ed Cubbon, athletic director at California Teachers College in California, Pennsylvania, to arrange for the Penn State freshman team to room at California. Higgins wanted Bruce to become the freshman coach at California. Bruce, who had played halfback at Washington & Jefferson for Andy Kerr, accepted the post. He came to the main campus in 1950 and remained on the football staff through the 1969 season, coaching the frosh team most of those years. Bruce continued to live in State College during his retirement.

The other addition to the staff was Jim O'Hora. In May Higgins wrote O'Hora and asked him to come on as an assistant to line coach Bedenk. O'Hora had been coaching high school ball before entering the service, and upon returning to Montaroy Township he was considering moving his family to New Jersey to find a better income. Moving to State College and working on Higgins's staff, however, sounded much more appealing. O'Hora remained on the staff until he retired in 1976 and he, too, remained in State College thereafter.

What O'Hora didn't realize when he joined the staff in 1946 was that he was also taking on a second job — that of "housemother" to the varsity players. Players had been scattered around the campus in fraternity houses and dorms for several years, but as fraternities re-activated following the war it became even more difficult for athletes to find beds. It was also a headache for Higgins to try and keep up with their whereabouts. Casey Jones answered the bell again and with other Pittsburgh alumni raised the funds to purchase the old Theta Kappa Phi house.

O'Hora and his wife and a newly-born son were having trouble finding an apartment. Higgins suggested that they move into the players' residence and that O'Hora become the head of the house. O'Hora had little choice but to accept.

"Boy that was tough," O'Hora said. "A bunch of guys would come and go and just throw their clothes where they wanted. Now I'm responsible for getting the grass cut, and sometimes you have to sweep the dust in your rooms, and we had this big lounge area and you have to put some wax on these floors. Now and then we need light bulbs and toilet paper. Red Moore was my sergeant. He'd go around and tell the guys what to do."

Moore, who hadn't played since the 1943 season, returned from the service for his senior season in 1946 and was named captain. A dozen other players returned on the GI bill as well. John Potsklan, who had survived in a German prison camp, hadn't played since 1941. Manny Weaver had been away just as long. Steve Suhey, Larry Joe, John Wolosky, Leo Nobile, Joe Colone, Jeff Durkota, Bucky Walters and Bob Weitzel hadn't played since 1942. Bobby Williams and Ed Czekaj hadn't played since 1943, Petchell since 1944. The GI bill enabled these deserving veterans to return to school and play football without the financial pressures they had endured before the war.

Sergeant Suhey had served in the Army Air Corps for forty-two months. He reported initially to Fort Niagara in February 1943 and moved on to flight school in Miami, Florida. He spent the last eighteen months in the hectic Pacific Theater, including time on Okinawa, where by an extreme coincidence he encountered two of his best friends from Cazenovia,

Bob Colligan and Don Washburn. Suhey served on the 440th Bomb Squadron in the 319th Bomb Group. He was a gunner in a small two-man attack plane and saw plenty of action.

Because of an exemption for farm boys Suhey could have chosen to miss the action and remain in State College. Suhey was the first person in his family who was born in the U.S., the first high school graduate, and the first to attend college. As difficult as was his upbringing in Cazenovia, the door was always open to opportunities that could improve his stand in life. A deep patriotism forever burned in Suhey and he never considered missing the war. "I wouldn't have been able to get up in the morning and look at myself in the mirror," Suhey said.

At one point in Suhey's war stint a boil-like infection had doctors discussing the amputation of one of his arms. But just before the planned removal of his limb a nurse mistakenly bumped into it, causing the wound to open and the infection to spray out. His arm soon healed.

After the U.S. dropped the atomic bombs and Japan surrendered, Suhey was in one of the first planes to land on the war-ravished island.

Suhey seldom spoke of the war. Years later, son Larry asked his father why he didn't talk about it. Suhey replied, "If you saw your best friends die, you wouldn't want to talk about it, either."

Higgins's daughter, Ginger, and Suhey wrote each other before he went overseas. They had become acquainted when Suhey lived at the Higgins home his freshman year. Ginger was a sophomore in high school then, but upon Suhey's return to Penn State both she and Suhey were sophomores in college. Both majored in physical education. They began to date.

Meanwhile, Suhey and Red Moore roomed together at the players' house. "He was my best friend," Moore said. "He'd do anything for you. If you needed help, he'd be there to help."

Suhey had a good sense of humor but he generally wasn't one to initiate practical jokes. Once, however, as Moore studied at the library, Suhey moved all of Moore's belongings — everything from razor blades to clothes and furniture — into another room. Suhey couldn't keep a straight face or the secret for long as Moore scratched his head and looked curiously about the room.

Suhey started at right guard on the 1946 team, which was flooded with talent. Moore was the left tackle. Walters, Nobile, Kosanovich, Nolan and Potsklan rounded out the line, supported by Tamburo, Rutkowski and Czekaj (who kicked extra points and field goals). A wave of backs included Weaver, Williams, Joe, Durkota, Colone, Petchel, Triplett and Weitzel.

Two more touchdowns and Penn State would have been undefeated. The 6-2 record included heartbreaking losses to Michigan State, 19-16, and Pittsburgh, 14-7. Injuries hampered Penn State throughout the season.

One of the biggest wins came late in the year at Navy, 12-8. Petchel scored two touchdowns, one of them on a twenty-yard run with an interception. The defense held Colgate to minus twenty-seven yards rushing in a 6-2 win. It was a sign of things to come the following season. Petchel had an outstanding game passing and running in a 26-0 win over Temple. Petchel led the team in rushing with 373 yards, averaging five yards a carry. He ran for seven touchdowns. He was also the leading passer, completing sixteen of thirty-seven for 287 yards and two touchdowns.

Penn State didn't get to play the final game on its schedule. The team was supposed to travel to Florida and play Miami, but Hurricane officials requested that Penn State leave its two black players home so as not to disrupt "arrangements for the game." The black players were halfback Triplett and end Dennie Hoggard. Higgins conferred with Dr. Carl Schott, dean of the School of Physical Education, and they agreed not to make the trip. Schott issued a statement: "We advised Miami that two Negroes are regular members of the Penn State football squad, and that it is the policy of the College to compete only under circumstances which will permit the playing of any or all members of its athletic teams."

It was a noble stand, and foreshadowed a similar racial incident that occurred the following season.

The next spring Higgins and his staff marveled at the number of talented players on the practice field. Positions were two, three and even four players deep. But that summer the news that lineman Leo Nobile was going pro rocked Higgins.

He wrote Last Man Douglas about the episode.

> July 28, 1947
> Dear Jim:
> At first I was quite upset about the Washington Redskins taking my good guard Nobile, because (George Preston) Marshall and Turk Edwards know me. Marshall has been in my dressing room asking me to introduce him to good boys and Edwards writes to me anytime he thinks I can do something for him. They have had this boy signed to a contract since last February, and you would think they would have had the decency to tell me about it, but it first came to my knowledge when I read it in the paper. I am going to give it to Marshall and Edwards the first opportunity I have, and I expect to have lots of them.
> Sincerely yours,
> R.A. Higgins
> Football Coach

Higgins needn't have worried. He had plenty of excellent guards still on the roster, including the best guard in American football, Steve Suhey.

§ 15 §
A Peak At Penn State

ALMOST FIFTY YEARS AFTER Steve Suhey's All-American performance at guard in 1947, his team-mates still had vivid recollections of his greatness and leadership, both on and off the field.

"Steve and I were the only New Yorkers on the team," said co-captain and tackle John Nolan. "He was from Cazenovia and I was from Glens Falls. We used to thumb home together. I can remember some cold days on the road. I would consider him my best friend on that 1947 team.

"He was a very strong, agile individual, and he was tough. I don't think he ever felt that he was as good as he was. He just worked awfully hard. He was a very fine pulling guard. I can remember he had the most enormous hands of any indi-vidual I ever saw. When you shook his hand your hand just disappeared inside there. He wasn't a tremendously large individual but he gave the impression of being much bigger because it seemed his muscles were so very well developed."

Guard Joe Drazenovich said, "Steve and I were room-mates on the road. I never knew Steve to be anything but a commendable individual. He went out there and did the job. He was extremely sound fundamentally. He pulled a lot and so did I. It was always nice pulling out behind him because he cleaned out everything in front of you. On defense with him in the middle there wasn't much coming through. He had big hands, meat hooks. He'd shake your hand all the way up to your shoulder."

End and kicker Ed Czekaj recalled Suhey's leadership in the huddle. "We'd run that off tackle play and if he missed the block he'd come back in the huddle and say, 'Run that damn play over because this time I'm going to put him on the sidelines.' When he spoke we listened. When he spoke he meant it. When he put that hand in your face you lost daylight."

"He had great speed," said tailback Bill Luther. "He would pull and here was 220 pounds coming fast. He knocked people on their backs. He was a fierce competitor. He could be loud if things weren't going right. He was a leader in the huddle. His anger on the football field was enough to spur everybody back to work. If you were going to war, you wanted him on your side. And we went to war every Saturday and he was on our side."

Suhey's coaches thought of him as a model player. O'Hora said, "Steve was the ideal guard. He had very quick feet. His quickness, from the snap of the ball and the pulling, the act of leading the interference and coming around on the linebacker on an off tackle play, that was his strength. Also his ability to block off the ball, straight ahead. And he played great defense as well."

Suhey spearheaded one of the greatest defenses in college football history. The 1947 Penn State defense still holds NCAA records for fewest yards allowed rushing per game at just seventeen yards (153 yards in nine games), and for fewest yards per rush, 0.64 (153 yards in 240 rushes). The 1947 defense also continues to hold the NCAA record for fewest total yards allowed in one game: minus forty-seven against Syracuse on October 18.

Higgins frequently ran a 5-3-2-1 defense. Suhey was the heart of that defense at middle guard. The starting linemen on defense (with height and weight as listed in the game programs) were co-captain Potsklan (5-11,183) at left end, co-captain Nolan (6-3, 228) at left tackle, Suhey (5-11, 205) at middle guard, Norton (6-1, 215) at right tackle and Tamburo (6-2, 185) at right end. Left, middle and right linebackers, respectively, were Chuck Drazenovich (6-1, 215), Joe Drazenovich (5-11, 200) and John Wolosky (5-11, 205).

The defense only gave up twenty-seven points during the regular season, and shut out six opponents. It manhandled opponents with acts of aggression not yet common in college football. It frequently blitzed the middle linebacker to the left or right of center with the noseguard going in the other way. It blitzed the outside linebackers either inside or outside of the ends. It also allowed the tackle, end and outside linebacker to work out a scheme. "You had some guys who really were headhunters," Joe Drazenovich said. "They had a good periphery of the game. They played winning football and they were all good individuals. They could smell the pass, they could smell the run. They covered up for one another."

At times the defense went to a six-man line with two linebackers, and a seven man line with a single linebacker. "We were well molded together," Wolosky said. "We were a quick ball club. We had a lot of talent. We liked each other." On offense Wolosky moved to center. With the single wing's unbalanced line, usually heavy to the right side, Suhey was at right guard, Norton and Nolan at the tackles and Potsklan at right end. Joe Drazenovich was at left guard and Tamburo was the left end.

The offensive and defensive lines had a wealth of backup talent in ends Czekaj, Fred Bell, Bob Hicks and Dennie Hoggard; tackles Bill Kyle and John Finley; guards John Simon, Paul Kelly and Robert Ross.

Williams returned punts and Joe ran back kickoffs.

The NCAA had liberalized substitution rules and Higgins took advantage of the change. He was a master at having the right people in the game at the right time and used various combinations of backs on offense and defense (the team ranked seventh nationally against the pass).

Chuck Drazenovich started every game at quarterback or blocking back. Joe (5-9, 185) started the majority of games at left halfback with Petchel, Williams and Bill Luther coming in. Triplett (5-10, 169) usually opened up at right halfback or wingback with Jeff Durkota and Cooney coming in. Colone (5-11, 190, who also punted) and Francis Rogel took turns starting at fullback and backing up each other. Durkota also played some fullback. Other contributors were fullbacks Weitzel and Clarence Gorinski, left halfback Clarence Hummel, and quarterbacks Ray Ulinski and Bill LaFleur, in addition to several others who saw action during a season laden with lopsided contests.

Higgins's single wing attack averaged thirty-five points per game and gained 364 total yards per game, three-hundred of it by running. While in seasons past Higgins's teams threw with some regularity, this one threw the ball just seventy-eight times and ran it 527 times.

But merely crunching numbers — as impressive as they are — doesn't tell the whole story of Penn State's 1947 squad. "There were two components to that team," co-captain Nolan recalled. "There were the older ones who had been at Penn State and gone overseas to the war and had come back, people like Potsy and Suhey. Then there was a group of us in the service who really hadn't gone away. We were the younger component. When we voted for captain it was split that way. The older people knew Potsy and the younger ones knew me."

Several of the "older" veterans — Potsklan, Suhey, Joe, Wolosky, Colone, Durkota, Williams, Czekaj — had returned in time for the 1946 season and had been able to sharpen the gridiron skills that had dulled during the layoff. As the 1947 season began they were raring to go. Several players — the Drazenovich brothers, Norton, Simon, and Hicks — rejoined the team for the 1947 season after time in the service. Halfback Luther, also coming out of the service, was a newcomer to the squad.

A third element of the team were the incoming sophomores from Bruce's freshman squad at California Teachers, which had gone 9-0 in 1946 and won the state teachers' college championship. Topping this list was bruising fullback Francis Rogel, 5-10, 195. He had played high school ball at North Braddock, Pennsylvania. Casey Jones was responsible for bringing him to Penn State. Jones had attended a North Braddock game to scout another player on the opposing team, but was so impressed by Rogel that he went into the North Braddock locker room after the game to inspect Rogel's legs. He looked like a fullback to Jones, who proceeded to lure Rogel to State College.

In addition to Rogel, California produced Chuck Beatty, Paul Kelly, Bob Ross, Clarence Hummel, Clarence Gorinsky and several others who made immediate contributions to the 1947 team.

Penn State's amazing collection of players didn't go unnoticed by the media, causing Higgins to comment: "Maybe we shouldn't play out our schedule. If what these boys say is true, it's a waste of time. Look, here's a fellow who says we won't have any trouble until we hit Navy and Pitt. And here's another fellow who thinks this is the best football team Penn State has played since the undefeated teams of 1920 and 1921. I hope our boys don't read any of this stuff. It won't do them any good."

Of course many of these players were anything but "boys." They were war-hardened men, twenty-four and twenty-five years old. Higgins loosened the reins. "We didn't want to be coached as much," Wolosky said. "We were pretty much just wanting to play."

"Hig was talking to a mature bunch of individuals," Drazenovich said. "He really couldn't treat them like he had treated other teams before. He put them in the right places and turned them loose. He was wise enough to do that. If they wanted to go downtown and have a beer, they could do it."

"It was always positive with Hig," Drazenovich added. "I never heard him chew anybody out. He complimented you when you did a nice job. When you weren't doing the job he'd say we needed to pull ourselves up and get going. He taught you other things besides going out there and blowing somebody apart. I used to wear a hat and I can remember him saying to me, 'When you wear a hat you've got to know the responsibilities of wearing a hat.'"

Penn State jumped all over Washington State, 27-6, in the opening game at New Beaver Field. Twelve players ran the football for the Nittany Lions. A key play came in the second quarter when Penn State blocked a Cougar punt in the end zone and Bill Kyle recovered for a touchdown.

A report of the game addressed Higgins's pleasant predicament: an abundance of backs. "It is obvious that Bob Higgins's major problem is one of selection. With the possible exception of Drazenovich, the blocking back, it is difficult to imagine a Lion backfield player staying on the field for any length of time. Petchel, the smallest, can do more things well. Larry Joe is the strongest and the fastest. Bobby Williams, a good passer, directs the team well. He's at his best when the boys need steadying down. Bill Luther, the tallest of the tailbacks, is potentially one of the best. Because of his kicking and defensive play it is difficult to keep Joe Colone out of the starting lineup. Yet, Rogel is the surest ground gainer."

After the first game Higgins simply responded, "What more can a coach expect in an opening game? Several of our sophomores served notice on the regulars that first team jobs are far from secure."

During the following week's rout of Bucknell, 54-0, Rogel only carried one time before Higgins shuffled in the backups. Rogel wasn't happy about it.

"I was going to quit the team after the Bucknell game," he said. "They took me out after two plays. I was crying and I told my brother the hell with this, I want to play in the easy games, too. I stayed because they promised I'd play in all the games."

Penn State held Bucknell to eighteen yards rushing. The game was never in doubt from the moment Joe took the opening kickoff and dashed ninety-five yards for a touchdown. Nolan intercepted a pass and ran thirty-four yards for a touchdown. Petchell threw forty-two yards to Hoggard for another score. Czekaj converted six of eight extra points.

The outcome of the following game prompted a public apology from Higgins to Fordham head coach Ed Danowski during a New York football luncheon on the Monday after the game. Penn State had buried Fordham 75-0 at the Polo Grounds, accumulating 572 total yards. Fordham, only a few years removed from winning the Lambert Trophy, rushed for twenty-six yards.

Higgins said he did everything possible to hold down the score. He had agreed to shorten the final two quarters. He had allowed the clock operator to keep the hands moving even when the ball was dead. Penn State didn't throw a pass in the second half.

In the first half Penn State's offense scored every time it possessed the ball and scored twice when Fordham had it. The Lions scored forty points in the second quarter. Durkota had a big day, running sixty-nine yards on a reverse for a touchdown, catching passes from Williams and Petchel for touchdowns and intercepting a pass and running twenty-seven yards for a score.

Young halfback Luther passed for two touchdowns and ran for another, but one of the touchdown passes drew a frown from Higgins. Penn State had already scored seven times when in the second quarter Luther passed to weak side end Hoggard who handed the ball to wingback Triplett who scored the touchdown. The play covered seventy-two yards. Luther recalled: "I come out of the game and Hig says, 'Why in the heck did you call that play? I was saving it.' It was diagrammed the next morning in *The New York Times* sports section."

The Penn State defense caved in on Syracuse the following week in State College. Syracuse lost 107 yards trying to run the football. The defense caused four Syracuse fumbles and the Lions cashed in on each of them. Petchel threw to Durkota for the first score of the game in the second quarter, completing a twelve-play, 81-yard drive. Rogel rushed for two touchdowns. Once again Colone had an outstanding day punting, averaging forty-two yards on eight boots.

Despite the differences in age and experience, the Penn State players were jelling as a unit. A major reason was the leadership of co-captains Potsklan and Nolan. A seemingly innocent incident brought the team together behind the captains, as Nolan recalled.

"We were having trouble with the food they were serving at the training table. Johnny Potsklan and myself as the co-captains went to the Hig and told him that some of the players were complaining. He said, 'Give me their names and I'll make sure we get them right the heck off this team.' So Potsy and I handed him a piece of paper with everybody's signature on it. Hig looked at it and said, 'Well, on second thought, maybe we better talk about it a little bit.'"

Higgins expected his captains to lead as they saw fit. "I think that as Potsy and I looked at it, a lot of what had to be done in so far as being successful as a football team, we had to do. We had a couple of guys who weren't blessed with discretion and thought maybe they were a little bit better than the team itself and possibly got out of line. We had two or three team meetings and Potsy and I went in and it was basically concerned with, 'Hey, we're all in this together and if we're going to accomplish anything we all need to do it together.'

"If a guy stepped out of line we let him know about it. We'd do the same thing on the field during the game. When we were behind against West Virginia, we had a timeout and we were talking about the possibility of running one play in particular. One player says, 'I haven't got a good angle on that guy.' We told him, 'We don't care whether you've got a good angle on that guy or not. Just get him!'"

West Virginia, coached by Bill Kern, came into State College undefeated and known for its passing attack. More than twenty-thousand fans turned out. The crowd was one of the biggest in Penn State history to that point. Penn State scored on a 64-yard drive in ten plays following the opening kickoff, but West Virginia rebounded with two touchdowns in the first quarter and led 14-7. Two pass interference penalties on Penn State, at its twenty- and its three-yard-line, aided the first Mountaineer score.

The second score came after West Virginia partially blocked a Colone punt, which slithered out of bounds at Penn State's 21-yard-line. With Suhey leading the defensive charge, West Virginia lost four yards in three running attempts. But on fourth down at the twenty-five, Mountaineer receiver Bernard Huntz leaped high over two Penn State defenders in the back of the end zone and caught the touchdown pass from Russ Combs. West Virginia led 14-7. Suhey and the Penn State linemen didn't hide their feelings from the secondary.

Still in the second quarter, Petchel, who was often inserted to punt when Penn State needed a coffin-corner kick, put one out of bounds at the West Virginia one. Penn State got the ball back with Petchel returning the Mountaineer punt sixteen yards to the twenty-four. Gorinski ran for twelve yards, a penalty moved the ball to the one, and Gorinski scored. Czekaj's point after tied the game at half 14-14.

Penn State had several opportunities to put points on the board in the second half, but did so only once. In the third quarter, at the West Virginia forty-seven, Petchel dropped back and threw a strike to Triplett who raced in for the game-winning score. Czekaj's extra point kick provided the final margin. The Penn State defense kept West Virginia so backed up in the second half that the Mountaineers couldn't go to the pass. For the game West Virginia had only six first downs and fifty-one total yards. Penn State amassed 405 total yards, 340 of it rushing. Rogel led the way with 114 yards on seventeen carries.

Suhey's play at guard was drawing national recognition and he appeared headed for All-American status. Line coach Bedenk summarized Suhey's role on defense. "Suhey's job is to smash through, hurry the kicker and passer, or nail the ballcarrier. He can do anything because of his strength and quickness."

Of the often brutal play in the trenches, Suhey said, "The Hig teaches us to play it clean. I think a player messes up his assignments when he tries to slug an opponent, because every team stresses timing and that doesn't give you the time you need to take out your man."

Higgins called Suhey the best guard in the country. "He's fast enough to pull out and lead interference on wide runs and deep reverses. He's one of the first men down under punts and kickoffs. He is a good diagnostician of plays. And it takes plenty of opponent to move him out."

Higgins's daughter, Ginger, listened closely to her dad's praise. She and Suhey were still dating.

One of the places they went in State College was to visit their friends Bob and Jean Urion, who lived in the "veterans trailer park," a residential area occupied by many of the returning war veterans. Bob first came to Penn State through the Navy V-12 program and returned to State College after the war. The Urion home was considered an "open house" to many of the football players. Jean was a special favorite of Higgins's, who remarked that she was like a mother to the young players.

By now Penn State was ranked in the top ten and kept climbing steadily the rest of the season. Colgate lost sixteen yards trying to run the football and fell to the Nittany Lions 46-0. Higgins used six tailbacks, four quarterbacks, three wingbacks, four fullbacks and a stream of linemen. Durkota was the leading rusher with ninety-seven yards.

Penn State ranked first in the nation in total defense and total offense when it played at Temple. Rain, wind and mud served as the great equalizer as Penn State squeaked out a 7-0 win. Neither team completed a pass. Temple had just two first downs.

With a scoreless tie at halftime, Higgins calmly outlined to his players the strategy for the third quarter. Penn State would kick off, force Temple to punt and try to gain possession in Temple territory. Penn State would conservatively power its way down the field for the touchdown. That's exactly what happened. After Penn State held, Temple punted and Williams returned it twelve yards to midfield. Then in one of the more memorable drives in Penn State football history, Williams and Rogel ran the ball sixteen times to paydirt. Most of the time they ran behind Suhey. The sequence of gains was this: Rogel, one; Williams, five; Rogel, three; Rogel, one; Williams, nine; Williams, one; Rogel, seven; Williams, two; Rogel, no gain; Williams, three; Rogel, four; Williams, five; Rogel, two; Rogel, three; Rogel, one; and Williams for two yards and the touchdown.

It was a bruising contest. Suhey hurt his knee and received a cut to the face that required twelve stitches, though he kept playing. Petchel and Wolosky were also banged up.

In spite of these injuries, Suhey played the full sixty minutes the next week at Navy. From his middle guard post Suhey battled Navy center Dick Scott. Both made All-American following the season and Suhey called Scott the best lineman he ever faced.

Penn State won 20-7. Navy, however, had some success against the nation's best defense, rushing for 120 yards and passing for 123. But two long touchdown runs on reverses by Jeff Durkota were the difference. Tamburo threw key blocks on both plays. On the second touchdown Suhey nailed a Navy defender at the line and then raced downfield and took out the final Navy pursuer. Williams scored the other touchdown as he carried the ball seven straight times beginning at the Navy thirteen. The scoring drive was set up by Joe's 59-yard burst.

Two days before the season-closer at Pittsburgh, Higgins received a letter from Bill Hollenback, who had coached the last unbeaten, untied Penn State team in 1912. Higgins had played for Hollenback's 1914 team as a freshman.

Dear Bob:

Robert, I want to congratulate you and your team on your splendid victory over Navy last Saturday and we shall all be looking forward to the results of the contest against Pittsburgh on Saturday. On the record of the two teams, I have no doubt, myself, of the outcome and that it will be in your favor. The team under your guidance has brought glory and prestige to Penn State and it means so much for the team to win and finish the season with an undefeated record. I know you will leave no stone unturned to win the game and I am extending my best wishes for success to you and your team.

Bob, here is a little story that may interest you. In 1912 at Pittsburgh, when we had finished the season undefeated, two great old Penn Staters, alumni members of the Football Committee, came up and slapped me on the back. Of course we were all feeling elated at the 38 to 0 victory. These two Penn State immortals, Bill Heppenstall and Pud Reed, were so enthusiastic they were overwhelmed. When they slapped me on the back I stepped right into the center of the field and said: "Take a look at this picture and drink it in to the fullest extent because today is one of the greatest days Penn State will ever see." My prediction held good for 35 years. But this coming Saturday, after you twist those Panthers' tails, you will surpass the record.

So, Robert, this is just a little message from the old football coach of 1912, thirty-five years back, to his illustrious pupil who has made such a glorious record.

Bill Hollenback

Before nearly 48,000, Penn State devoured Pitt 29-0 to finish the regular season at 9-0. Pitt gained just one yard in the first half and the Lions led at half 13-0 on two short touchdown runs by Williams. Penn State scored in the third quarter when Rogel bulled his way for twenty yards and then, with Pitt players all over him, pitched to Petchel who scooted another twenty yards for the touchdown. Hoggard scored the final touchdown when he charged into the Pitt backfield, snatched a fumble in mid-air and coasted twenty-five yards to the end zone. Czekaj added a 21-yard field goal.

Penn State fans rushed the field, hoisted Higgins on their

shoulders and escorted him to the locker room. Other fans took down the goal posts. It was the crowning moment of Higgins's career as head coach at Penn State. Sixteen years earlier in 1931 his Penn State team had lost to the likes of Waynesburg and Dickinson and finished with a 2-8 record. Against tremendous odds, Higgins had rebuilt the program and driven it to new heights.

Following the season, brothers Victor and Henry Lambert awarded the Lambert Trophy to Penn State as the top team in the East. The brothers had established the award in 1936 in memory of their father, August Lambert, a New York jeweler who was heavily involved in youth sports. Penn State would win its next Lambert Trophy in 1961 and dominate the award thereafter under another great Lion legend, Joe Paterno.

Statistically, Durkota led the team in scoring with ten touchdowns. Rogel scored six times. Czekaj accounted for thirty-five points and made thirty-two of forty-seven extra point attempts.

Rogel led in rushing with 499 yards. Petchel was the leading passer with 353 yards on eighteen completions, five for touchdowns. Luther led the squad in interceptions with five.

Colone averaged forty yards with his twenty-eight punts. He had a knack for booting fifty to sixty yarders when Penn State was backed up to its goal line.

The Associated Press ranked Frank Leahy's Notre Dame number one in the nation with a 9-0 record. Irish back Johnny Lujack won the Heisman Trophy. Michigan, coached by retiring Fritz Crisler, also went undefeated. Fullback Bob Chappuis paced the Wolverines. The AP ranked once-tied Southern Methodist, led by sophomore sensation Doak Walker, third in the country and put Higgins's Penn State at number four. All of those teams could lay claim to the national title, but SMU and Penn State would fight for their claim on the field as second-ranked Michigan was Rose Bowl-bound and Notre Dame didn't play in a bowl game.

The Cotton Bowl in Dallas quickly signed on SMU and hometown hero Walker who, by the end of his career, was the most popular football player in America. Suhey and

Walker, in fact, as All-Americans on undefeated teams, represented the best of the returning war veterans and the new younger players who shared the spotlight in the great 1947 season. At the Cotton Bowl, the media made much of photographing the handsome young Walker talking with the more seasoned but equally-talented Suhey.

Cotton Bowl officials, of course, wanted Penn State to play SMU, thereby giving them the top-ranked post-season game in the country. But they hadn't forgotten that Penn State cancelled the Miami game in 1946 because of the two black players, Triplett and Hoggard. The two were still on the team in 1947, and both were big contributors to the perfect season.

SMU wanted to play the best team available, black players or not, so the Cotton Bowl extended the invitation. Penn State, which had made only one bowl appearance in its history, the New Year's Day Rose Bowl of 1923, accepted the invitation. But manager Ike Gilbert soon found out that no Dallas hotels would take in blacks. The only place Gilbert and Higgins could find for the team to stay, set up through an officer in Harrisburg, was the Naval air station, which was fourteen miles from the city of Dallas. Higgins had already told his team the trip would be no picnic and that two practices a day would be the norm. Now this latest news caused some concern among the players.

The team departed by train for Texas several days before Christmas, stopping en route in St. Louis. Higgins had them practice on his old stomping grounds, Francis Field at Washington University. "See these gray hairs," Higgins told the press. "Don't you think I didn't get a lot of them here."

The players had questioned the accommodations upon hearing about them back at State College. Now as they entered the Naval station their jaws dropped and their blood boiled. Here they were, many of them combat veterans and most with service stints, supposedly enjoying the fruits of bowl participation and Southern hospitality, but instead they were surrounded by a fence in the middle of nowhere. Much of the base was closed down for Christmas, except for the mess hall. "We ate chicken with the feathers still on it," Rogel said.

Higgins understood that many of his players were veterans and that they frowned upon being "back in the service."

But this was the hand they had been dealt. The positive side as Higgins saw it was that the base was an excellent place to practice football, away from the typical bowl disturbances. It was a good field with plenty of tackling dummies.

"It was a good facility for football, but it was bad for morale," assistant coach O'Hora noted.

"It was like punishment," said starting center and veteran Wolosky. "We couldn't even get out of the base."

O'Hora did chaperone the squad on a couple of afternoon outings by bus. They went atop the tallest bank building in the city and viewed the hustle and bustle of the big time metropolis. The activity below only stirred the adrenaline of the bottled-up players and they convinced O'Hora to stop the bus at a nightclub. "It was still early so there wasn't much going on," O'Hora said. "But I'm not so sure Petchel and a couple of other guys didn't hustle off to the bathroom and end up at the bar for a beer."

After knocking heads all day on the practice field, several players slipped away for a night on the town. "Suhey and some others escaped many times," O'Hora said. "Being a coach you try not to know too much about what they're doing. We knew there were things going on, but everybody seemed to be in good shape and ready to go the next day at practice."

But ill feelings over the poor accommodations may have carried over into the first half of the Cotton Bowl game on New Year's Day 1948. "We were lax in our performance, maybe still a little irritated at our treatment down there," Joe Drazenovich said.

"We were dissatisfied," end Tamburo echoed. "We weren't mentally set for the game."

"People were in the wrong frame of mind," Rogel added. "We were thinking, 'Why should we play down here? They're not treating us right.'"

Playing against Doak Walker was no time to let down. Walker had finished third in the Heisman vote in 1947 as a sophomore. He would win the coveted award in 1948. He made All-American teams each of his varsity seasons from 1947-1949. During the 1947 season Walker ran 163 times for 653 yards and eleven touchdowns; completed thirty of fifty-two passes for 344 yards and two touchdowns; caught eight passes for 132 yards; returned twenty punts for 258 yards; returned ten kickoffs for 387 yards; intercepted two passes and punted eleven times for a 34.4 average. He also kicked eighteen extra points and a field goal.

Walker backed up those numbers with his performance in the first half before 47,000 fans with temperatures resting just above freezing. Late in the first quarter, with the wind at SMU's back, Walker threw a bomb to Paul Page who caught it for the first touchdown of the game. The play covered fifty-three yards.

Twice in the second quarter SMU moved the football, but both times Penn State held. SMU, winning the battle of field position, returned a Penn State punt to the Lion thirty-eight. SMU drove and Walker scored on a three-yard run. A strong rush by Wolosky foiled Walker's extra point attempt.

SMU had dominated play, but Penn State got back in the game with a score just before halftime. Starting on the Penn State thirty-five, Petchel hooked up with Hicks for eighteen yards. Petchel then ran for fifteen yards to the thirty-two. A short pass completion and a penalty on Penn State moved the ball back to the thirty-six. After two incompletions, and with only seconds remaining in the half, Petchel found Cooney racing in the clear at the SMU ten and threw to him for the touchdown. Czekaj's extra point cut the lead to 13-7.

SMU nearly took the ensuing kickoff all the way back. Walker received the kick and handed off to Page on a reverse. Page broke containment and was running free when Suhey caught him from behind at the forty.

Penn State players were furious at themselves in the locker room. And no one was angrier than Suhey.

"That was probably the only time I saw Steve angry at half time," Drazenovich said. "He chewed everybody out. It amounted to this: 'Hey, we can beat these guys and we're not doing the job here. Forget what the hell has happened. Let's get going and do what we have to do.'"

Suhey's future father-in-law Higgins walked in the locker room and calmly uttered one statement: "This is something you'll remember the rest of your life."

Suhey and the defense racked up Walker and company in the second half. SMU rushed for only fifteen yards and completed just three passes for twenty-four yards in the final two stanzas.

Penn State drove early in the third quarter to the SMU one. The Mustangs held, but the poor field position hurt SMU. Penn State's Joe returned a punt to the SMU nine-yard line. Rogel carried twice for five yards down to the four, and then Petchel darted left and passed to Triplett in the end zone for the touchdown.

With Williams holding for the extra point, Czekaj kicked high and the official called it wide right. The score remained tied 13-13.

"We had a good feeling as soon as he kicked it," Luther recalled. "There was a long delay before the call."

Drazenovich said, "To this day, I honest to God believe this — there's no question in my mind that the extra point was good. The snap was good, the placement was good, the blocking was good, and Ed popped it in there. Those posts weren't very high. The official called it after it curved away."

Czekaj's response, upon trotting to the sidelines and being asked by Higgins if the kick was good, has become famous: "I don't know, coach, you always told me to keep my head down."

As it turned out, the missed extra point cost Penn State legitimate bragging rights to the national title. But plenty of football was left to be played and Penn State had chances to score again.

In the fourth quarter Tamburo blocked Walker's punt and Suhey recovered near mid-field. The Nittany Lions drove the ball to the SMU twenty, but a fourth down reverse lost yardage and the ball turned over. Penn State's Beatty intercepted a pass at the SMU thirty-two, but two plays later SMU intercepted Petchel's pass.

Late in the game Walker intercepted Petchel at midfield, but Penn State held at its own forty and took possession one final time. With seconds remaining, Hicks made a circus catch of a Petchel pass at the SMU thirty-seven. On the final play of the game, Petchel rolled right and heaved the ball into the end zone toward Triplett and Hoggard who were covered by two SMU defenders. The Mustang players leaped high and one of them deflected the ball off Hoggard. The Lion receiver desperately grabbed for the ball but it fell to the earth as the game ended.

The two teams played to a tie. The statistics were nearly even with both teams grinding out twelve first downs. Penn State gained 258 total yards to SMU's 206. Rogel led all rushers with ninety-five yards on twenty-five carries. Walker gained fifty-six yards in eighteen carries and was five of nine passing for sixty-nine yards. Petchel hit on seven of fifteen passes for ninety-three yards.

Since taking over a program at the very bottom, without the attraction of financial aid in the midst of the Great Depression, Bob Higgins had brought Penn State back to the top. He had done it as a player and now as a coach. It was one of the most amazing upward marches the college game had ever known.

Penn Staters never forgot Bob Higgins and the football class of 1947.

§ 16 §
Out On A High Note

ON JANUARY 28, 1948, STEVE SUHEY received a letter from Walter Davenport of *Collier's Magazine* notifying him that he had been selected as a Grantland Rice All-American. The *Collier's* All-American team was still regarded at the most authoritative. Walter Camp had selected it for the publication from 1889-1924. The great sportswriter Rice, who had chronicled Higgins and the A.E.F. Championship years earlier, took over the honorable task in 1925.

Suhey, upon learning of his selection to Rice's 1947 All-American first team at guard, humbly asked, "Did any of the other boys make the team? They are the ones who deserve the honors as much as I do. After all, we played together on the line and I only did my part." It sounds almost corny, but this is the way Suhey is recalled by virtually everyone who ever knew him — humble, unassuming, a team player.

The Associated Press and International News Service also named Suhey to their All-American first teams. Suhey became the second Higgins player at Penn State, after Leon Gajecki, to be named All-American.

Rice's first team included Columbia's Bill Swiacki and Southern Cal's Paul Cleary at the ends, Notre Dame's George Connor and Georgia Tech's Bob Davis at the tackles, Penn State's Suhey and Army's Joe Steffy at the guards, Navy's Dick Scott at center, Notre Dame's Johnny Lujack at quarterback, Kansas' Ray Evans and Penn's Tony Minisi at the halfbacks, and Michigan's Bob Chappuis at fullback.

All-American status suddenly placed the New York farm boy in the bright lights of the Big Apple when Suhey and 100 college football stars attended the annual Winter Ball at the

Waldorf-Astoria in New York City.

But it was a celebration on February 5, 1948 in Cazenovia that Suhey always held closest to his heart. After hitchhiking from State College to the outskirts of Cazenovia, Suhey walked into town and couldn't believe his eyes. A large banner draped across Main Street said, "Welcome Home All-American Steve Suhey."

"We were very proud of Steve," said Don Mansfield, who was mayor of Cazenovia at the time and instrumental in putting the event together. "He was a popular kid in high school. He worked hard on his farm and he was a great football player. We watched him all the way through Penn State."

Another Cazenovia citizen, Gurdin Freeborn, also worked on Steve Suhey Day. "We went big on it," Freeborn said. "The whole community went for it. He was well thought of."

Three-hundred people turned out for the banquet at the Cazenovia Central High School gymnasium. Suhey's parents attended, as did Penn State line coach Bedenk, Suhey's prep coach Max Buckley, high school principal Doc Lowe, Colgate Director of Athletics William Reid, and Syracuse Athletic Director Lewis Andrews. Both Reid and Andrews were still shaking their heads over the one that got away.

Bedenk stated, "I haven't seen a better guard than Steve Suhey. You can't say anything bad about the guy." Suhey found it difficult to believe that such a fuss was being made over him.

The crowd retired to outside of the gym where a 1948 Oldsmobile coupe was presented to Suhey by the citizens of Cazenovia. He was shocked. He invited his parents to join him for a ride, and then indicated to the gathering that Virginia (Ginger) Higgins back at State College would be the first non-family member to accompany him in the new automobile.

All-American status continued to pay dividends when Suhey received the following letter dated April 30, 1948.

Dear Steve,

The fifteenth annual All Star football game will be played at Soldier Field the night of August 20 against the Chicago Cardinals, champions of the National Football League. I would like to have you as a member of the All Star squad. The Chicago Tribune Charities, Inc., will assume all your expenses from the time you leave for training camp until you are returned to your home or place of employment. In addition, we will pay you $150.00 for your services, the same as we pay every other member of the squad.

The team will assemble at Northwestern University about August 1 and will be quartered in fraternity houses. All the workouts will be held in Dyche Stadium. The squad again will be handled by five of the nation's most widely known college coaches. The net proceeds will be donated to charity as always.

We have contracts with both the National Football League and the All America Conference which entitle us to use any players who may be under contract to teams in those organizations.

Cordially,
Arch Ward
Sports Editor
Chicago Tribune

Penn State tackle Nolan joined Suhey on the all-star team, and so did Higgins as an assistant coach. Notre Dame's Leahy headed the staff. Workouts were intense and a concussion sustained by Nolan during a scrimmage put him in the hospital instead of the starting lineup. It was all downhill for the all-stars, who lost to the Cardinals, 28-0. The Cardinals, led by former Georgia great Charlie Trippi, had defeated Philadelphia to win the title.

Philadelphia had beaten Pittsburgh in an Eastern Division playoff game for the right to play in the championship. On that Pittsburgh team was Suhey's close friend and former Penn State star, Bill "Red" Moore. As Suhey had sparkled on the college gridiron in 1947, Moore made first team All-Pro at guard in his rookie season.

Moore was a member of the last football team coached by Jock Sutherland, the long-time peer of Higgins. Sutherland had ventured into the pro ranks after making his impressive mark as head coach of the Pittsburgh Panthers from 1924-1938. Pittsburgh Steelers' owner Art Rooney had hired Sutherland for the 1946 season. On April 11, 1948, Sutherland died of a brain tumor. Rooney, who had paid $2,500 for the franchise in 1933, tapped John Michelosen, a former Sutherland pupil at Pitt, as the new head coach.

Despite invitations from the San Francisco 49ers and several other teams, Suhey preferred to play in the state of Pennsylvania so he could return to Penn State in the off-season to see Ginger Higgins and continue his undergraduate work in the School of Physical Education. Suhey joined the Steelers and resumed his friendship with Moore. The two roomed together on the road. Moore's wife, Eleanor, and Suhey and Ginger became companion couples and would remain so long after Moore and Suhey's playing days had ended.

"The pressure was very great in the pros, a lot greater than it was in college," Moore recalled. "After the season started we'd go up to Forbes Field early in the morning and do individual drills, then get together for a full scrimmage. We'd go in and shower, go out and have lunch and then come back and have chalk talk until about three o'clock every day.

"Back in those days you played both ways, and most guys played three, four years at the most and then went on to their life's work. Linemen made four or five thousand dollars a year."

The 1948 Pittsburgh Steelers football guide listed Suhey at 5-11, 215 and, not surprisingly, stated that he "Probably has the biggest hands in pro ball."

Suhey was an immediate starter at guard for the Steelers during the post-war period when pro football produced some of its greatest players ever. Steve Van Buren led the league in rushing in 1948 with 945 yards. Los Angeles' Tom Fears topped the league in receptions with fifty-one. All-pros included the Cardinals' Trippi and Cleveland backs Otto Graham and Marion Motley. Sammy Baugh played quarterback for Washington. The Bears may have had the three greatest quarterbacks ever to play on the same team—Sid Luckman, Johnny Lujack and Bobby Layne.

Meanwhile, Suhey and Moore continued to root hard for their alma mater and Bob Higgins. Higgins put together another national title contender in 1948, despite the departure of Suhey, Nolan, Potsklan, Wolosky, Durkota, Williams and Czekaj from the 1947 Cotton Bowl team.

But several 1947 starters returned, including tackle Norton, guard Joe Drazenovich, end Tamburo, quarterback and linebacker Chuck Drazenovich, and halfbacks Triplett and Joe.

Petchel was back at halfback as were fullbacks Colone (who was captain), Rogel and Gorinsky. Beatty stepped up to the starting role at center, Simon moved in at guard and Luther at halfback. Backs Chuckran and Cooney returned, as did ends Hicks and Hoggard, tackles Ross and Finley, and guards Felbaum and Kelly. Less familiar names in tackle Don Murray and ends Dalton Rumberger and John Smidansky joined the fray.

Tamburo had been looking forward to the season from the moment the Cotton Bowl game had ended. He felt Penn State had the much better team that New Year's Day against SMU and that the Naval station situation had distracted the players. "It was the worst game I ever played," Tamburo said. "I didn't get mentally ready. I decided as soon as the game ended that it would never happen to me again."

The press picked the Nittany Lions to compete for the national championship, and convincing wins over Bucknell, Syracuse and West Virginia met expectations. Triplett scored twice in the Bucknell game, Petchel and Rogel once. Triplett rushed for 143 yards against Syracuse in only eight carries. He scored another touchdown, while Rogel scored two and gained ninety-two yards running. Triplett ran for 103 yards against West Virginia and scored twice, once on a 54-yard dash and again on an 85-yard punt return. Petchel hooked up with Tamburo for their second touchdown tandem of the young season.

The defense, as expected, didn't dominate like the 1947 team. Syracuse passed for 181 yards. West Virginia gained eighteen first downs, rushed for 124 yards and passed for 145 yards. But the defense was solid.

The following homecoming clash with Michigan State drew 24,000 fans, which was the largest crowd in Penn State football history at the time. Michigan State went ahead 7-0, but Petchel completed an eleven-yard pass to Smidansky for a second quarter touchdown. Carl Sturges kicked the tying point.

In the same quarter Penn State put together an eighty-yard drive to the Michigan State six. With ten seconds remaining in the half, Petchel tried to hit Tamburo with a pass, but the Spartans' George Guerre stepped up, made the interception and dashed 100 yards for what appeared to be a touchdown. But Michigan State had clipped, the ball came back and the half ended in a tie.

Michigan State scored quickly on a 47-yard pass in the third quarter, but Penn State drove eighty-three yards in fifteen plays to tie the game at 14-14. The touchdown came on a pass from Petchel to Tamburo, who then faked a handoff to Rogel and handed the ball to guard Simon who plowed over for the score. The play covered twenty yards.

Michigan State drove deep into Penn State territory five more times, but interceptions by Cooney, Triplett and Rogel and big-play tackling kept the Spartans out of the end zone. Higgins gambled in the final period when on fourth and one on Penn State's own thirty-two he opted to go for the first down. Rogel's run came up inches short. The game ended in a tie with Penn State gaining 274 total yards to State's 263.

After four games the Penn State defense had given up forty-five first downs. The 1947 defense allowed only forty-eight the entire season. But Penn State's unbeaten streak had extended to fourteen and wins over Colgate and Penn stretched it even further.

More than 71,000 attended the Penn State-Penn contest at Franklin Field in Philadelphia. Penn's football program had come on strong since 1945, losing only four of thirty-one games. Penn was led by All-American center Chuck Bednarik.

The Penn State defense played its best game of the season, holding Penn to nineteen yards rushing. Rogel rushed for seventy-five yards and scored both of Penn State's touchdowns, one of them on a 44-yard run off tackle. Petchel completed eight of fourteen passes for 121 yards, including a scoring strike to Rogel. Kelly and Finley excelled on the line.

A 47-0 rout of Temple advanced the unbeaten string to seventeen going into a road game at Pittsburgh. Rogel had another outstanding game against Pitt and in fact played one of the best games of his career, carrying the ball thirty-one times for 116 yards. But Pitt stopped him short of the goal line on the final play of the game to preserve a 7-0 upset and end the Penn State streak.

Trailing 7-0 late in the final period, Penn State took possession near midfield. Two first downs, one of them aided by a Pitt pass interference, moved the ball to the twenty-two with thirty seconds left. Petchel connected with Cooney for another first down and Petchel passed to Smidansky for nine yards to the two-yard line. As the clock ran out, the left side of the Panther line rose to the occasion and stopped Rogel.

"Fate was unjust to connect young Rogel with this final failure," a report of the game stated. "It is difficult to find words to express his really heroic contribution."

Penn State had dominated the contest with 242 yards rushing to Pitt's seventy-nine and fourteen first downs to Pitt's four. Pitt's score came early in the final period when a deflected Petchel pass was intercepted and returned twenty-three yards for the winning touchdown.

The defeat stung Higgins and broke his players' hearts. They grudgingly flew to Tacoma, Washington to close the season against Washington State. Penn State won 7-0 as Cooney's 18-yard reverse accounted for the only score. The 7-1-1 record placed Penn State eighteenth in the country.

On the season Rogel led with 602 yards rushing, while Petchel threw for 628 yards and nine touchdowns. Tamburo was the team's leading receiver with seventeen catches for 301 yards and three touchdowns.

Tamburo had held true to his commitment following the Cotton Bowl. He was prepared for every game and played with great intensity on every snap. His performance, offensively and defensively, earned him first team All-American selections at end from *Collier's* and International News Service. He became the third All-American player under Higgins, following Gajecki and Suhey.

The season-ending game against Washington State had meant little at the time, but it turned out to be Higgins's final game as head football coach. During the past couple of years Higgins had toyed with the possibility of retiring because of bouts of angina. He was tired, not of football, which he dearly loved, but tired from being a head coach for so long.

He was turning fifty-five years old. He had been a college head coach for twenty-six years, the last nineteen at Penn State. He sensed that the game was becoming something a little different — more specialized on the field, more of a big business off of it. He was of the old school, one of the last of the single wing men. If college football had entered a new era, Higgins seemed content to let younger men take the charge.

Indeed, fresh faces with great football minds had come on the scene since the second world war: Bear Bryant at Maryland and Kentucky, Bud Wilkinson at Oklahoma, Johnny Vaught at Ole Miss, Bobby Dodd at Georgia Tech, Woody Hayes at Denison. In a sense Higgins, as one of the last in that great crop of coaches who had helped to define, shape and popularize college football, was passing the torch. Pop Warner had bowed out after the 1938 season at Temple with 313 victories, which at the time put him at the top of the all-time wins list. Amos Alonzo Stagg finally retired after the 1946 season at Pacific with 314 wins, one more than Warner. Who knows how many games Rockne would have won, but he was long gone, having died in a plane crash on a Kansas farm on March 31, 1931. He was only forty-three years old when he died. He had coached Notre Dame to a near-unbelievable 105-12-5 record in thirteen seasons, and won five national titles. Pitt's Jock Sutherland had left the college game after the 1938 season, Dana Bible had called it quits after the 1946 season at Texas, as had Andy Kerr at Colgate. Fritz Crisler had retired at Michigan following the 1947 season.

Higgins had outlasted them all. His twenty-six years as head coach at West Virginia Wesleyan, Washington University and Penn State had produced a 123-83-16 record. His nineteen-year mark at Penn State stood impressively at 91-57-11. He had lost forty of those games at Penn State in his first nine years, when the no-scholarship policy devastated recruiting. Higgins and his alumni friends such as Casey Jones worked hard to reverse the effects of the policy and rebuilt the program to the point that Higgins went 62-17-7 over his last ten years. Even that mark was hindered by three war years when rosters fluctuated almost daily. From 1939 to 1942 and 1946 to 1948, Higgins's teams won forty-six, lost eight and tied six. His teams had lost but one game in his final two seasons. He had fielded the best-ever defense against the run in 1947. His team had shut out Washington State 7-0 in the final game of the 1948 season. Why not make that game his swan song? Why not go out on top?

Higgins mulled it over for three winter months, often thinking on it while cradling his first grandchild, Robert Higgins Lyford, born to his eldest daughter, Mary Ann, and Ralph Lyford, a Penn State grad and a member of the Blue Band in his day.

Perhaps sensing he was going to call it quits, Higgins requested autographed photos from several of his coaching peers during these months. One photo came from Stagg, who wrote the following:

May I congratulate you most heartily on the remarkable records your teams have made. As you probably know, I have been at Susquehanna University with A.A. Junior during the Falls of 1947 and 1948 and have read many fine comments about your great teams.

With many good wishes, I am,

Sincerely,

A.A. Stagg

On March 12, 1949, Higgins announced his resignation. He stated, "I haven't felt as good as I should the last few years, and I think football has been largely to blame. My family has worried about me, and I haven't liked that."

The news stunned college football. Higgins would become a professor of physical education and serve the college as somewhat of a goodwill ambassador. Letters poured in by the hundreds.

March 17, 1949

Dear Bob:

I noted in the papers and in The Collegian that you have resigned as Head Football Coach to devote your time to other duties in the school.

I can't blame you for this move, particularly since I understand your health is not too good, which of course I am sorry to learn, and evidently it is worse than I had anticipated.

It is not easy to let loose of work one has been doing for so many years, but the time comes for all of us to step aside and turn the more arduous tasks over to someone else to carry along. I know the College and the many boys who have played under you have benefited by your contributions to them. The first few years, with the woeful lack of material, were very difficult for you, but you hung on and the sky got brighter—and your record became enviable.

I want to thank you, not only as an officer of the College but as an individual, for the many good things you have done for Penn State. May you live happily in your new work and enjoy your family, which I know you will.

With best wishes to you and Mrs. Higgins for the future, I am

Sincerely,
Pete Mauthe
Vice President

Pete Mauthe was one of the greatest fullbacks in Penn State history. He played from 1909 to 1912 and was captain of Bill Hollenback's undefeated 1912 team, which went 8-0.

March 16, 1949
Dear Bob:

I was very much surprised Sunday morning when I read in the newspaper where you had resigned as football coach at your Alma Mater. I sincerely am sorry to see you giving up the coaching profession for I have always had the highest respect and admiration for you, and I know that everyone in the coaching game will miss you as a coach of the Nittany Lions. I feel that the football players and students at Penn State will also miss not seeing you at the head of your football teams, leading them to great achievements.

Sincerely,
John P. Michelosen
Head Coach
Pittsburgh Steelers

March 13, 1949
Dear Bob:
I read with considerable regret of your resignation in this morning's paper. Over the years you have certainly given Penn State the best in football. Particularly pleasing to an alumnus have been the comments I have heard from officials who from time to time have handled State's games. They have told me on several occasions what a clean cut bunch of boys represented State and that their coach was a great fellow to work with. After the game's over this is what really counts.

I see by the papers that you are to be a "good will" man. May I suggest two jobs: 1. Get Penn on our schedule every year. 2. Keep the Pennsylvania boys where they belong—at Penn State. Those two jobs could probably keep you going for years.

Sincerely,
Dick Wills

March 14, 1949
Dear Professor:
Congratulations on your decision to take a rest. I hope you enjoy a well deserved rest.

We are certainly sorry to see you leave the active coaching ranks, but you left a marvelous record behind. The memory of each and every boy who played under you is something which will live long after you and I are gone.

Now that you will have a little more time to enjoy life, bring Mrs. Higgins and come to Allenberry for several days. You know the latch string will always be out and we would love to have you.

With kindest personal regards to you and Mrs. Higgins.
Sincerely yours,
Charles A.B. Heinze
Heinze's Fine Foods

March 15, 1949
Dear Bob:
Yesterday's papers carried the announcement of the changes at Penn State. This is just to let you know that all of us here send our very best wishes for the years to come as you

enjoy the very much earned relaxation you so deserve. I'm sure no other Peddie man has ever contributed so much to the world of sports as you since leaving Peddie.

Congratulations from all of us and don't forget that the latch string is always out here in Highstown.

Sincerely,
Donald Rich, Jr.
Alumni Secretary
The Peddie School

March 14, 1949
Dear Bob:

Like a great many other people, I was sorry to read the announcement of your resignation as head coach of football. I think it is very important to have a man of fine character as well as coaching skill to head football at an important college. I think it has been distinctly to the betterment of Penn State all along the line to have had you for Head Coach for the last nineteen years.

At the same time, of course, I am glad that you will remain with us as a member of the faculty; and from one point of view, I am glad that you will be relieved of the strain and anxieties of the annual football season.

With best regards,
Sincerely yours,
H.P. Hammond, Dean
School of Engineering

March 15, 1949
Dear Bob:

I was sorry to hear that you retired from active coaching at the college, but if it's a matter of your health I believe you are doing the right thing. You surely had them clicking the past two years and deserve only the best.

Very truly yours,
Eddie Marlin
Sinclair Refining

March 15, 1949
Dear Bob:
We carried the story of your resignation and your picture in the Sunday paper with mixed emotions. It marked the step-down of a guy who was a big name when I was a kid and you hate to see these men retire.

But at the same time, now that I am older and have done a turn or two in the hospital, I'm not so strong for that silly theory of working until you drop. You step down at the peak of your career.

Like Crisler, you have a fine sense of timing.
Sincerely,
Leo Riordan
Executive Sports Editor
The Philadelphia Inquirer

March 13, 1949
Dear Bob,
The Sunday Herald-Tribune carries the news that you are giving up coaching. As one of your sports page followers let me congratulate you on your fine record and wish you well. As an old W & J man I "adopted" Penn State in football seasons since we dropped down to the Bethany-Waynesburg classification.

Let me explain why I have taken an interest in your good work. Back in World War I days I happened to be the senior instructor of musketry and bayonet at the Third Corps School at Clamecy, France. My assistants liked your work and so to your disgust you were picked off as an instructor. I told you I would try to get you released and succeeded. What you probably did not know was that Col. Friedendahl-now General-was tough about men trying to get out of teaching which we all tried to do, and so the only way I got you out was by explaining that you were too damn dumb to teach. Our whole gang watched the Stars and Stripes accounts of divisional football in which you frequently figured.

After nearly 40 years I still have pleasant recollections of State College and the old Beta House I visited as district chief from 1909 to 1912.

Hope you will really begin to enjoy life now that you have

laid aside the strain of football coaching.

    Cordially yours,
    Sharrard Ewing
    Manville, NJ

    March 13, 1949
    Dear Bob,
    Your decision to ease up a bit on front line duty is a wise one. You have done a genuinely grand job thru these many years, and every State man can thank you for what you have done for State. But you have earned a blow, which will in turn permit you to redirect your energies, making it possible for you to go for many years to come. And I too think it will be a delightful change for Mrs. Higgins.

    You will miss it at first but adjustments can be made surprisingly quick, at the same time be delightfully surprising.

    Now don't get ambitious and go farming for that tough assignment. Rather get yourself a second handed accordion or fiddle, take a few lessons, and you're ready to go. I recall very clearly what a contribution you made in that Old Track House quartet with your clear bell-like tenor. And then do you recall the talk you gave to the Peddie boys after a Penn game? Listen boy, it is in your family to be evangelists.

    I think it is timely for State to have an ambassador like yourself to go into the high schools and preparatory schools to carry to them what is so desperately needed on their part— a challenge for good citizenship and clean living.

    Good luck, Bob, and God bless you and yours.
    Loyally and sincerely,
    Bill Wood
    Staten Island, NY

    The announcement of Higgins's retirement coincided with the naming of line coach Bedenk as the new head coach. The Athletic Board's selection came down to Bedenk and ends coach Edwards. The two assistant coaches were known to have their differences with each other through the years. Higgins endorsed Edwards as his replacement, but the board voted for Bedenk. Higgins felt especially bad that Edwards had

Penn State's Gridiron Legacy

missed out.

"Bob had it all lined up for Earle Edwards to be the next coach and Earle would have been a fine coach. But it didn't work out," recalled Jim O'Hora, who stayed on with Bedenk as an assistant. "Bedenk had had success doing what he did. Jim Gilligan on the athletic board said to me that his philosophy was Bedenk is one of the oldest coaches and he should have a crack at it."

Edwards resigned following spring practice and joined Biggie Munn's staff at Michigan State. Bedenk added Sever Toretti as a line coach and former Pitt star Frank Patrick as a defensive backfield coach. Patrick had played for Jock Sutherland's 1936 Rose Bowl team and unbeaten 1937 squad.

Higgins and Casey Jones had to shake their heads and chuckle when just two months following Higgins's resignation the athletic program approved tuition scholarships for football and other sports. The no-scholarship policy had begun just prior to Higgins's first year as head coach in 1930, and now its abolishment came nineteen seasons later as Higgins bowed out. The irony was thick, but Higgins wasn't one to bemoan the course of events. He had met the challenge and successfully worked through it. Given the purist policy predicament, his coaching effort was one of the finest in the history of college football.

§ 17 §
A Quieter Life

ON MARCH 5, 1949, a week before Higgins announced his resignation as head coach, his daughter Ginger married his former All-American guard Steve Suhey in Auburn, New York. Ginger had received her degree from Penn State in 1948 in physical education. The couple moved to Pittsburgh for the 1949 football season. Suhey again started at guard for the Steelers. The team improved to a 6-5-1 record and finished second in the Eastern Division. Philadelphia repeated as division and league champion, defeating Los Angeles 14-0 in the title game. Philadelphia's Van Buren set a single season rushing record with 1,146 yards. The year also saw the abandonment of the All-America Football Conference after a four-year existence.

As the season progressed Suhey considered getting out of pro football. He made numerous life-long acquaintances during his brief stint in the pros, but the post-World War II game's animal-like nature with minimal financial rewards didn't appeal to Suhey. He was anxious to complete his undergraduate requirements, go after his master's degree and pursue a career in coaching. A knee injury late in the season during a game with Los Angeles helped convince Suhey that the time had come to hang up his playing cleats.

Suhey and his wife returned to State College in 1950 and with great pride Suhey finished his school work and received his degree from Penn State in physical education. It was a crowning moment for the poor farm boy from Cazenovia. He would demand of his children in coming years that they also receive college diplomas.

Meanwhile Joe Bedenk's first year as head football coach in 1949 was also his last. Bedenk's true coaching love remained baseball. The football team fell to five wins and four losses and was soundly whipped by Villanova, Army, Michigan State and Pitt. Bedenk relinquished the head post in the spring of 1950, though he remained on the staff as the line coach for another season. The development proved that Higgins's preference for Edwards as his successor had been the correct one. However, had Edwards gotten the post instead of Bedenk, Charles "Rip" Engle and Joe Paterno might not have come to Penn State and begun five decades of exemplary football leadership.

Suhey entered the master's program in the fall of 1950 and became a graduate assistant for the new head coach, Engle, who had established a solid football program at Brown University during the 1940s. Before going to Brown, Engle had coached Waynesboro High School in Pennsylvania for eleven seasons after graduating from Western Maryland. Engle kept assistants Bedenk, Michaels, O'Hora, Bruce, Toretti and Patrick on the staff. He also added an unknown name — Joe Paterno, who had been Brown's senior quarterback and star defensive back in 1949.

The Suheys and their infant son Steve, Jr. had moved into a two bedroom apartment in State College. Paterno initially lived with head coach Engle but wanted some off-the-field distance from his mentor. Steve Suhey invited Paterno to rent their second bedroom and Paterno accepted. This seemingly minor development probably kept Paterno at Penn State. He had been bound for law school when at the last moment Engle asked him to come along as an assistant coach. Once at State College, Paterno wasn't particularly happy and was thinking of leaving. Then the Suheys welcomed him in.

"I think in a way it was beneficial to him," Ginger Suhey said. "He didn't know any young people; the coaching staff was a little older then. We divided everything into thirds. He was very, very nice and considerate. We introduced him to a lot of our friends."

"We were young and poor," Paterno recalled. "Steve and Ginger were trying to get by on a graduate assistant stipend. Steve was working on his master's degree. But we had a lot of fun. I used to kid Ginger that she made the greatest Spanish rice in the world because we'd eat it for about a week at the end of the month. Steve and Ginger were very popular. People would gravitate to them. On football weekends there would be eight to ten people sleeping on the floor, people that played with Steve. We'd sit up until God knows what hour talking football, arguing football and talking about all kinds of things. I didn't think I'd like Penn State. I had talked to Coach Engle about leaving as soon as the season was over. But as the season went on and I got to know these people, that feeling drifted away and I decided to stay."

The Suhey-Paterno relationship deepened through the years as three of the Suhey sons starred on the local high school gridiron and went on to play for Paterno at Penn State. Ginger Suhey became close friends with Paterno's wife, Sue.

One thing Steve Suhey and Paterno immediately had in common was their love of a "good discussion" about almost anything. "They would start arguing with each other and they'd turn around and start arguing the other side," Ginger Suhey recalled.

"Steve was a very positive, outgoing guy and I was, too," Paterno said. "Steve had very strong opinions as I did. Sometimes they were different opinions. We'd end up laughing and I'd say 'How dumb can you be, honky.' And he'd say 'Dago, you don't know what you're talking about.' We had a great relationship."

The Suheys weren't long for State College as Steve accepted the head coaching position at Waynesboro High School in the summer of 1951. Engle, who had coached at Waynesboro, helped Suhey get the job. Suhey coached Waynesboro for three seasons and then became the head coach for Kingston High School near Scranton for one season in 1954.

A former Kingston player recalled one afternoon when practice had begun to drag and the players on the blocking sled seemed to have forgotten everything Coach Suhey had taught them. Suhey waved the boys aside, got down in his stance and hit the sled so hard that it fell apart. Lack of hustle was not a problem for the rest of the season.

By now the Suheys had five children including Steve Jr., Kathy (born in 1951), Betsy (1952), Larry (1954) and Nancy (1955). The joke in the family was that Ginger had fared poorly in following the planned parenthood philosophy of her aunt

Margaret Sanger.

At a sports banquet not long after the birth of his fifth child, Steve encountered an officer of L.G. Balfour Co., which sold class rings and represented Taylor Publishing yearbooks. Suhey received an offer to become a salesman which would allow him to move the family back to State College. Suhey considered his growing family along with the low wages associated with the coaching profession, and signed on with Balfour.

"I always felt bad because I think he really loved coaching," Ginger said. But Suhey always put his family first regardless of his personal goals. Though he would never again serve in an official coaching capacity, Suhey's football expertise and general guidance would be called upon time and time again.

By the time the Suheys returned to State College in 1956, Bob Higgins had settled into retirement with his wife, Virginia, and Virginia's mother, Grace, who lived on the third floor of the Higgins residence on McKee Street. Higgins greatly admired his mother-in-law, who was very active and loved to travel.

When Higgins wasn't traveling to Delray Beach in Florida or visiting his sister Margaret in Arizona, he enjoyed playing golf and bridge and had a passion for reading. Former players and Beta Theta Pi fraternity brothers constantly dropped by the house to visit.

One Beta brother with whom Higgins kept in close touch through the years was Alan Helffrich, who was the world's fastest middle distance runner in the 1920s. Helffrich was captain of the Penn State track team in 1924 and later that year won the Olympic gold medal in Paris running in the 4x400 meter relay. The U.S. foursome set a world record of 3:16, with Helffrich running his leg in forty seven seconds. Helffrich, who had gone to high school in Yonkers, New York, won the 600 meter run at the internationally famous Millrose Games in New York City five years in a row. He held as many as nine indoor and outdoor world records. Though Helffrich graduated several years after Higgins, their paths crossed frequently at fraternity functions and they struck up a friendship. Higgins attended many of Helffrich's races in the 1920s and later attended major track and field meets in the Northeast for which Helffrich officiated. Higgins's love of track had remained strong since his Penn Relay years at Peddie Institute.

Helffrich's son, Alan Jr., also a Beta, graduated from Penn State in 1952 and spent many hours in the Higgins home. "They were one of the most fascinating couples I ever met," said Alan Jr. of Bob and Virginia Higgins. "You get a guy like the Hig and Casey Jones together and they start telling stories to the undergraduates, and Virgie had a way of bringing things back down to earth. 'Now boys, let's not get carried away,' she'd say. She was a fabulous woman."

Alan Jr. took many of his fraternity brothers to meet "Uncle Bob."

"He reigned supreme," Helffrich said. "He was a living legend to me. He and my dad were a lot alike in that they both gloried in talking to young men and training young men and in teaching them to be the best."

The young Helffrich once asked Higgins how his dad, Alan Sr., a relatively small man, had become such a great runner. "He was an iron man," Higgins said. "He was a winner. He'd single out the next best runner in the race and beat him."

One of young Helffrich's trips to McKee Street paid off in a big way. He met his wife-to-be, Fritz Alderfer, daughter of Dr. Harold Alderfer, a respected political scientist at Penn State. Fritz Alderfer was best friends with Higgins's daughter Nancy.

Higgins officially stepped away from his position with the college in late 1951, which was his third season off the sidelines. Letting go of coaching was a difficult adjustment for Higgins, tougher than he had thought it would be, particularly when the fall rolled around and college football filled the air. He made himself available to Bedenk and then Engle, but he never interfered. He questioned whether an old single wing coach had any knowledge that could be put to much use toward T formation football. He continued to attend every home game and several away games each season.

After resigning as head coach, Higgins continued to help

with the recruiting program and with fund-raising. In 1950 Penn State as usual hosted the State Interscholastic Track and Field Meet at Beaver Field. Paterno was escorting around a big high school lineman named Roosevelt Grier who also had track and field aspirations. Paterno, the youngest assistant coach under Engle, introduced Grier to Higgins. Higgins sized up the big kid and then looked over at Paterno. Later Higgins met up with head coach Engle. "Rip, I don't know whether we can get the big guy, but I'm sure we can get the little guy. But do we really want the little guy?"

Engle informed Higgins that the "little guy" was assistant coach Paterno. Rosy Grier, of course, played at Penn State and became a great lineman for the New York Giants and Los Angeles Rams, a media personality, and later a confidante of Robert Kennedy.

Assistant coach O'Hora recalled a Quarterback Club meeting during the 1950 season. The lights were out and the game film was running with Paterno narrating the action. Penn State had just intercepted a pass when a high squeaky voice in the audience, unmistakably Higgins's, spoke up, "Hey young fella, what do you coach?"

"I coach interceptions," Paterno replied. "Didn't you see that one?"

O'Hora reflected: "Bob loved a great comeback. He loved the fact that somebody would give a retort that would please him. From that point on, you see, Bob knew who Joe was."

Of course the Last Man's Club continued to meet annually and Higgins enjoyed the camaraderie immensely. Members, now into their fifties, wrote to each other with as much regularity as when they were just out of World War I.

December 1, 1949
My dear Shive:
It was good to have a chance to visit with you at the Army-Navy game and I did enjoy your dinner at Jack Hammitt's old hangout behind the Bellevue. Virginia said you didn't think the food was very good; I thought it was excellent. The reason could be that I was prepared for it and you weren't. The part of our visit I enjoyed most was being next to you at the game. I realized for the first time that I have missed a lot of inside

football in the past thirty years by not having you on my coaching staff, at least in an advisory capacity. The many many times that you called the right play that was coming up next amazed me, and the people for several seats around us were also impressed with your flow of accurate conversation. Was sorry you had to catch an early train.

Good luck and best wishes.

Sincerely,

R.A. Higgins

March 22, 1950

Dear Bob:

It's good to hear from you. Now that you have more leisure, you should write more often. I don't know of any one in the world I would rather hear from than you.

I dislike to admit any temporary weaknesses to you, however, I have had one hell of a time for the past six or seven weeks—upper jaw bone. It hit me out of a clear sky with a thud about two months ago during the middle of the night in a hotel in Washington. Since then, I have been in the hands of two good doctors and eleven specialists. The two good doctors, independent of one another, agreed on a diagnosis. The eleven specialists all had different theories of the trouble—each theory supporting a six or seven months treatment by that particular specialist. My family dentist, on the basis of his own X-rays, diagnosed my difficulty as a cyst on the upper jaw. His diagnosis coincided with that of a friendly doctor in Washington. I finally made up my own alleged mind and ended all the bull and misery by having a surgeon go up there and chisel out the damned cyst. It was a right good sized cyst for a boy from Vinton County to have. When the doctors asked if I had ever been hit on the mouth, I told them never but once and that was by you when I had my back turned.

As ever, with love,

Shive

March 27, 1950

Dear Shive:

The main purpose of this letter is to tell you that the position of Head Coach of Football at Penn State is open and

I would appreciate it very much if you would consider the position. I will promise to keep out and give you a free hand.

Regards and best wishes.

Sincerely yours,

R.A. Higgins

March 29, 1950

Dear Bob:

I wish I could give the Penn State job more consideration. I do appreciate the fact that your motive is good when you offer it to me. It goes without saying that you would not have to give me "a free hand" if I took the job—I would take two free hands. I wear no man's collar. At the same time, I would rather carry slop in a bordel than be Head Football Coach at Penn State. I say this Robert because you have made it too tough for any one who succeeds you during the next ten or fifteen years. Besides, I don't like football coaching. I like only football coaches. And I like you.

As ever, with love,

E.C. Shively

February 13, 1951

Dear Jim:

In the past month I have had delightful visits at the home of three members of the Last Man's Club, namely McWane and Dirom of Lynchburg and Smith of Greensburg. Virginia and I were returning from the Southwest and we happened to be near Lynchburg, so I called Henry's home and Fan answered and I have never had a more cordial invitation to come visit. The fact that Virginia was with me put me on my good behavior.

Vince had a birthday party a week ago last Saturday, and Smith does not fool. It lasted from Friday until Sunday. Virginia says everybody in the Last Man's Club has got a big home except Higgins, and of course you know that I have got a small home with a big mortgage and six shirts with the collars turned. Shively of Ohio has two homes, one in the borough of South Charleston and the other at the farm. I have been in both. Some guys get all the breaks.

It is my opinion, Jim, that Smith should not cross swords

with Shively in letter-writing. He might beat him in another kind of a contest, but I have my doubts if he can do it by mail.

Virginia sent me down to the store for a pound of hamburg the other day and I saw a sign that read "We will buy all fats for 6 cents a pound." To me that is the handwriting on the wall. Mr. Truman says the U.S. is not at war, but I believe he is mistaken. This Korean job is probably the toughest one we have ever had. Ninety-five per cent of all the soldiers in Korea are Americanos. I have never been in Korea, but the fellows that I know who have been there say it is a stinking place. February 1951 bears a splendid resemblance to February 1941. Things have changed very little in the past 10 years, except that now we are a little more familiar with the problems. Most of us are holding our hats and saying "Here we go again." Suppose the boys in Korea get back up to the 38th parallel again. How are they going to hold it, just sit on it? Are we going to leave another army there and for how long? We have had an army in Japan since 1945. It is my opinion, that we ought to pull out of Korea right now and save face. We will lose if we stay there much longer. We can lick Russia.

Regards and best wishes.

R.A. Higgins

Higgins took on the label "The Pied Piper of McKee Street" during his retirement because of his evening strolls with his grandson which always attracted other youngsters in the College Heights neighborhood. Ross Lehman wrote the following article in *The Centre Daily Times* newspaper:

Bob would take his grandson by the hand, and around the block they would march. Bob was attired generally in shorts, and his gnarled knees — and stocky, footballish legs — looked slightly ludicrous as they resembled two tree trunks encircled in burlap.

Soon the pair would be joined by another child, then another, and another, until there was a gang of eight to twelve toddlers in the parade. As they marched, the Pied Piper of McKee Street would be exuding his charm; he told ridiculous, simple stories, he roared with laughter until his Chinese elms shook, he even sang them some Irish ditties, and he cajoled them and teased them in an easy, familiar fashion, one that invited the children into his enchanting circle.

One night, when Bob and his entourage swept by our corner, he suddenly decided to bring them all into our living room. They busted in, like a gusty wind, and Bob soon had them sitting cross legged on the floor.

Then he delivered a mighty, roof-shaking oration. It was "Casey at the Bat." His Irish voice rose and fell, developed suspense in the youngsters, and carried them to the awful climax. When mighty Casey struck out, and the hearts of Mudville were saddened, the young ones of McKee Street shed a few tears, too.

But in a twinkling, Higgins had them up on their feet and dancing into the street again. They swirled and pranced around him, like capricious leaves around a mighty oak.

Grandchildren seemed to be crawling out of the woodwork and into Higgins's lap. His three daughters provided him fifteen grandchildren — eight boys and seven girls. His youngest daughter, Nancy, graduated from Penn State in 1953 and in 1957 married Penn State graduate and football center Jim Dooley. The Dooleys had their first child in 1958.

Dooley had started at center for Engle's teams in 1951 and 1952. He was an Associated Press second team All-American in 1952. Dooley played in the Blue-Gray and Senior Bowl all-star games following his senior season. After playing high school ball for South Williamsport, Dooley was recruited by Dick Lowe, the same man who helped bring Steve Suhey to Penn State. Dooley's freshman class of 1949 was actually the first to receive scholarships at Penn State since the late 1920s. That class went 7-2-1 as seniors in 1952.

Higgins's first decade out of coaching was a time for others to recognize his career on the gridiron. On October 16, 1954, at halftime of the West Virginia-Penn State homecoming game at Beaver Field, the National Football Foundation and College Hall of Fame held an induction ceremony for Higgins. A record home crowd of 32,384 attended the festivities. The College Hall of Fame, which had begun its program in 1951, inducted two other former Penn Staters that year: Dick Harlow and Hugo Bezdek.

Ernie McCoy, who had succeeded Carl Schott in 1953 as director of athletics and dean of the college of physical education and athletics, had recommended Higgins for induction into the Hall of Fame in a letter to George Little, executive secretary of the Hall of Fame.

April 21, 1954
Dear George:
If this name has not already been brought to your attention, I should like to recommend very strongly that the name of Robert A. Higgins be added to the many celebrities who now belong in the Football Hall of Fame.

I feel that not only the great contribution which Bob has made to the game of football as a player and competitor but his long and honorable association as a coach certainly qualify him for consideration for this very signal honor.

I am enclosing information that may help to fill in his background. If there are any other steps that I should take, I shall be more than happy to hear from you.

Best personal regards and with all good wishes for your continued good health, I am
Sincerely yours,
Ernest B. McCoy, Dean

The following January 14, 1955, Higgins returned to his high school, Peddie Institute, now named The Peddie School, in Highstown, New Jersey. He was one of fourteen Peddie alumni to be honored for outstanding successes in their fields since the school's chartering in 1865.

The year 1958 was a joyous one for Higgins. He attended two major functions that recognized his coaching successes. In early November he attended a dinner hosted by the College Football Hall of Fame. Hall of Fame executive secretary Harvey Harman followed up with a letter to Higgins.

November 14, 1958
Dear Bob:
You and the other famous football players and coaches elected to the Hall of Fame honored us with your presence. I hope you will come back to next year's dinner.

It was certainly a pleasure to see you. I am almost ready to forgive you for catching that pass thrown from behind the goal line in the 1919 Pitt game.

Cordially yours,
Harvey Harman

Perhaps the most enjoyable occasion Higgins experienced during his retirement, outside of his grandchildren, was the reunion banquet of the Cotton Bowl team in State College in 1958, which was the first of many gatherings held through the years by this exceptionally close-knit team. Speakers included Chet Smith, veteran sports editor of the *Pittsburgh Press*, Casey Jones, alumnus and recruiter-extraordinare, and Higgins. The reminiscing revealed the special bond between the players and coaches on the unbeaten 1947 team, which played SMU and Doak Walker to a 13-13 tie on New Year's Day 1948. Tears flowed along with the constant laughter.

Sportswriter Smith, who served as toastmaster, introduced Jones: "Casey is one of the institutions, one of the landmarks at Penn State. He came here in 1914 and his heart has stayed here ever since. He has possibly shanghaied more football players than anybody in the history of America. But he has made everyone of them happy after they got here."

Jones spoke only briefly, typical of his style to remain in the background. "It's one of the happiest moments of my life to come here," he said. "I looked at the list of players and I had something to do with eleven kids."

In his introduction of Higgins, Smith said, "I've had three great friends in football coaching. One was Bob, one was Jock Sutherland and the other was Knute Rockne. They were all fine gentlemen, fine football coaches.

"Bob had some bad years at Penn State. He didn't have you fellas to work with. He'd come down to Pittsburgh and get his brains beat out. Finally he began to get some football players and he began to win. All he needed was a few horses and he went to town. In my book, Bob Higgins is not only one of the fine football coaches in this country, but he is the greatest gentleman who has ever been connected with the football game."

Higgins's warmth and humor permeated the audience.

With a touch of his Irish ancestry, his voice rose with emphasis as he went from player to player and recalled a memorable story. He repeatedly apologized for possibly excluding a player or two in his discourse, but, in fact, he overlooked no one.

"We had so many great tailbacks," Higgins said. "All of them were mad at me because they couldn't play. But we had six of them. How are you going to get six tailbacks in the game?"

Higgins called Francis Rogel one of the greatest fullbacks he'd ever seen. Higgins always blamed himself for not publicizing Rogel enough as an All-American candidate. Higgins remembered: "Frannie Rogel is going down for a touchdown and somebody hits him and he goes down on one hand, recovers himself and the ref blows the whistle. Frannie says, 'Hey ref, never blow a fast whistle on me, I'm never down, I'm never down.' I'll never forget Francis Rogel."

He recalled Steve Suhey living at the Higgins home. "Steve had to do some work around our house. I don't mean he would cut the lawn or anything like that, but he would take care of the furnace. When it was zero weather he would let the furnace go out and when it was hot he would have four pounds of steam on."

He remembered Larry Cooney: "Sixteen years old and he makes the varsity. Holy catfish. He and some of you fellas at Syracuse drove me crazy. We go up to Syracuse and honest-to-Christmas we order a baked potato and steak and they're marching out with the flowers. I said, 'Where are you going with those flowers?' They said they were going to give them to the cigarette girl. I said, 'Put those flowers back there.' And then I caught them smoking. I could hardly believe my eyes."

Of end Dennis Hoggard, one of two black players on the team: "Dennis missed a forward pass in the Cotton Bowl that hit him right in the navel over the goal line. But let me tell you, it was deflected. I've dropped many of them. It's a good thing you did drop it, Dennie, cause I believe Texas would have seceded from the union."

Of fullback and punter Joe Colone: "I felt sort of like a father to him. He got us out of many, many difficult positions where he would go back and boot that ball. It was easy for him, too. He was a natural."

Of Elwood Petchel: "It's a wonder I didn't kill Elwood Petchel. I had many occasions to do it. I checked on him rather closely on his grades. I called all these professors and said, 'Watch Petchel, if he isn't going to class let me know.' So I said, 'Hey Elwood, how are you getting along, did you go to class today?' He said, 'Sure.' I said, 'You didn't go to class today, the professor called me up. Why didn't you go?' He said it was raining."

Of Casey Jones: "If it wasn't for Casey Jones we wouldn't be here today. We roomed together in school and we were in the first World War together. It's a friendship that's lasting and is good. Everybody has done a good many things for me because I'm sort of a helpless guy. Casey, I appreciate it very much."

Higgins closed his speech by saying, "My intention was to run our whole football relations on the basis of a big nice family. We tried to do that and we got along well doing that."

Co-captains John Nolan and Johnny Potsklan made presentations to Higgins on behalf of the squad. Nolan presented Higgins the petition signed by the team during the 1947 season in protest of poor food and too few game tickets for the players. "As the Hig said, we were sort of a big happy family," Nolan commented. "But like every family, every once in a while something happened that had to be ironed out." At the time, hearing of the disgruntlement, Higgins had threatened to kick several players off the team until Nolan pulled out the paper and showed him the long list of signatures.

Potsklan presented a tape recorder to Higgins, who had expressed a desire to put his memories in writing, though he never did. Potsklan referred to Higgins as "a great gentleman, a great coach, and a father to most of us."

Two years later, in 1960, Higgins suffered a severe stroke (cerebral thrombosis) that paralyzed his left arm and left leg. The NCAA Coaches Association was meeting in Pittsburgh at the time. Its president, Rip Engle, received word that Higgins had suffered a stroke. Engle called for a minute of silence.

Higgins eventually fought his way out of bed, and with

the aid of a cane and a wheelchair, and with his speech still intact, continued to make the rounds and be as sharp as ever. Engle welcomed him to practice and would call the team together and introduce them to the old coach. Engle was always thankful to Higgins for never second-guessing him. "He was a man of great courage and integrity," Engle said of Higgins.

Higgins, the once-powerful physical specimen, was never heard to complain about his setback.

§ 18 §
A Hero's Final Triumph

STEVE AND GINGER SUHEY spent the 1960s raising a large Catholic family in State College, Pennsylvania. Two more sons, Paul, born in 1957, and Matt, born in 1958, increased the sibling total to a lucky number seven.

In 1960, the Suheys moved into a new house they had built on Sparks Street, only a short walk from State College Area High School, where Larry, Paul and Matt would excel in football, wrestling and other sports from 1968 to 1975. The house on Sparks Street became a hub for high school and university players, coaches, families, fraternity brothers and old teammates.

"Ever since I can remember, on a Friday night before a game or on a Saturday after the game, we always had thirty or forty people around," said Paul Suhey, who captained the great 1978 Penn State team. "We had a five-bedroom home, but for seven kids there wasn't much space. We were often farmed out to somebody's house to stay for the weekend. It was always a very festive time — lots of stories, lots of food, people showing up, always cars out front."

The person in the middle of it all was Ginger Suhey.

"She kept everybody together," Paterno said. "People were all over the place, eating, sleeping, and Ginger would always be cooking. She's so gracious. They used to have a great big kitchen table and people would come in and out a group at a time."

For Ginger the lively football atmosphere and constant companionship was all she had ever known growing up in the Higgins household.

Paterno was forever grateful to Ginger for taking his wife,

239

Sue, under her wing. Paterno married Suzanne Pohland in 1962, the same year she graduated from Penn State. Paterno was still a few years away from becoming the head coach. "Ginger took her over as if she were her kid sister," Paterno said.

Bob Higgins was a regular attraction at the Suhey residence. Grandchildren battled him in checkers, tested his memorization of U.S. presidents and vice presidents and gladly accepted candy from him. One afternoon behind the Suhey house, as the grandchildren were scampering about, Higgins pointed to young Matt and said, "You see that kid? Look at those huge legs. He's going to be a great athlete." In this case, as in hundreds of others down through the years, Higgins was an astute judge of athletic talent. Time would show just how great an athlete Matt Suhey would become.

Larry Suhey remembered returning home after a full day of play at Rec Hall on the Penn State campus and his mother telling him to go and say hello to his grandfather.

"Larry, what have you been up today?" Higgins asked.

"I went to Rec Hall, Gramps," Larry said. "I'm trying to get better, working out, lifting weights. But they keep throwing me out. I got thrown out six times today."

Higgins grimaced, "Next time you tell them you're the grandson of Bob Higgins. For sure they'll throw you out."

Steve Suhey enjoyed the weekends as he spent long hours on the road during the week selling class rings and yearbooks. Though his hands were huge, he was good with them and he refinished and built furniture, and with beeswax and a straight pin decorated eggs Ukrainian style. He enjoyed his daughter Betsy's jewelry-making and wanted to learn to cut gemstones, though he died before he had the chance. He frequently played golf with Dean McCoy and Homer Barr, the latter a close friend who had been a champion wrestler at Penn State and coached the high school wrestling team. Steve Jr. often caddied for the group.

Steve Suhey was an extremely thoughtful and positive person who remained deeply devoted to Penn State, the school that had provided him an escape from the farm and its hardships. The athletic powers at the university often came to Suhey for advice.

Neither was he shy about volunteering his opinions. When close friend Barr wasn't offered the position as head wrestling coach at Penn State, as Suhey had expected, Suhey invited Dean McCoy into the office of the golf pro prior to their next outing on the links. Voices lifted behind closed doors. It was one of the few times Suhey wasn't happy with his alma mater.

Another incident on the golf course showed that the toughness Suhey learned on the farm and the football field never left him. Suhey was lining up a putt when a man in the group behind him yelled, "Come on fat boy, putt the ball!" Suhey walked up to the man, grabbed his shirt with one giant hand and lifted him off the ground. "Who are you calling fat boy?" Suhey asked calmly.

Suhey didn't demand that his children play organized sports at an early age. He did believe that if they chose to do so they should be prepared to give their all and attend every practice. He didn't feel obligated to attend every game his children played since his work schedule made that difficult. Son Larry once asked him why he didn't come to more games like so many other fathers. "Larry, when it counts, when it really matters, I'll be there," Suhey replied. The father would live up to those words.

"My father was a pretty straight-laced, straight-forward guy. You knew there was a line you never crossed with him," said Matt Suhey. "The way my parents raised us, you were thankful for what you had. You worked hard. You were honest. You were humble and gracious in your winnings. You kept your mouth shut when you lost. You took the blame and that's the way it was."

The role of Bob Higgins and Steve Suhey in the Penn State football tradition became known to Larry, Paul and Matt, the family's three future Penn State football players, only when they saw large photos of Higgins and Suhey in Rec Hall.

"I knew my grandfather had been a coach and that my dad played some, but it was low key, no understanding of the significance of that," Paul said. "We used to sneak into Rec Hall when I was in grade school. I was running through there one day and in the front entrance they had big five-foot photos of Penn State All-American football players. I stopped and looked and said, 'Hey, that's my dad's name and picture. And my grandfather's is there too. Son of a gun, dad was an All-American. Gramps was an All-American.' It wasn't a big topic in our family."

It was a big topic in other families, particularly those families whose sons might benefit from Steve Suhey's coaching. Dave Joyner was a first-team All-American offensive tackle at Penn State in 1971. It probably wouldn't have happened without Suhey's assistance. Early in his junior season in high school, Joyner was sitting with his family watching television one evening when the door flew open and Suhey, a close friend of the family's, marched in.

"I can't stand it anymore," Suhey said, pointing at Joyner. "You and me up in the living room."

Joyner was a big kid, but not very mature. Suhey believed Joyner had lineman potential but was not living up to it.

"He came over two or three nights a week from then on during my high school career," Joyner said. "He and I would go to the living room and he'd work with me and teach me certain moves and show me tricks on how to block. He was an excellent coach. He was very patient. The way he related things to me were very easily followed, and at that point I hadn't been very coachable. His wealth of knowledge about line play had a great depth to it."

When word came following the 1971 season that Joyner had made All-American as a Penn State senior, one of the first congratulatory telephone calls came from Suhey. "Welcome to the club," Suhey said. "It feels pretty good, doesn't it."

Joyner added: "Steve Suhey was a legend to me. He was a guy who had a big heart and was tough and would tell you what he thought right off the bat."

While Suhey was getting Joyner's act together in high school, Paterno was taking over from Rip Engle as head football coach in 1966. Engle's sixteen teams had produced an outstanding 104-48-4 record and won the Lambert Trophy three times. The 1962 team was Engle's highest ranked nationally, ninth in both polls with a 9-2 record. All-Americans during this period included guard Sam Valentine, quarterback Rich Lucas, end Bob Mitinger, end Dave Robinson, half-back Roger Kochman and center/middle guard Glenn Ressler. Lucas in 1959 and Ressler in 1964 won the Maxwell Award as the nation's outstanding college football players. Lucas finished second in the 1959 Heisman Trophy vote to LSU's Billy Cannon.

One of the more famous names to play under Engle was Lenny Moore, who played from 1953-1955 and became the school's leading career rusher with 2,380 yards. Moore starred for the Baltimore Colts from 1956-1967 and was inducted into the Pro Football Hall of Fame in 1975. Milt Plum, who had a long and distinguished pro career, played quarterback for Engle in 1955-1956. Galen Hall, later head coach at the University of Florida, was quarterback in 1960-1961.

Bob Higgins was glad to see that the football program under Engle had built on the foundation he had worked so hard to establish. The Hig lived for the college football season.

"I can't remember from the early 1960s all the way through until his death in 1969 that he ever missed a football game," said grandson Steve Jr.

Steve Suhey's eldest son fondly remembered the times he and his dad picked up Higgins every Saturday shortly after noon and drove to Beaver Field. "I really got to know him then," Steve Jr. said. "He was extremely interested in how we were doing in sports. He would talk about competing and disciplining yourself and doing the best you can, despite however you finished."

The Suheys would escort Higgins up the press box elevator and get him settled in Dean McCoy's box. Higgins watched the games with binoculars and kept up to date on the varied formations, plays and specialty teams coming into football in the 1960s.

As good as it was for Higgins being with his grandchildren during this period, every year seemed to invite the dark news that another loved one had passed away. In April 1964 fellow Last Man member Ted Crane died in Delray Beach, Florida at age sixty-eight. Crane had been president of D. Van Nostrand Company, a book publisher in Princeton, New

Jersey.

Crane had planned on attending a Last Man's dinner to be held at the Old Stone House in Greensburg on July 17. In preparation for that dinner, Smith, the attorney from Greensburg, had written member Henry McWane a letter with the travel schedule and sadly added, "Formally closed my office today. I have no secretary and no typewriter. From now on you are the chairman of the Last Man's Club."

The Club's original members were down to Higgins, Douglas, Dirom, McWane and Smith. Higgins's buddy Shively had died in 1956. The 1964 gathering appears to have been the last one in which all surviving original members were in attendance.

Higgins lost another close friend on July 28, 1966. Claude Aikens, a prominent businessman in State College and publisher of *The Centre Daily Times* newspaper, died at age seventy-four. Higgins had invited Aikens into the Last Man's Club and they frequently traveled to the outings together. Aikens had been an ardent hunter and fisherman, sometimes accompanied by Higgins. Aikens had seen to it that Higgins and the Penn State football program received plenty of positive ink through the years.

Higgins received another blow when his sister, Margaret Sanger, died of arteriosclerosis on September 6, 1966 at age eighty-two in Tucson, Arizona. She had been ill for several years. The founder of the birth control movement had continued to travel worldwide expounding on her cause. As late as age seventy-five, Sanger was president of the International Planned Parenthood Federation. During her career she made nine trips to Japan, three to India, countless journeys to Europe and lectured throughout the U.S. regularly. "Birth control" had meant to her the right of every woman to control the size of her own family. She had lived to see her dream realized not only in the U.S. but in much of the world, and is recognized today as one of the most important visionaries of the twentieth century.

Tragedy of an unexpected nature struck the following year, 1967, when Steve Suhey suffered a near-fatal heart attack at age forty-five. He had traveled to the Pittsburgh airport in May with one of his daughters, Kathy, to pick up a

large shipment of yearbooks. The heart attack hit Suhey after he loaded the yearbooks on a truck and began to drive
back to State College. He drove until the pain engulfed him
and he felt himself passing out. His daughter, who was too
young to drive, checked him into a hotel. A physician suspected the pain was merely indigestion and Suhey slept
awhile. With the inner-fortitude that had become a Suhey
trademark, he drove the remainder of the 145-mile trip home.
He slept much of two days, but his color and his condition
continued to worsen and his wife called for an ambulance.
His life hung in the balance, but he pulled through.

"You have a man who is 5-11, 235 pounds and now he's
reduced to 185 pounds," said Steve Jr. of his father's recovery
during the summer. "He couldn't pick up a suitcase. He had
to quit smoking. He had to be treated with kid gloves. It was
a difficult time for him."

Doctors told his wife he could live another ten years.
Suhey would say to his family that he felt grateful to still be
alive and that he was lucky to be living on borrowed time.

Bob Higgins did not have another ten years. He had
grown old with dignity and during his twenty years out of
college football had become one of the game's legends. He had
lived a remarkable life, rich in historic value — the son of a
poor Irish philosopher and stonecutter, the brother of one of
this century's greatest figures, a hero of the Western Front in
World War I, an All-American of the college gridiron, a pioneer of pro football, a primary molder of the Penn State football tradition, a father-figure to hundreds of players, a story-
telling comrade to so many friends, a beloved family man who
felt that the most important thing in life was to live it with
zest and be thankful for the opportunity.

The last Penn State football team Higgins witnessed
rushed through ten games without a defeat during the regular season and beat Kansas in the Orange Bowl. The 1968
team produced Penn State's first undefeated season since
Higgins's 1947 team had stonewalled opponent after opponent. Higgins knew how head coach Joe Paterno felt.

One of the players on the 1968 team was junior fullback
and kicker Don Abbey. Abbey grew close to Higgins near the

end of Higgins's life. Abbey, like Higgins, was a Beta Theta Pi. Abbey was responsible for picking up Higgins's wife, Virginia, who was the fraternity's house mother, and driving her over to the frat house so she could chaperone during weekend festivities. Abbey enjoyed coming to the Higgins home so much that he always arrived a couple of hours early.

"I would listen to the coach tell stories," Abbey said. "He talked about the old Canton Bulldogs and Jim Thorpe. He never got out of his chair. He used to sit there and line his cigarettes up one by one on the flat part of his chair and line his matches up right next to them. He'd go right down the line, smoking cigarettes and telling stories. It was like you were listening to Moses."

In late May 1969, Higgins suffered another stroke at home that left him totally paralyzed and nearly comatose. He lay in Centre County Hospital in nearby Bellefonte for several days as his wife and family frequented his bedside. His eldest daughter, Mary Ann Lyford, leaned over and asked of her dad, "Can you hear me?" The 75-year-old Higgins blinked to let her know that he could. Many years earlier Higgins's father had suffered a stroke and he, too, could only communicate by blinking.

On the morning of June 6, Steve and Ginger Suhey attended their son Steve's graduation ceremony at the private prep school, Kiski, in Saltsburg. Watching over the Suhey home and children at State College were Paul and Judy Johnson. Paul was a starting defensive back on the undefeated 1968 and 1969 Penn State teams. He was from Cazenovia as was Steve Suhey. The Suheys often looked to the young couple to babysit.

Late in the morning, the Johnsons received word from Virginia Higgins that her husband had died at 11:45 a.m. The Suhey kids came and went during the day but the Johnsons felt obligated to hold back the information until Ginger and Steve returned. Judy continued to hem a prom dress for Ginger's eldest daughter, Kathy.

Late in the afternoon Steve and Ginger arrived home, still unaware of Higgins's passing. Johnson pulled Steve aside and told him. Steve then took Ginger into their bedroom and told her.

Kathy was uncertain if she should still go to the prom, but Ginger said, "I can't think of anybody more than your grandfather who would want you to go."

Services were held for Higgins on Monday morning, June 9, at St. Andrews Episcopal Church. The Rev. James Trost officiated at the ceremony. Higgins was buried at Centre County Memorial Park in State College. Most of the unbeaten 1947 team returned for the service. Hundreds of university and townspeople attended, as did hundreds of friends whom Higgins had touched along the way of his fascinating journey through life.

Joe Paterno later said, "Bob Higgins always had an air about him. He was a born leader. He had that confidence. When the Carnegie Foundation came out and Penn State was one of the few schools to do what they were asked to do — give up athletic dorms, give up athletic scholarships — they cut back and didn't have any players. Bob Higgins inherited that and slowly with several great assistants like Earle Edwards and Al Michaels literally nickeled and dimed their way into it and built the program back. Bob Higgins was absolutely the right guy at the right place. He had the patience, the support of the alumni, he had Penn State people around him. He was Penn State all the way. He believed in Penn State and Penn State football. Bob set a tone."

In June 1966, three years before he died, Higgins received the Lion's Paw medal, an award established the previous year to recognize those personalities who promoted the welfare and traditions of Penn State University. These words were read to Higgins during the presentation of the award:

"To Robert A. Higgins, for many years of dedicated service to Penn State; for his contribution to football as a great competitor and a highly successful teacher; for his beneficial influence on countless young men; for his sense of humor in the face of adversity; for the great courage manifested throughout his life—a true embodiment of the Penn State Spirit."

§ 19 §
The Boys Become Men

PATERNO'S NITTANY LIONS put up perfect 12-0 records in 1968 and 1969, including Orange Bowl victories over Kansas and Missouri. All-Americans poured out of the program. Ted Kwalick won the honor as a tight end in 1968 and went on to play with San Francisco and Oakland. Dennis Onkotz was an All-American linebacker in 1968 and 1969. Mike Reid was an All-American defensive tackle in 1969, and also won the Maxwell Award and Outland Trophy. He became an All-Pro with the Cincinnati Bengals. Halfback Charlie Pittman and safety Neal Smith also made All-American in 1969.

The defensive lineup changed very little during those two years. The tackles, Reid and Steve Smear, doubled as captains both seasons. John Ebersole and Gary Hull played the ends. Onkotz was at inside linebacker along with Jim Kates. Pete Johnson and Mike Smith played outside linebacker along with future Pittsburgh Steeler and pro football Hall-of-Fame inductee, Jack Ham. Neal Smith, who intercepted eighteen passes in 1968 and 1969, was joined in the secondary by George Landis and Paul Johnson. In 1970 NFL teams drafted six of those seniors players — Reid, Onkotz, Smear, Ebersole, Kates and Paul Johnson.

Chuck Burkhart methodically and successfully directed the team at quarterback for twenty-four consecutive victories. Pittman led the team in rushing both seasons (a combined 1,656 yards). He ran for twenty-four touchdowns and rushed for more than 100 yards in seven games. A couple of running backs named Franco Harris and Lydell Mitchell stepped up as sophomores in 1969.

In the midst of this college football frenzy in State College, Steve Suhey's second oldest son, Larry, came of age as a great running back and wrestler at State College Area High School. Larry appeared to be headed for private school until State College High School hired Jim Williams, an assistant coach at nearby Bellefonte High School, as the new head football coach. Williams, a State College native, had played center and linebacker at Penn State in the early 1960s. Steve Suhey wanted Larry to play football for Williams.

Larry was nothing less than a bull toting the football. At an early age his strength was complemented with an in-depth understanding of the game, thanks to years of instruction from his father. As an eighth-grader playing ninth-grade football Larry had his running and blocking assignments down pat.

"My dad would go through all the plays and tell me what my job was," Larry recalled. "He'd say, 'This is the I formation. These guys are going to block these guys. When you get to the line your block is coming from the tight end on the linebacker, so you want to fake to the right.' He'd tell me when I should run right at the linebacker and when I should fake him. He'd tell me when to use the stiff arm. When I got in the game everything happened exactly like he said it would. It was like slow motion."

As good as Larry was at football by his sophomore season in high school, statewide recognition came first in wrestling, which in Pennsylvania had as big a following as football. Steve Suhey provided important guidance. "You're going to go far, but there's only one way to do it and that's the right way," Steve said. "You have to dedicate yourself to what you want to achieve in life. You can't go half way. Get your sleep, eat right. If you want it, you've got to pay the price."

As a sophomore Larry reached the semifinals of the state wrestling meet before losing for only the second time during the season. He proceeded to win back-to-back state titles in the 180-pound class his junior and senior seasons. The turning point came his junior year after he was pinned for the only time in his career during a seasonal meet with Clearfield

High School.

"It was in State College and the place was packed," Suhey said. "I made a wrong move and the kid pinned me. I was really bummed out. I go to the locker room. Everybody is all upset. My dad comes in and I'm sitting there almost in tears. It's the only time my dad ever came to the locker room. He has a big smile on his face and starts laughing. He says, 'Larry, that's the funniest thing I've ever seen. What a fluke. Put it behind you and it'll make you a better athlete.' I started laughing too. He was right. It was the best thing that ever happened to me. It made me realize I was human and had to work harder."

As Steve Suhey had told Larry years earlier, he would be there when his son needed him the most.

Larry, who was just under six feet tall, didn't lose a match the remainder of his high school career, compiling an incredible three-year mark of 64-3 and carving his name as one of the state's great high school wrestlers.

After Larry won his second consecutive state title at Harrisburg in the spring of 1972 in a tough 6-5 bout, his wrestling coach, Ron Pifer, commented: "I think I respected Larry more for the way he wrestled in that final match than anything else. There were several times that it could have gone either way and Larry just wanted it more. It's a little tougher the second time around. That puts a different kind of pressure on a boy. He either has to win or disappoint people. I thought Larry met a boy who was at his best and beat him. That's the mark of a champion."

Meanwhile, behind Suhey's power running — which frequently turned dive plays into long gainers — State College Area High School under coach Williams began to establish a dynasty. When discussion rolled around to great Pennsylvania high school football teams, these teams were always mentioned.

"It was one of those eras, in a five-year period, if you had to pick the twenty best football players ever to play at State College High School, probably eighteen of them went through there at that time," Williams said.

The program turned around in the middle of Larry's sophomore season when, after a 3-3 start, coach Williams threw out the existing offense and defense. He shifted personnel on offense, including switching Larry from tailback to fullback. He implemented a 4-4 defense. The team won its remaining three games of the season over undefeated foes.

In Larry's junior year, 1970, the starting quarterback was Mike Archer, who later became head coach at LSU. That team lost only one game, which was the next-to-final game of the season. The Lions didn't lose again until the middle of the 1974 season, a winning streak of thirty-six games.

Back at tailback, Larry dominated the gridiron his senior season and made All-State. A typical performance was his 249 yards rushing and two touchdowns against Huntingdon. Larry exploded through defensive lines and no lone defensive back could slow him down. The quarterback and safety of the unbeaten 1971 team was Tim Curley, who became athletic director at Penn State in 1994.

The high school football team received tremendous support from the community. As usual the Suhey family was in the middle of it. "Steve was a very strong person," Williams said. "He with a couple of other parents had a lot of impact when they would go to talk to people when things had to be done, like when the football field had to be worked on. They had some respect from those people."

Larry mentioned the closeness of several large football families such as the Suheys, the Curleys, the Ellises and the Sefters. The high school soccer field behind the Suhey home became a second practice field to many of the players, especially during the summer. Steve Suhey would come outside and assist the boys as they worked out. Ginger kept the growing boys well-fed.

"Mr. Suhey was an intimidating figure because he was so big physically," Curley recalled. "But I think down deep he had a soft spot and really looked after not only his sons and daughters but the people they associated with.

"I have really good memories of spending time with the Suhey family. There was always a group of people that hung out over there. Ginger was so great to us. I can remember Ginger giving me a ride home many times after I'd been there all day. I ate a lot of peanut butter and jelly sandwiches at the Suheys."

December 17, 1971
Dear Larry:
Our Pitt football program is striving to build teams that are the best in the country. To achieve this goal, we need a very special and highly selected type of young man.

My coaching staff and I have carefully studied your athletic, academic, and personal characteristics. We are certain that you are the outstanding type of young man we need, and I am pleased to offer you the maximum amount of athletic scholarship permitted under NCAA rules.

This Special Aid Award consists of full tuition, fees, room and board, free loan of books, and $15.00 per month for personal expenses. The award, which is subject to your admission and enrollment, fully protects you under NCAA rules and cannot be cancelled because of injury.

Sincerely,
Carl DePasqua
Head Football Coach

It would have been a great coup for Pitt, but Larry stayed the family course and accepted a scholarship from Penn State. Unfortunately, in pre-season practice his freshman season, Larry tore ligaments in his right knee. He had already experienced some knee problems in high school.

Penn State redshirted Larry. He would never again be the bruising, dominating player he was in high school, but his impact on the Penn State football program grew in other ways.

Larry's injury enabled him to keep a closer eye on his younger brothers, Paul and Matt. Paul was at linebacker and fullback when State College High School went undefeated in 1972, his sophomore year. The team put up another perfect mark in 1973, Paul's junior year and Matt's sophomore year.

Paul, the tallest of the brothers at 6-1, played with great intelligence and awareness. He credited his dad with bringing him along at the right pace.

"Larry and Matt were great high school athletes, but I was the kind of guy who made the team my sophomore year, played some more my junior year and peaked my senior year. My dad did a nice job with me and understanding my ability and understanding that Matt and Larry were a lot better athletes than I was. I never felt any pressure.

"My dad kept things in perspective. He wasn't one of these dads that was a raving fanatical father. I can remember coming home after a lousy game and he'd say, 'Aw, come on. You didn't play that bad.' He'd point out some good things and you'd feel better about yourself. I can remember some other days coming home and thinking, 'I'm the best thing in the world,' and he'd knock you down to size in a hurry."

Paul's greatest sports accomplishment in high school occurred on the wrestling mat in the spring of his senior year when he won the state title in the heavyweight division to complete an undefeated season. His brother, Larry, told him before the season he could win the championship.

"Larry took me to the wrestling room and worked me to death," Paul said. "He pushed me unbelievably, had me out running hills at night, climbing ropes, doing pushups and situps. Once I won it I found out that it wasn't that hard if you just have the drive and someone to push you. I was lucky because not many people have brothers who are like that. The work ethic I learned from him carried over into my life."

Paul was recruited by several schools including Pitt, Maryland, Virginia, North Carolina State and, of course, Penn State. Initially he leaned toward attending another school besides Penn State. He even told his parents he planned to sign a letter of intent with NC State, which was coached by Lou Holtz, who had been a visitor in the Suhey home. Paul's parents told him to go where he would feel most comfortable.

"The next day I get called out of one of my classes and there's Joe Paterno in the principal's office," Paul said. "He said 'I want you to do what's best for you, but why go eight hours away when you can come here and be a part of this tradition.' I think my mom might have talked to Sue Paterno."

Paul thought it over some more. A conversation with Larry finally pulled him back to Penn State.

"Larry really put it in perspective. He said, 'You realize you could be a link in a chain here. Why break it unless you really want to go away?' I said, 'You're right.' I'm glad I made that decision."

While Paul enrolled at Penn State, Matt continued to

run rampant on the high school gridiron. Bob Higgins had been on the money when he pointed to a young Matt Suhey and said this was a boy with natural talent. Matt is remembered as one of the greatest — if not *the* greatest — high school tailbacks in Pennsylvania's history.

"He's the best high school football player I ever saw," said his coach, Williams, who later joined the Penn State staff and recruited for the Nittany Lions. "I don't remember going to a game and watching someone dominate it the way Matt Suhey did in high school."

Matt, playing at 5-11, 200 pounds, was selected as an All-State player three times. He rushed for a staggering 4,557 yards and scored fifty-nine touchdowns.

"I learned a lot from my father," Matt said. "He had great knowledge. But more important than the basic instruction was his intensity and his work habits. He emphasized honesty and goals and making a commitment to play the game. Preparation was a big deal for him. Whether it was football or wrestling or track or schoolwork, once you made a commitment, let's do it. Let's work.

"I had an experience in track my junior year when a bunch of guys quit. I came home and said to my dad, 'None of my friends are there. Maybe I'll just work out and get ready to play football.' He said, 'Absolutely not. Just because those guys aren't doing it, there's a lot you can get out of track, there's a lot you can see.' I went to the Penn Relays in Philadelphia, I went to Virginia, to Ohio, did a lot of traveling and got to know a different group of guys in high school that I wouldn't have gotten to meet otherwise, which was important. He didn't push us, but he felt very strongly you should be involved in sports.

"I was lucky when I played high school football because we had a great coaching staff and a lot of great players. It mixed right in with the tradition of Penn State. Penn State really had some great teams in the 1960s when I was growing up and into the 1970s, some great, great teams and great players, and it so happened the high school was doing very well, which actually started with my brother Larry."

Paterno said that Matt was one of the four or five most highly-recruited players in the country.

"He was a very strong, very quick, very explosive football player," Paterno said. "He had been that way since junior high."

Penn State's recruiting battle against Ohio State for Matt's services is legendary. Matt's high school coach, Williams, remembered when Penn State recruiting coordinator Sever "Tor" Toretti, who had played under Higgins, called about the youngest Suhey brother. "Tor said, 'Jim, can you give us a little help with Matt? We think he's going to Ohio State.' I said, 'Tor, he told me two weeks ago he's going to Penn State.'"

Indeed, Matt kept people guessing. "It was really touch and go," Toretti said. "I kept saying to Joe, 'We can't afford to let this kid get away from us. The other schools will use it against us. Here are the Suheys with all their background. If he doesn't go to Penn State there must be something wrong.'"

"I wanted to go to Ohio State," Matt said. "There was this coach, Alex Gibbs, who recruited me for Ohio State. I liked him a lot. He wrote some nice letters concerning what was best for me and the academic side of it. I went out there and had a great visit. Then Woody Hayes came to my house and met my father. At the time my brother Larry was sharing playing time. My father felt he should be playing a little bit more. My brother Paul was kind of playing tight end, playing linebacker and bouncing around. I thought maybe it's a nice time for me to leave. I made my decision that I was going to Ohio State. I said it was what was best for me."

Paterno recalled: "I was having a little bit of a problem with Steve about Larry. Steve felt I hadn't done a good job with Larry. When Matt came along, I figured Steve and I knew each other well enough that I wasn't going to get into a big recruiting thing with him. It got tight. Matt was seriously thinking Ohio State. Steve and I had a breakfast meeting. He called me up and said, 'You and I better talk.' We went out to a Howard Johnson here, got into a little booth in the back of the room and he and I had it out. After that I thought Matt was all set. Steve had to get a couple of things out of his craw and once we talked that thing out I felt Matt would come to Penn State."

Matt remembered other intense moments.

"Toretti got me in a room after school one afternoon and started hammering me," he said. "He talked about my grandfather, talked about my father, talked about my brothers. And then Joe came to see me a couple of days later. My father and Joe got in a big discussion, a heated one at that, most of it about Nixon and foreign policy. My father and Paterno always debated the issues, and they were discussing Nixon more than they were me. Then Paterno got me in this room and hammered me for about ten minutes."

Larry's playing time may have been a point of concern for others, but Larry was adamant about Matt going to Penn State. "When Paul made his decision to go to Penn State, there was no way Matt was going somewhere else," Larry said. "I said, 'Matt, you're not going to Ohio State. You're not going to make mom and dad decide if they should go see you or Paul play.'"

Toretti recalled that very late in the recruiting season he approached Matt and said, "Let's quit fooling around. Let's make a decision on this thing." Toretti said Matt told him he wanted to go to Penn State, but he wanted Toretti to keep it to himself a few days. "I think Matt was enjoying watching everybody squirm," Toretti said.

Matt said, "My mom wanted me to go to Penn State. My father did, too. I knew it down in my heart. Fortunately Penn State was the best place for me."

Larry had been at Penn State for four seasons when Matt arrived on the scene for preseason practice in 1976. In 1972, the year Larry hurt his knee, Penn State went 10-2, losing to Oklahoma in the Sugar Bowl, and finished number ten in the Associated Press. Led by Heisman Trophy winner John Cappelletti, Penn State went 12-0 in 1973, beating LSU in the Orange Bowl. But pollsters ranked the Nittany Lions fifth in the nation, meaning that in three of the past six years Penn State had gone 12-0 and still hadn't been voted national champions. Penn Staters everywhere had legitimate reason to suspect poll and media bias.

In 1974, Penn State finished seventh in the nation with a 10-2 record, including a Cotton Bowl win over Baylor. In 1975, the Lions were voted tenth in the country, going nine and three and losing to Alabama in the Sugar Bowl. All-American players from these major bowl teams included defensive end Bruce Bannon, quarterback John Hufnagel, linebacker John Skorupan, halfback Cappelletti, defensive tackle Randy Crowder, linebacker Ed O'Neil, tackle John Nessel, defensive end Mike Hartenstine, kicker Chris Bahr, linebacker Greg Buttle and guard Tom Rafferty.

Larry had enjoyed the experience of playing in all the major bowl games, but ever since the knee injury his freshman season he had played mostly in a backup role. When his spirits sagged, his dad lifted them. Steve Suhey challenged his son to stick it out. In fact, Steve was a source of inspiration and a sounding board to many Penn State players who spent time at the Suhey house. Some problems never reached Paterno because they were nipped in the bud on Sparks Street. Steve Suhey may have had his differences with Paterno, but he remained loyal to the great head coach and always spoke well of him to the players who gravitated to the Suhey home.

With remarkable determination and grit, Larry was on the verge of winning the starting fullback position prior to his fifth and final season in 1976. In line for the starting tailback spot was freshman Matt Suhey, who had climbed rapidly up the depth charts. A freshman starting for Penn State was unheard of at the time. Paul, meanwhile, had lettered his freshman season in 1975 playing fullback, tight end and on the specialty teams. He was moved to linebacker for his sophomore season.

Late in preseason drills, the grim reaper again pointed to Larry Suhey. While running drills Larry spun off a player who held on to his jersey and fell across the back of Larry's left leg, causing ligament damage to the knee. A physician told Larry his career was over and called for an operation.

"I can remember Larry getting hurt, the look on his face when the trainers helped him off the field," Paul recalled. "He knew he had hurt his knee bad. It was very sad."

Yet again Larry fought back. He was determined to block for his younger brother in the Penn State backfield. He wanted his parents to watch three of their sons play for Penn State in the same game. He refused the operation, wore a cast several weeks and spent hours in the weight room. Nobody doubted he would be back. His father was Steve Suhey. His grandfather was Bob Higgins.

In one of the great twists of football fate, while Larry rehabilitated, Paterno moved Matt from tailback to fullback. Matt not only starred at fullback for Penn State for four seasons, but he would play ten years at fullback for the Chicago Bears. His blocking paved the way for Walter Payton to become the pro game's all-time leading rusher.

In the opening game of the 1976 season before 62,000 fans at Beaver Field, Matt rushed for 119 yards on twenty-three carries as Penn State nipped Stanford 15-12. It was one of the greatest varsity performances by a Penn State freshman since Bob Higgins had dominated the trenches in a 13-13 tie with Harvard in 1914.

But the 1976 season caved in on the Nittany Lions. Following the win over Stanford, Penn State lost tight ones at home to Ohio State and Iowa, and lost on the road to Kentucky. It was Penn State's first three game losing streak since the beginning of the 1964 season.

The Nittany Lions rebounded with six consecutive victories before losing the final game of the regular season at Pittsburgh, 24-7. Despite a 7-4 record, Penn State received an invitation to play in the Gator Bowl in Jacksonville, Florida. The opponent would be Notre Dame, coming off an 8-3 record. The contest would mark the first time these two prestigious football programs had met since 1928, when Hugo Bezdek's Penn State fell to Rockne's Notre Dame, 9-0, at Franklin Field in Philadelphia. On the Penn State sidelines that day in 1928 was ends coach Bob Higgins, who was two years away from becoming head coach at his alma mater.

The outcome on December 27, 1976 was no different, as Notre Dame won 20-9. But that Gator Bowl would forever hold special memories for the Suhey family.

Nearly 68,000 fans turned out for the game on a cool, breezy day. Notre Dame led 20-3 at half as Irish running back Al Hunter scored twice from the one-yard line. Paterno put Larry in at fullback for most of the second half with Matt running at tailback. Larry had struggled back from the knee injury and played sparingly in the last few games of the season. Now he would end his career like he wanted, playing alongside his brothers on national television with their parents sitting in the stands.

Penn State marched up and down the field on the Notre Dame defense, but mistakes and penalties stalled drives deep in Irish territory. Penn State finally scored in the fourth quarter on an eight-yard pass from quarterback Chuck Fusina to Matt Suhey.

At one point, not in the best playing shape because of the injury and layoff, Larry bent over in the huddle, coughing and gasping. "Are you going to die?" Matt asked. Larry grinned. "I'm all right. Just give me time."

The hurting had never felt so good. The sensation of blocking for his brother, the satisfaction he felt for coming back and finishing his career, the pride he knew that was now building in his parents as they watched him play, was all that mattered.

After the game Larry, Paul and Matt met with their father in his hotel room. Steve pulled out a bottle of Southern Comfort and offered a toast to his sons.

Twelve days later, on Saturday, January 8, 1977, Steve Suhey died of a massive heart attack as he knelt to put wood in his fireplace on Sparks Street. It was his fifty-fifth birthday. All seven of the Suhey children were in State College for the celebration, though they were all out on various errands. Ginger was preparing dinner in the kitchen when she heard her husband collapse.

As a snowstorm hit State College, services for Steve Suhey were held at Our Lady Of Victory Catholic Church. He was buried at Centre County Memorial Park. People from all walks of life came to say good-bye to this man who had moved them with his loyalty and his friendship.

Epilogue

S TEVE AND GINGER SUHEY'S seven children ful-
filled their dad's wish and graduated from college, six
of them receiving diplomas from Penn State University. Long football hours didn't keep Larry, Paul and Matt
from focusing on the importance of a college education.

After Larry graduated in 1977 he and his mother took
over Steve's Balfour ring business in central Pennsylvania.
Larry continues to run the business today. He travels the same
roads his father traveled. He eats at the same restaurants.
He and his wife, Chris, reside in nearby Boalsburg and are
raising a son and a daughter. The children spend a lot of time
at their grandmother's house on Sparks Street. Ginger Suhey,
as vivacious as ever, wouldn't have it any other way.

After three years at Penn State, Paul Suhey's football career still hadn't taken off. But in 1978, his senior year,
Paul won a starting post at linebacker. More importantly, his
teammates elected him co-captain along with quarterback
Chuck Fusina. "I saw a lot of upperclassmen affected by things
in 1976, and when I became a captain in 1978 I made it a
point to try to keep the senior class together," Paul said. "The
older guys are the ones you count on in a pinch."

Suhey's leadership and his play at linebacker contributed to Penn State's undefeated run through its eleven-game
regular season in 1978. A national championship slipped away
when Penn State lost to Alabama in the Sugar Bowl, 14-7.
The Nittany Lions finished fourth in the country.

"Paul was one of the finest captains I ever had," Paterno
said. "He had a lot of his father and a lot of his grandfather in

him. He was not a phony, he was not a hypocrite. He wa
absolutely honest. He knew who he was. He believed in him
self. He was willing to do what it took to lead by example a
well as being able to get people around him and talk sense t
them."

Paul graduated from Penn State in 1979. In the fall c
that year he served briefly as a graduate assistant coach fo
Paterno. Despite Paterno's urging that he could become a
excellent coach, Paul moved on and pursued a career in medi
cine. He graduated from the Philadelphia College of Ostec
pathic Medicine. Today he is an orthopedic surgeon in Jack
sonville, Florida. He and his wife, Carolyn, have two sons an
two daughters.

Matt Suhey became one of Penn State's greatest run
ning backs of all time and then played ten years with th
Chicago Bears. He led the Nittany Lions in rushing his sopho
more, junior and senior seasons. He rushed for 2,818 yard
and twenty-six touchdowns during his four seasons. When h
graduated he ranked second in rushing yardage behind Lydel
Mitchell. He ranks fifth on the all-time list today. Suhey ra
for more than 100 yards eight times, including five times hi
senior season. Against Army in 1979 he carried the ball twenty
three times for 225 yards and two touchdowns.

Matt was also on the 1978 team that went unbeaten dur
ing the regular season and lost to Alabama in the Sugar Bowl
At the Alabama goal line late in the game, Penn State, or
third and fourth downs, tried to run at the heart of Bea
Bryant's defense and came up short. The goal line stand i
regarded as one of the greatest moments in Alabama footbal
history. Matt Suhey attempted to go over the top on thirc
down. Paterno said, "You'd have a tough time telling anybody
that Matt didn't score." Indeed, the game films leave plenty
of doubt that his plunge was short of the end zone.

Matt Suhey was a model of consistency. In 1978 and 197£
he led the team in all-purpose yardage (rushing, pass receiv
ing, kickoff and punt returns) with 1,131 and 1,127 yards
respectively. He set a Penn State record for punt return yard
age in a game with 145 against North Carolina State in 1978

Matt started in four bowl games — Gator, Fiesta, Sugar and Liberty — and rushed for 276 yards.

As did his grandfather Bob Higgins, Matt lettered four years in football at Penn State.

In May 1980, as Suhey prepared to graduate in marketing, State College mayor Arnold Addison proclaimed Matt Suhey Day. Four-hundred people attended the celebration dinner at Gatsby's. Jim Williams, who was Suhey's high school coach and was on the Penn State staff when Matt played for Penn State, was one of the speakers. Williams said, "Maybe Matt's most impressive accomplishment is the way he earned the respect of his teammates and the job he did academically at Penn State."

Matt's mother, Ginger, received two standing ovations during the dinner.

"Looking back, Penn State always did things the polite way, the intelligent way, the efficient way," Matt said. "Nice and clean. Not a lot of big talking, always humble, always playing hard. It's going to be a long day if you want to beat Penn State.

"One of the best compliments I ever had was when talking to the pro scouts for the Chicago Bears. They said when you look at Penn State you know you're getting a smart football player who won't make big mistakes, and you're also getting a smart human being, a good solid human being, a person with character. And that says much more beyond football. I think that tradition started with my grandfather and was accentuated through Paterno."

The Chicago Bears drafted Matt in the second round in 1980. He was Chicago's highest running back pick since Walter Payton was selected in the first round in 1975. Playing at 215 pounds, Suhey was the starting fullback for most of his ten-year career with the Bears.

The consistency and durability he displayed at Penn State continued in the pro ranks. He missed only one game due to injury. He rushed for 2,946 yards, which upon his retirement was sixth on the all-time Bears list behind Walter Payton, Rick Casares, Gale Sayers, Roland Harper and Willie Galimore. He ran for twenty touchdowns. His 259 career receptions placed him fourth on the Bears all-time list behind

Payton, Johnny Morris and Mike Ditka. He gained 2,109 yards receiving and caught five passes for touchdowns.

But Suhey is best remembered for his superb blocking. Walter Payton, the NFL's all-time rushing leader with 16,726 yards, had lots of occasions to praise his teammate's skill, power, and steadfast dedication.

The Bears, under head coach Mike Ditka, fielded powerful teams with Suhey at fullback, Payton at tailback, Jim McMahon at quarterback and Willie Gault at wide receiver. The defense included such stars as linebackers Mike Singletary and Wilber Marshall, tackle William "The Refrigerator" Perry, end Richard Dent and defensive back Gary Fencik.

Chicago reached the NFC Championship game in 1984 before losing to San Francisco. It all came together in 1985 as the Bears went 15-1 in the regular season, shut out the Giants 21-0 in the divisional playoffs, blanked the Rams 24-0 in the NFC Championship, and crushed the New England Patriots, 46-10, in Super Bowl XX in New Orleans. With the Bears ahead 6-3 in the first quarter, Suhey crashed in for the game's first touchdown and the rout was on.

Matt retired from the Bears following the 1989 season and today works with an investment firm in Chicago. He and his wife Donna have two sons and a daughter.

Eldest son Steve and his wife Louise have a son and a daughter, bringing the number of Ginger's grandchildren to eleven — six boys and five girls.

February 8, 1985
Dear Mrs. Suhey:
As Chairmen of The National Football Foundation's Board of Directors and Honors Court we have the honor of notifying you of your late husband Steve Suhey's election to The National Football Foundation's College Football Hall of Fame.

This is the greatest honor that can come to a former player or coach. Your husband will be honored at an on-campus ceremony at Penn State this fall.
Sincerely,
Vincent dePaul Draddy, Fred Russell

Thirty-one years following the induction of her father into the College Football Hall of Fame, Ginger Suhey sat in for her late husband, Steve, as he was inducted at halftime of the West Virginia game on October 26, 1985.

In November 1985 two of the original thirteen members of the Last Man's Club, Henry McWane and Guy Dirom, both lived in Lynchburg, Virginia. Both were patients in Virginia Baptist Hospital. Both men lay near death.

McWane, Dirom and their 80th Division buddies had formed the Last Man's Club in 1918 during a break in the brutal warfare on the Western Front in France. The club had met at least once a year until 1964. The festive occasions always concluded with a formal dinner at which the unopened bottle of rum was placed in the center of the table. A French interpreter had purchased the rum only moments after one of their comrades in the 80th Division had fallen. They pledged to leave the bottle unopened until all but one man had passed away. At that time, the last man would open the bottle and drink to his comrades.

Three of the original members — Frank Clemmer, Clovis Moomaw and Tingle Culbertson — had been killed during the war. The remaining members of the club, all extremely successful in their endeavors following the war, had slipped away with time — Charles Sweeney, Sidney King, Earl Shively, Ted Crane, Jack Hammitt, Bob Higgins, Jim Douglas and Vince Smith.

McWane and Dirom had become especially close since they lived in the same city. McWane's sister had married Dirom's brother.

At the age of eighty-nine, following a series of strokes, Henry McWane died in Virginia Baptist Hospital on Thursday, November 7. The next morning, in another room of the hospital, Dirom's family informed him of his friend's passing. Many years before, upon fellow Last Man member Ted Crane's death, Dirom had written to the other members: "I can't see any advantage of being the Last Man left on this side of The River."

Dirom, also eighty-nine years old, had been ill for some time and suffered from a kidney ailment. He knew his time was short. On November 11, the Monday following McWane's death, Dirom and McWane family members brought the bottle of Rhum Negrita to Guy Dirom's room. McWane had been in possession of the bottle and when he died his son Hank found it in one of his father's drawers.

"I just wish I felt a little better," said Dirom as he prepared to taste the rum in his bed.

Thirteen plastic champagne glasses — one for each original member — were placed on a tray. Wrapped in cellophane, its label faded, the bottle released a pungent aroma when Dirom's nephew, Mac Dirom, unscrewed the cap. The nephew filled the thirteen glasses. Dirom's daughter, Joanne Hayes, slid the tray in front of her father.

His voice weak, Dirom uttered, "I'll need a straw."

His daughter provided one and Dirom sipped the rum. "No more," he said with a wince after a brief taste.

The names of the other twelve members were read. Dirom's mind roamed back to the trenches of France, and on to the years of companionship, laughter and love that followed.

Guy Dirom died eighteen days later, on Friday, November 29, 1985, the day after Thanksgiving. The last man was gone.

Several years ago Jim Dooley, Bob Higgins's son-in-law, attended a Lehigh-Colgate football game at Lehigh University in Bethlehem, Pennsylvania. Dooley, who had received his ticket from a business associate and Lehigh alumnus, sat on the fifty-yard-line. An elderly gentleman sitting next to Dooley asked if he was a Lehigh alumnus, as Dooley had such an excellent seat in the alumni section. Dooley said he hadn't gone to Lehigh but that he knew of someone who possibly attended Lehigh in the same era as the older gentleman. Dooley asked the man if he knew a Dick Higgins. The man thought a moment and responded, "No, I didn't know a Dick Higgins, but I knew a Bob Higgins. That S.O.B."

Dooley smiled and told the man that Bob Higgins was his father-in-law and that Dick Higgins, who had played baseball at Lehigh, was Bob's brother.

"Sir, why did you refer to Bob Higgins as an S.O.B.?" Dooley asked with great curiosity.

The elderly man explained that he had graduated from Bethlehem High School and gone to West Virginia Wesleyan to play football when Bob Higgins was head football coach. As a freshman the man participated in a scrimmage. Because of a shortage of players, coach Higgins dressed out that day with the team. Higgins was fresh from his playing days with Jim Thorpe and the Canton Bulldogs.

Attempting to impress the head coach, the freshman from Bethlehem tried to throw a block on Higgins.

The elderly man paused, shook his head, and said, "Bob Higgins put a lick on me that knocked me all the way back to Bethlehem."

Bibliography

Books

Baker, Dr. L.H. *Football: Fact and Figures*. New York, NY: Rinehart & Co., Inc., 1945.

Bezilla, Michael. *Penn State, An Illustrated History*. University Park, PA: The Pennsylvania State University Press, 1985.

Durant, John and Etter, Les. *Highlights of College Football*. New York: Hastings House, 1970.

Geiger, Carl. *The Peddie School's First Century*. Valley Forge, PA: The Judson Press, 1965.

Gilbert, Bob. *Neyland: The Gridiron General*. Savannah, GA: Golden Coast Publishing Company, 1990.

Kamper, Erich. *Encyclopedia of the Olympic Games*. New York, NY: McGraw-Hill Book Company, 1972.

Kaye, Ivan. *Good Clean Violence*. Philadelphia, PA: J.B. Lippincott Company, 1973.

Kessler, Kent. *Hail West Virginians!* Parkersburg, WV: Park Press, 1959.

Koger, Jim. *National Champions*. Columbus, GA: Atlantic Publishing Co., 1970.

Lader, Lawrence. *The Margaret Sanger Story*. Garden City, NY: Doubleday & Co., Inc., 1955.

Libby, Bill. *Champions of College Football*. New York, NY: Hawthorn Book, Inc. 1975.

Mendell, Ronald and Phares, Timothy. *Who's Who In Football*. New Rochelle, NY: Arlington House, 1974.

Menke, Frank. *The Encyclopedia of Sports*. Cranbury, NJ: A.S. Barnes & Co., Inc., 1944.

NCAA Football's Finest. Overland Park, KS: National Collegiate Athletic Association, 1989.

Paterno, Joe, with Bernard Asbell. *Paterno: By The Book*. New York, NY: Random House, 1989.

Penn State In The World War, 1917-1918. State College, PA: The Alumni Assn. 1923.

Reeder, Col. Red. *The Story of the First World War*. New York, NY: Duell, Sloan and Pearce, 1962.

Riley, Ridge. *Road to Number One. A Personal Chronicle of Penn State Football*. Garden City, NY: Doubleday & Co., Inc., 1977.

Sanger, Margaret. *Margaret Sanger, An Autobiography*. New York, NY: Dover Publications, Inc., 1971 (reprint).

Schoor, Gene. *The Jim Thorpe Story*. New York, NY: Julian Messner, 1951.

Snyder, Louis. *The First Book of World War I*. New York, NY: Franklin Watts, Inc., 1958.

Stallings, Laurence and Wyeth, M.S. *The Doughboys*. New York, NY: Harper & Row, 1963.

Toland, John. *No Man's Land. 1918—the last year of the Great War*. Garden City, NY: Doubleday & Co., Inc., 1980.

Treat, Roger. *The Official Encylopedia of Football*. Cranbury, NJ: A.S. Barnes & Co., Inc., 1973.

Wallace, Francis. *Knute Rockne*. Garden City, NY: Doubleday & Company, Inc., 1960.

Werstein, Irving. *The Lost Battalion*. New York, NY: W.W. Norton & Co., Inc., 1966.

Whittingham, Richard. *The Chicago Bears.* New York, NY: Simon & Schuster, Inc. 1979.

Wilkinson, Bud. *Sports Illustrated Football: Winning Offense.* New York, NY: Time, Inc.,1987.

Major Sources

The Higgins-Suhey Articles and Memorabilia Collection
Bob Higgins personal correspondence files
Tape of Cotton Bowl team reunion provided by Ed Czekaj

Facilities and Sources

Auburn University Library
Auburn University at Montgomery Library
Cazenovia Central High School Library
Chicago Bears Sports Information Department
Corning Historical Society (John McCarthy)
Corning Public Library
Montgomery (Ala.) Public Library
National Football Foundation's College Hall of Fame (Ellyn Giordano)
National Football League Hall of Fame
Notre Dame Sports Information Department
Penn State Sports Information Department
Penn State University Archives Department
State of Alabama Archives and History
The Peddie School (Kay Hansen, research coordinator)
The Peddie School Library
University of Alabama Sports Information Department
University of Pittsburgh Sports Information Department
Washington University Sports Information Department
West Virginia Wesleyan College Sports Information Dept.

Periodicals-Guides

Collier's
Huddle
Penn State Annual Football Yearbook
Penn State game day programs
Pennsylvania State College student yearbooks (*La Vie*)
Pittsburgh Steelers Guide (1949)

Saturday Evening Post
Sports Illustrated
Time

Newspapers

Highfield Review
Peddie Weekly News
Penn State Collegian
Philadelphia Daily News
Philadelphia Record
Pittsburgh Press
Pittsburgh Sunday Sun-Tele-
graph
St. Louis Daily Globe-

Democrat
The Canton Daily News
The Centre Daily Times
The Montgomery Advertiser
The New York Times
The Ohio State Journal
The Washingtonian
The Washington Post
Waynesboro Record Herald

Interviews

Don Abbey
Ed Ammann
Earl Bruce
Earl "Sparky" Brown
Bill Colligan
Ray Conger
Tim Curley
Ed Czekaj
Jim Dooley
Nancy Higgins Dooley
Joe Drazenovich
Earle Edwards
Gurdin Freeborn
Leon Gajecki
George Harvey
Joanne Hayes
Alan Helffrich, Jr.
Paul Johnson
Judy Johnson
Dave Joyner
Lenny Krouse
Jack Livezey
Bill Luther

Mary Ann Higgins Lyford
Don Mansfield
Henry McWane, Jr.
Bill "Red" Moore
John Nolan
Jim O'Hora
Joe Paterno
Francis Rogel
Carl Stravinski
Betsy Suhey
Ginger Suhey
Larry Suhey
Matt Suhey
Paul Suhey
Steve Suhey, Jr.
Sam Tamburo
Sever "Tor" Toretti
Dallas Trammell
John Watkins
Wendell "Rabbit" Wear
F. Guy White
Jim Williams
John Wolosky